AF575478

William Blake's

Divine Comedy Illustrations

102 Full-Color Plates

William Blake

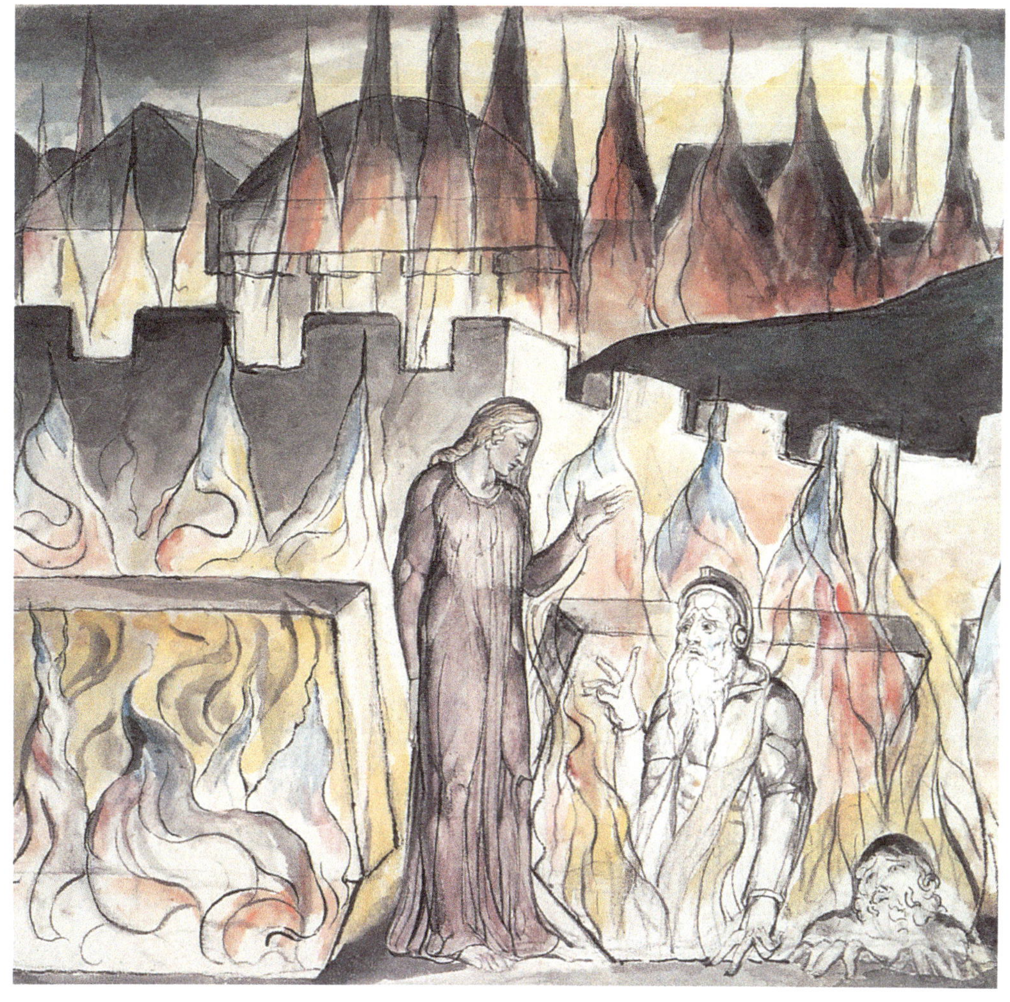

DOVER PUBLICATIONS
Garden City, New York

Copyright

Bibliographical Note

This Dover edition, first published in 2008, reprints all 102 watercolors by William Blake of scenes from *The Divine Comedy.* A Publisher's Note and captions have been specially prepared for this edition.

Library of Congress Cataloging-in-Publication Data

Blake, William, 1757–1827.
William Blake's Divine comedy illustrations : 102 full-color plates / William Blake.
p. cm.
ISBN-13: 978-0-486-46429-9
ISBN-10: 0-486-46429-6
1. Blake, William, 1757–1827. 2. Dante Alighieri, 1265–1321. Divina commedia—Illustrations. I. Title. II. Title: Divine comedy illustrations.

NC978.5.B55A4 2008
760.092—dc22

2008028679

Manufactured in the United States of America
46429604
www.doverpublications.com

Publisher's Note

William Blake's final artistic project is a stunning collection of illustrations for Dante Alighieri's masterpiece, the epic poem *Divinia commedia.* Born nearly 500 years after Dante, the English poet and artist nevertheless succeeds in bridging the centuries to provide a unique perspective on the medieval classic. It is a fascinating marriage, as Dante, although harshly critical of the Church and its adherents, was nevertheless a believer, whereas Blake was renowned for his iconoclastic stance against organized religion.

William Blake, born in London in 1757, was encouraged by his parents to study art, and he became an apprentice to James Basire, an engraver, in his early teens. After doing magazine illustrations, he opened a print shop in London with his wife, Catherine Boucher (whom he had wed in 1782) and brother; that business failed. In addition to his artwork, Blake wrote many poems, combining engravings with verse in *The Marriage of Heaven and Hell* (1790), *The Book of Urizen* (1794), and *Jerusalem* (1804–1818), as well as other works displaying his bold and unconventional literary and artistic sensibility. Although he received critical attention during his lifetime, Blake was often regarded as an eccentric, and he became detached from his supporters in his later years. He died on August 12, 1827.

In 1824, the painter and printmaker John Linnell offered Blake a commission to engrave illustrations for the Book of Job (c. 1825). Linnell then proposed that Blake illustrate the *Divine Comedy,* and Blake accepted, even learning enough Italian to grasp the gist of the original verse. Blake was in contact with the Reverend Henry Cary, whose 1814 translation of Dante was held in great esteem, and it is possible that the two discussed the poem at some point. Thus, Linnell provided the watercolor paper, and Blake proceeded with his illustrations. Blake was plagued by gallbladder attacks toward the end of his life, but he persevered with the project. By the time of his death, in 1827, Blake had created 102 drawings for the *Divine Comedy*—some were sketches; others were fully realized watercolors. (He also made seven copperplate engravings, falling far short of his goal to engrave the entire work.) The final count included seventy-two illustrations for *Inferno,* twenty for *Purgatorio,* and only ten for *Paradiso.* Linnell paid the artist £130 for his work. The drawings were not published at the time, but remained with Linnell.

The mid-nineteenth-century Pre-Raphaelite movement in England brought about an appreciation of Blake's work—unsurprising, as the Pre-Raphaelite artists and critics found an affinity with medieval culture (Dante's milieu) and a belief in the freedom of the individual (a tenet of Blake), and his drawings were exhibited in London's Royal Academy. Ironically, Blake had studied at the Royal Academy School in his early days. In 1913, the drawings were shown at the Tate Gallery. Five years later, the Linnell family sold their entire Blake collection at auction, and the Dante drawings were dispersed, going to public galleries in England, the United States, and Australia.

From the outset of their journey from the entrance to Hell to the ultimate reward of Heaven, Dante and Virgil encounter a multitude of grotesque scenes—and a number of transcendent ones. The expressive line and color of William Blake's vivid watercolors imbue these scenes, and their subjects, with pathos, pity, and terror, as well as luminous joy.

The Plates

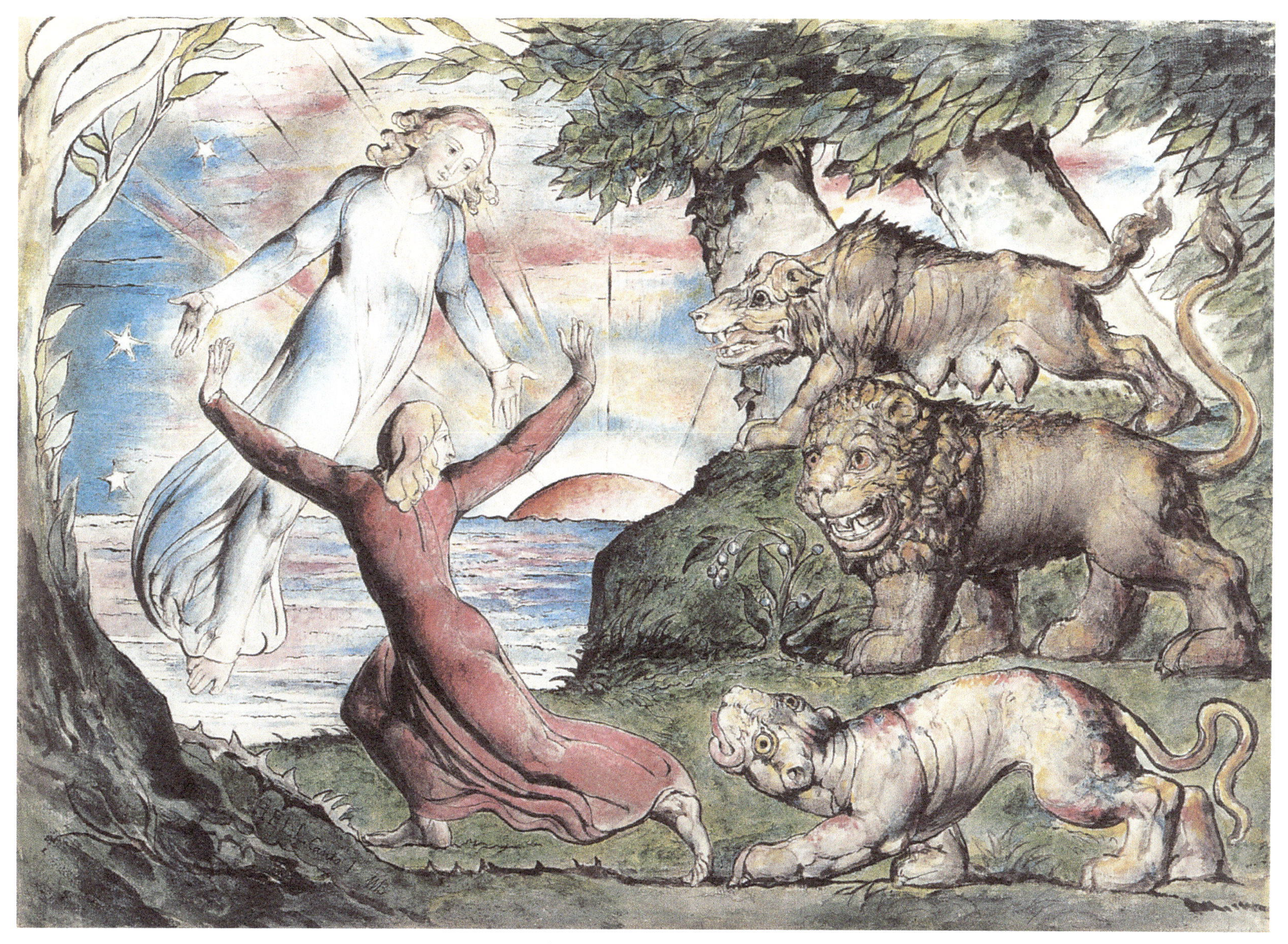

PLATE 1

After entering the dark wood, Dante is pursued by a panther, a lion, and a she-wolf.
They represent his vices: pleasure, pride, and avarice.
[*Inferno,* Canto 1, lines 1–90]

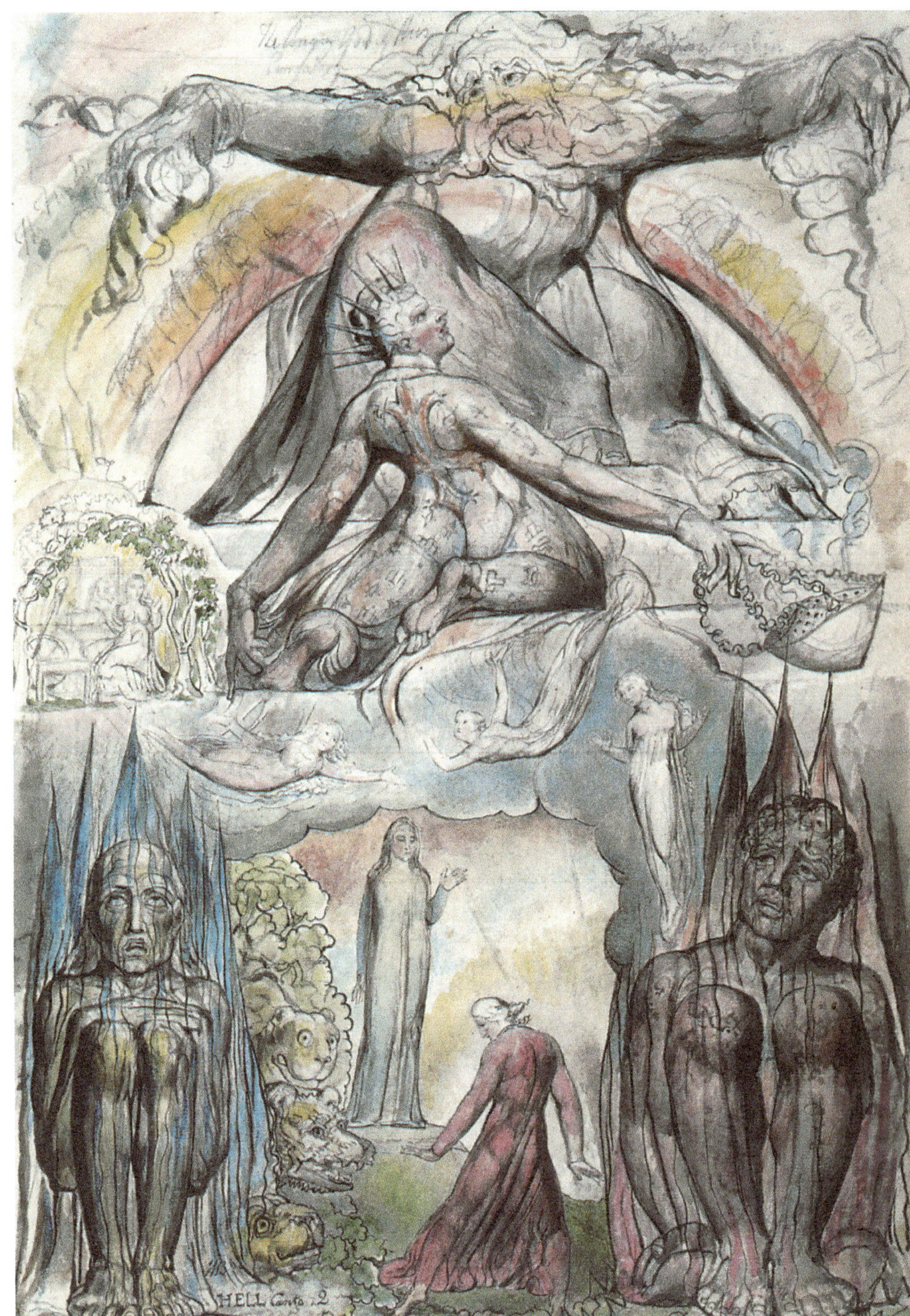

PLATE 2

Dante will be tested by God as he passes through Hell. The three beasts lurk below. [*Inferno,* Canto 2, lines 59–69]

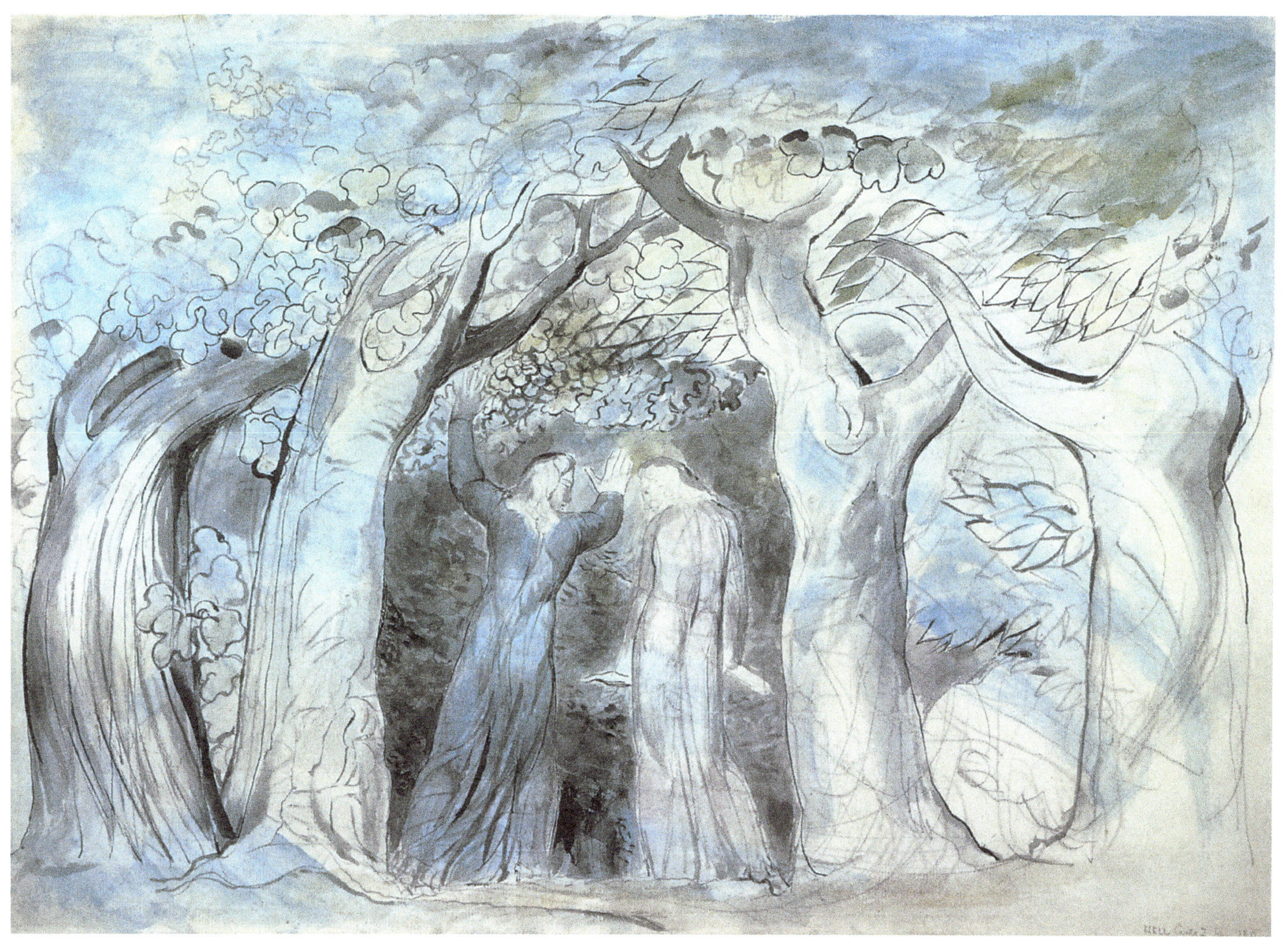

PLATE 3

Virgil, at the request of Beatrice, will assist Dante in his quest for divine wisdom.
[*Inferno,* Canto 2, lines 139–141]

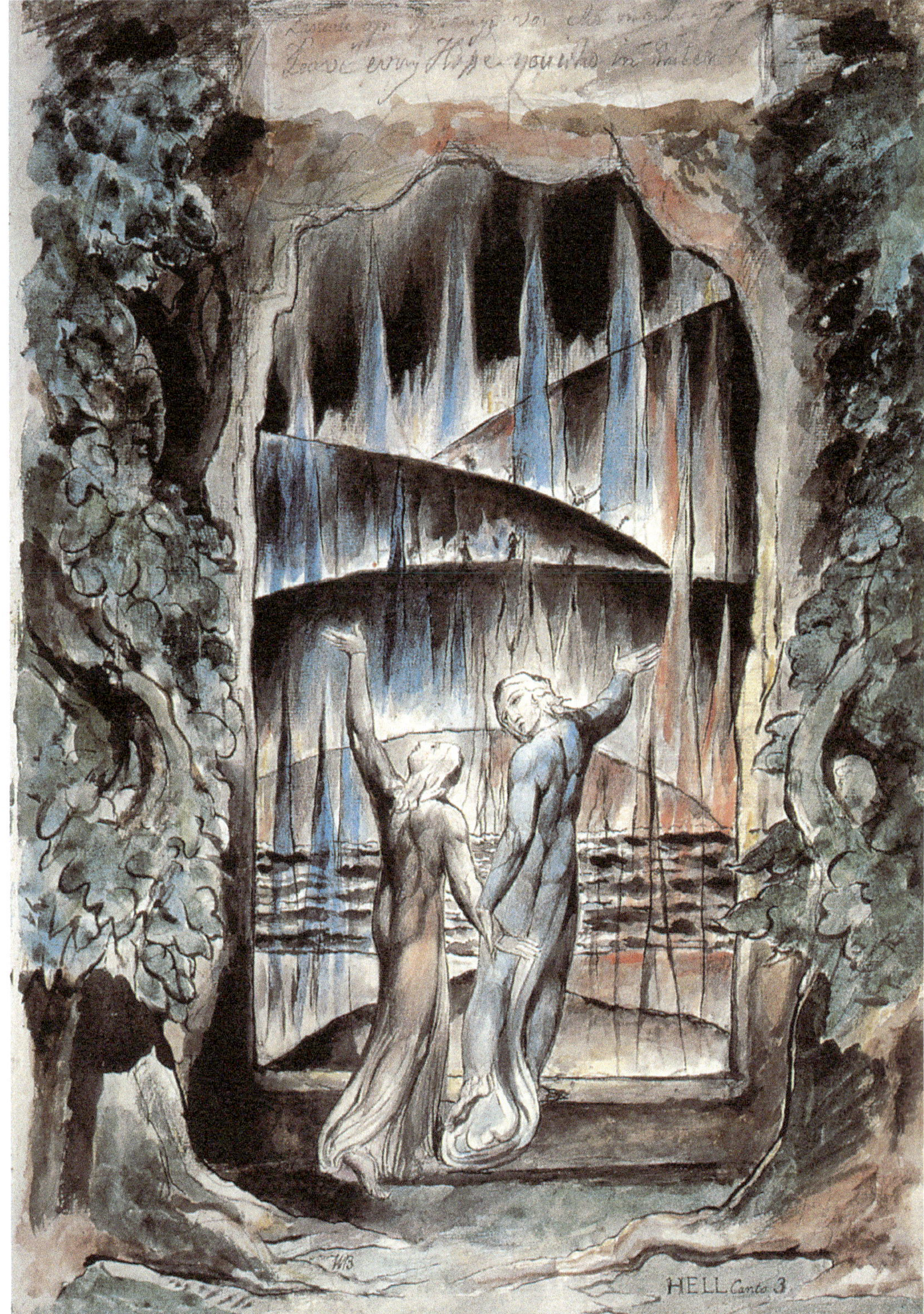

PLATE 4

As he enters the gate of Hell, Dante reads the inscription: "All hope abandon, ye who enter here."
[*Inferno,* Canto 3, lines 1–10]

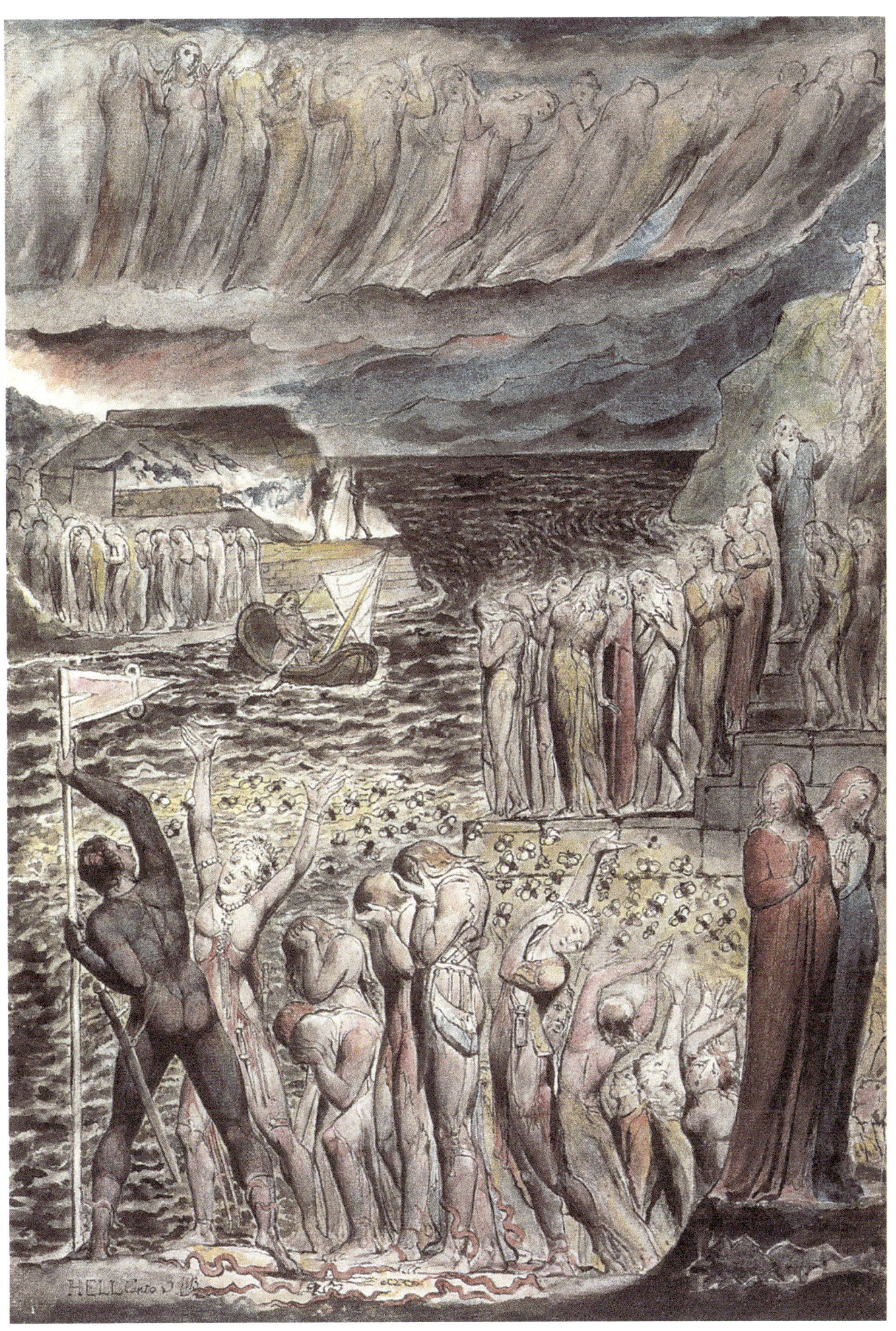

PLATE 5

Dante and Virgil join the souls who suffered from apathy in life. Charon's boat will take them across the Acheron.
[*Inferno,* Canto 3, lines 32–40]

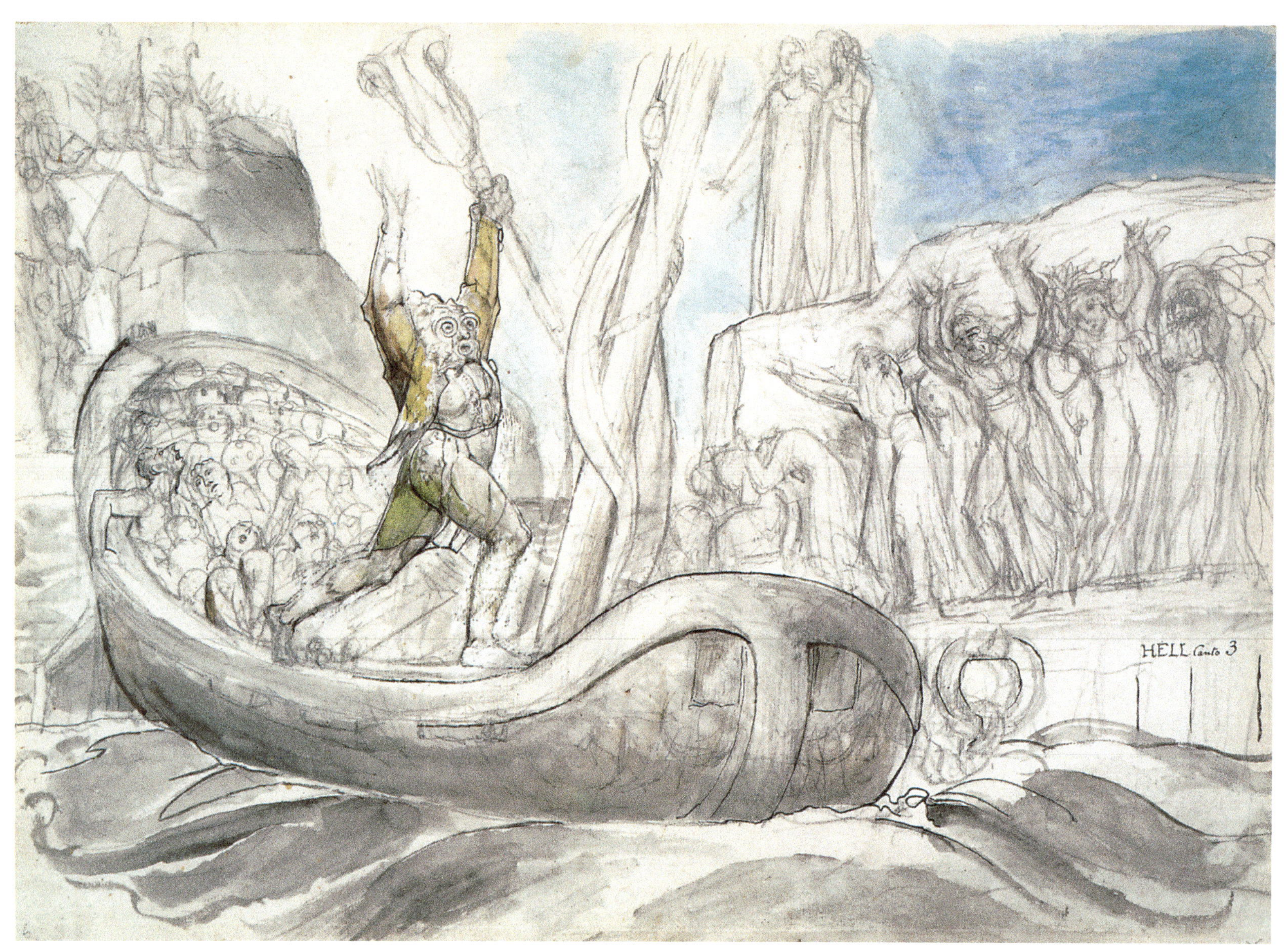

PLATE 6

Charon warns his passengers of the misery that awaits them.
[*Inferno,* Canto 3, lines 76–84]

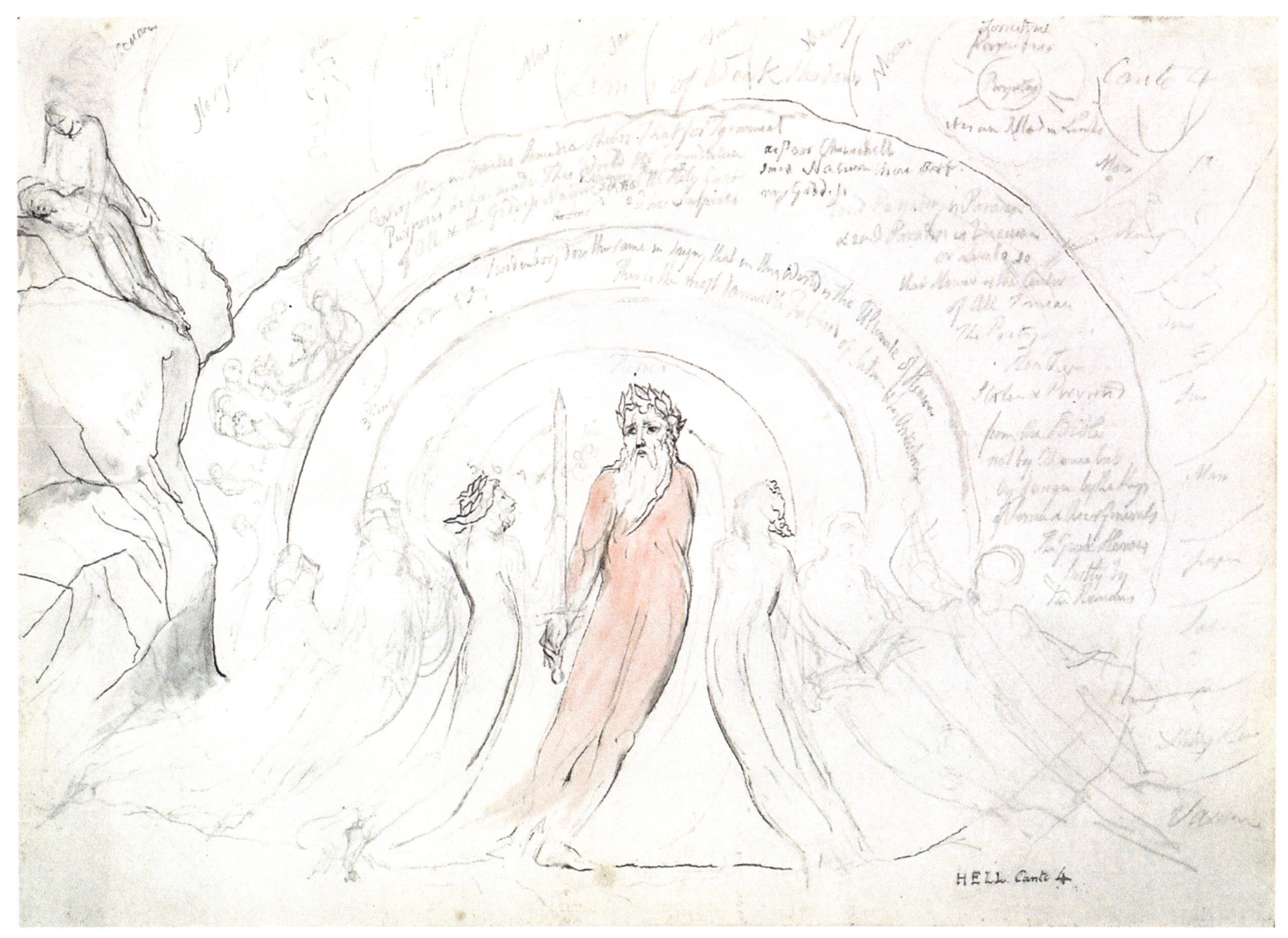

PLATE 7

Homer, symbol of classical culture, wields his sword.
[*Inferno,* Canto 4, lines 83–88]

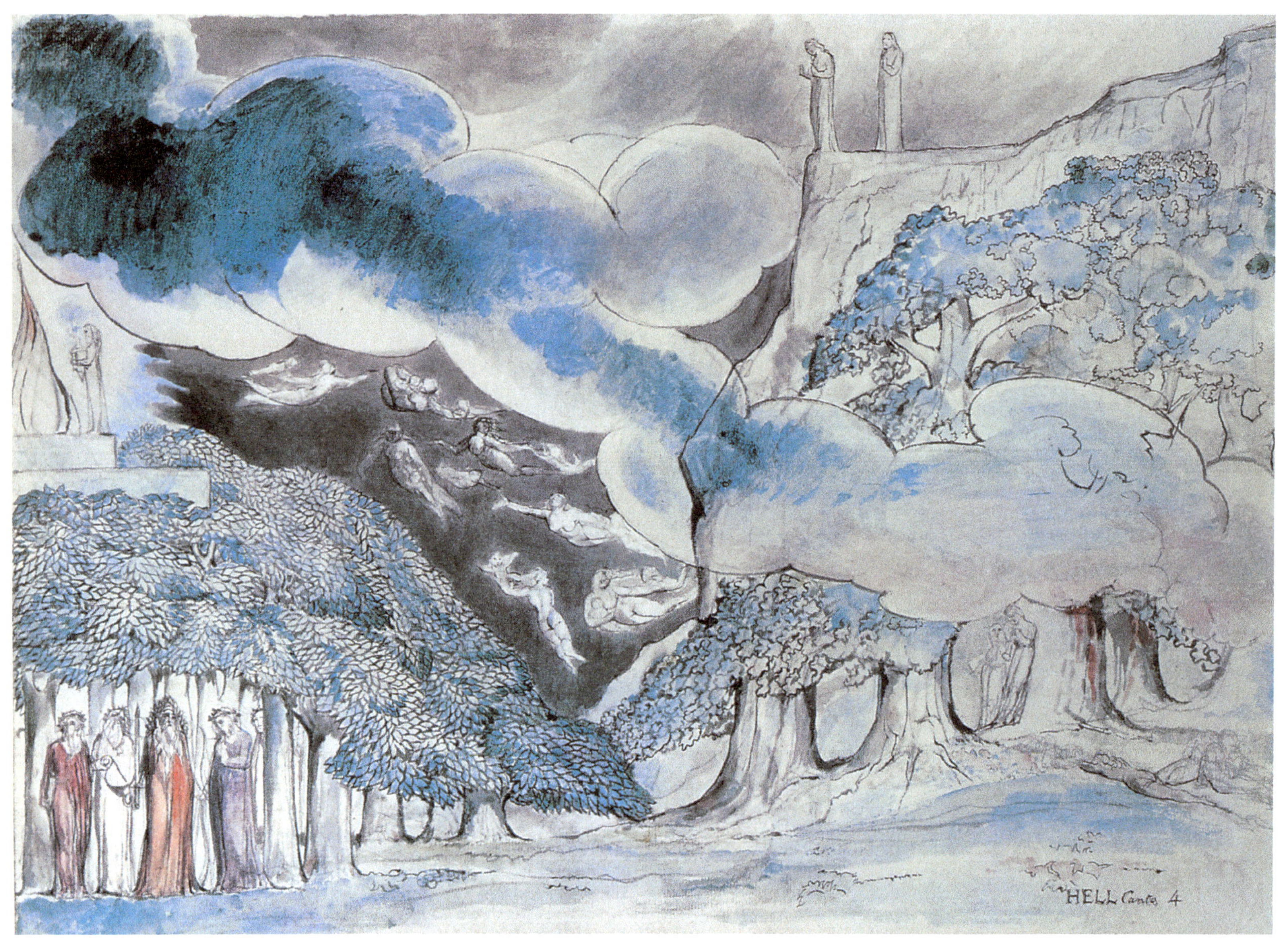

PLATE 8

Dante and Virgil view the ancient poets Homer, Horace, Ovid, and Lucan,
whose paganism denies them entrance to Heaven.
[*Inferno,* Canto 4, lines 89–95]

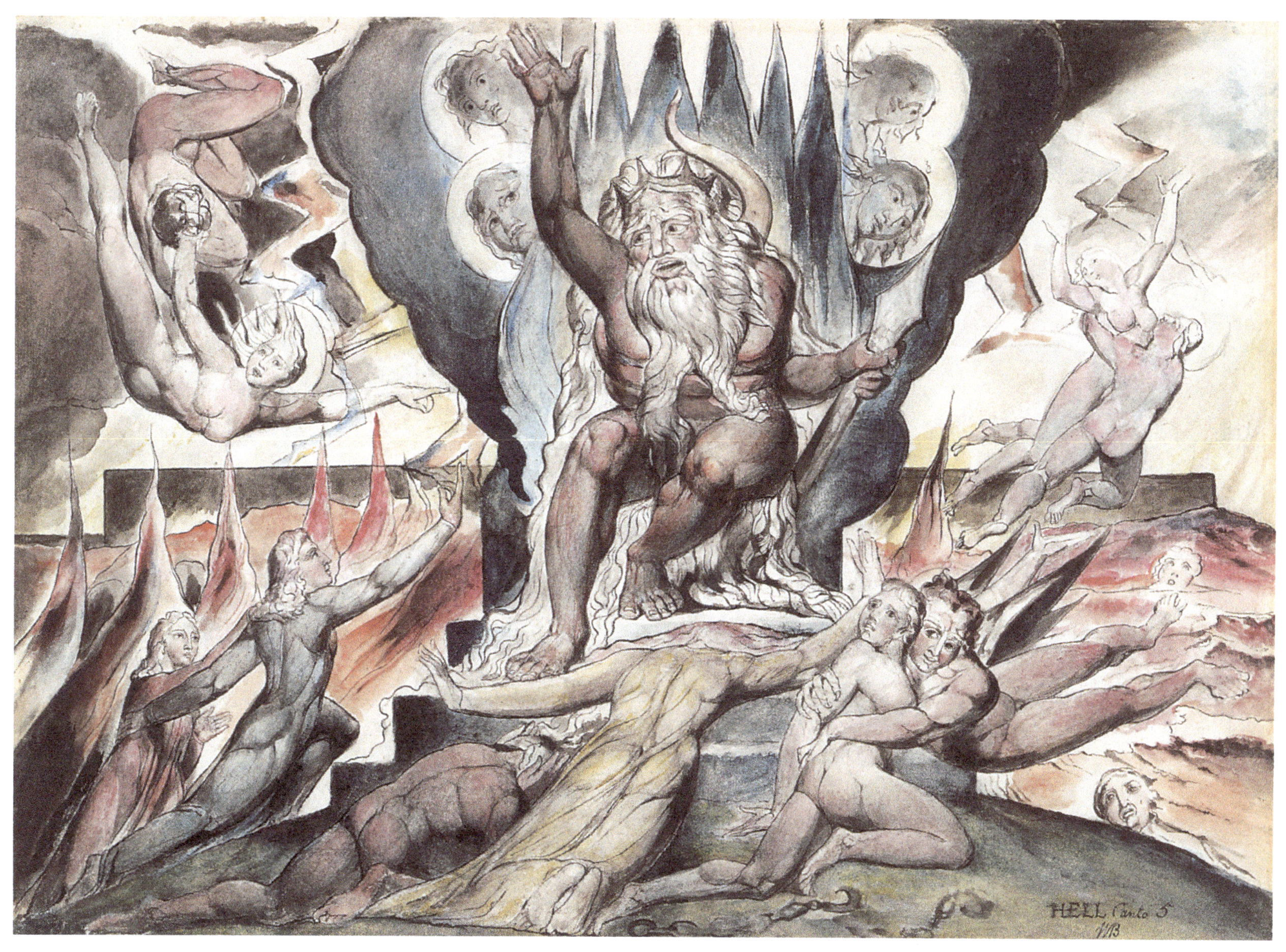

PLATE 9

Dante and Virgil encounter the vengeful judge Minos
in the second circle of Hell.
[*Inferno,* Canto 5, lines 4–24]

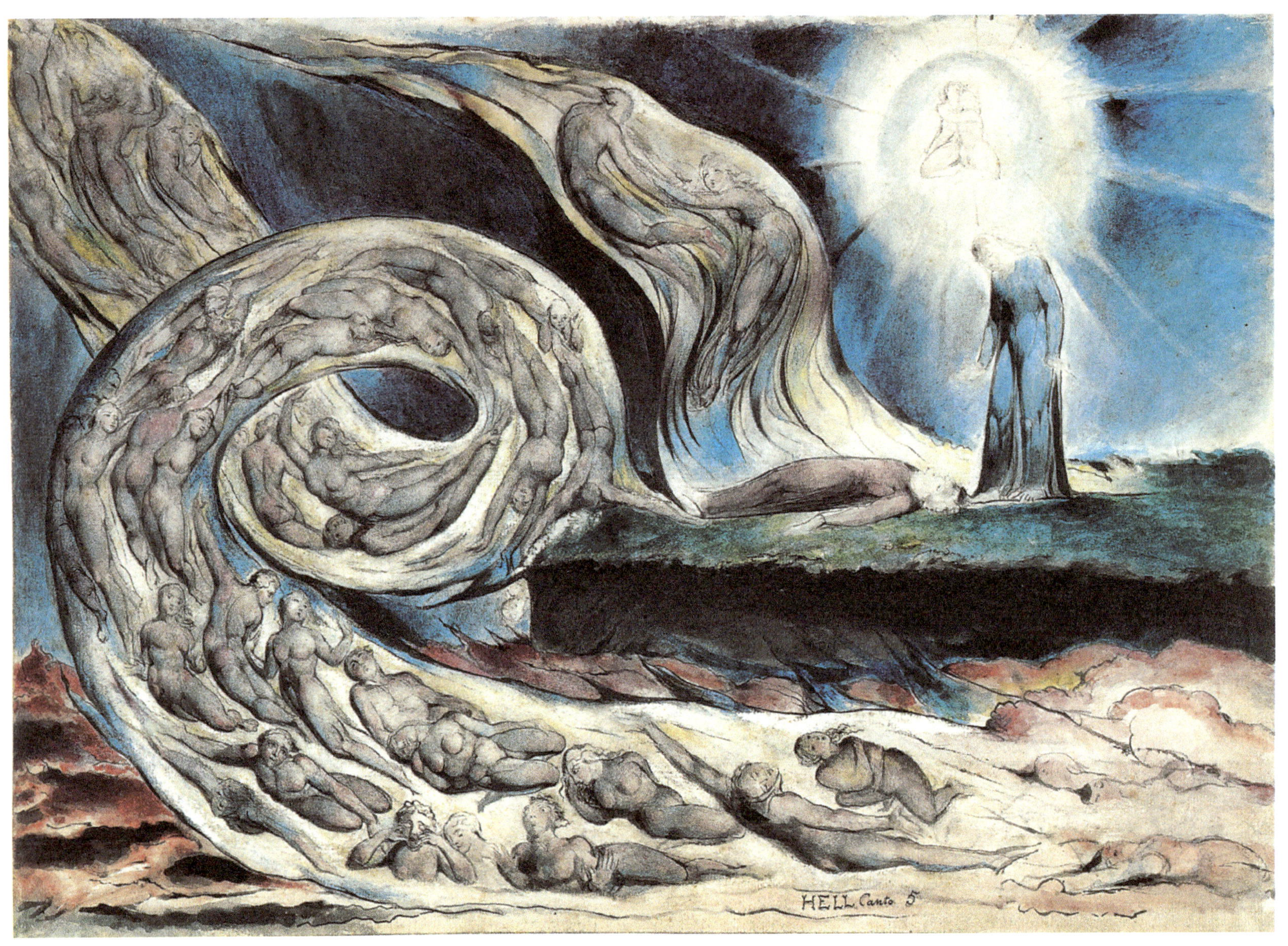

PLATE 10

Dante has fainted upon hearing Francesca da Rimini tell of her passionate encounter with Paolo. The lustful are condemned to be forever caught up by winds. [*Inferno,* Canto 5, lines 37–138]

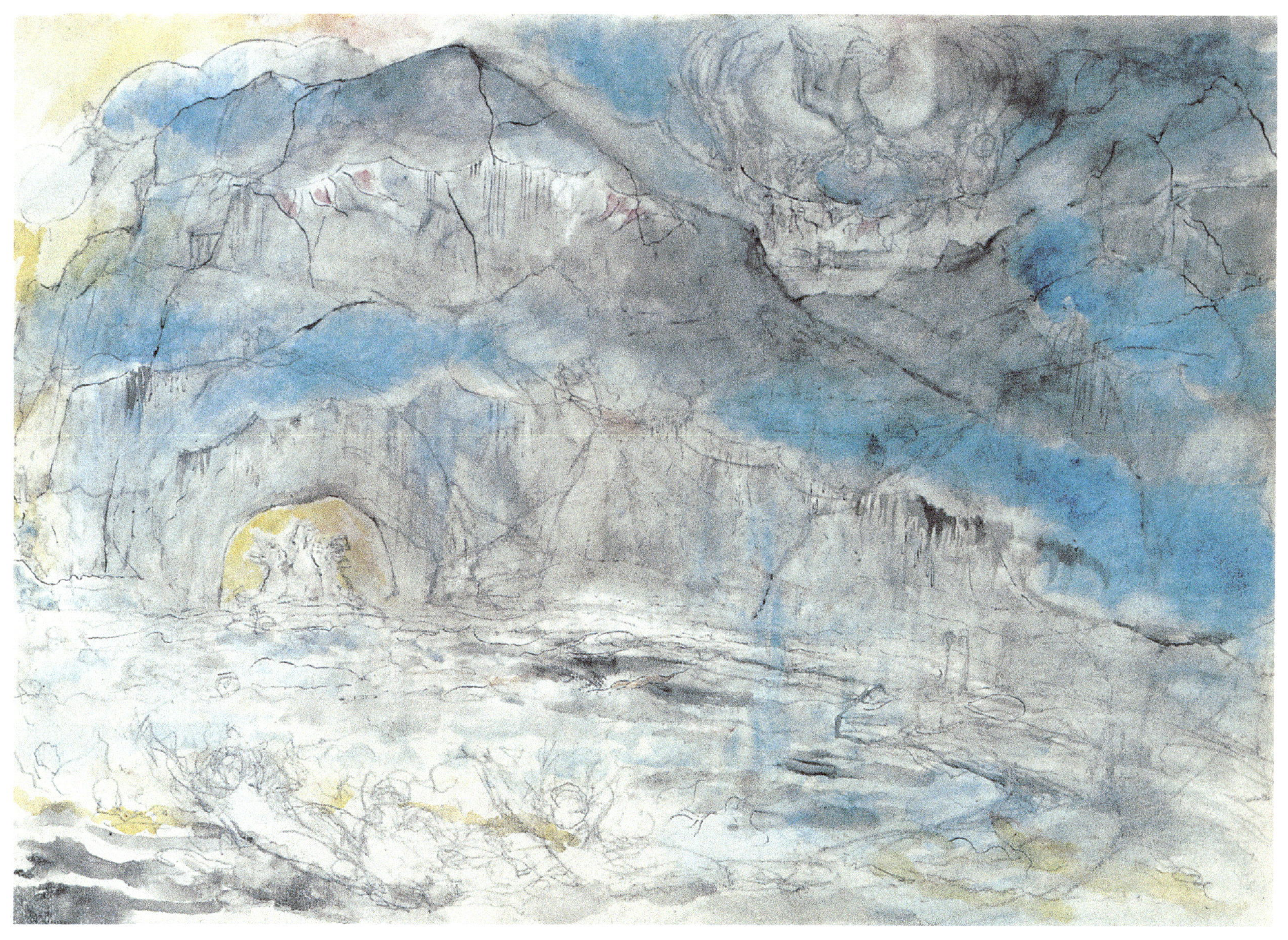

PLATE 11

The gluttons, watched by the three-headed Cerberus, are subjected to foul weather in the third circle.
[*Inferno,* Canto 6, lines 12–35]

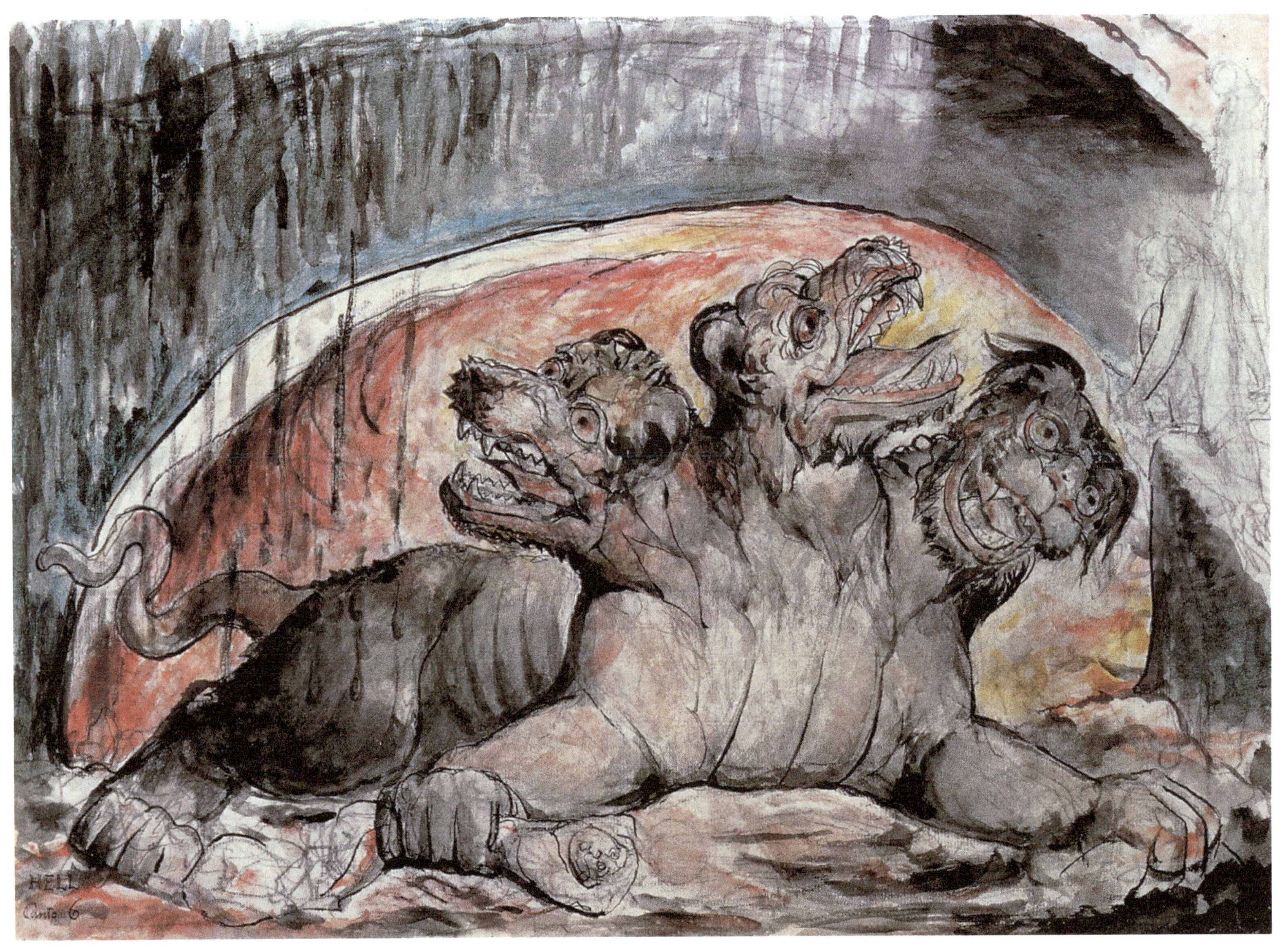

PLATE 12

The monstrous Cerberus pulls tormented souls from the water.
[*Inferno,* Canto 6, lines 12–35]

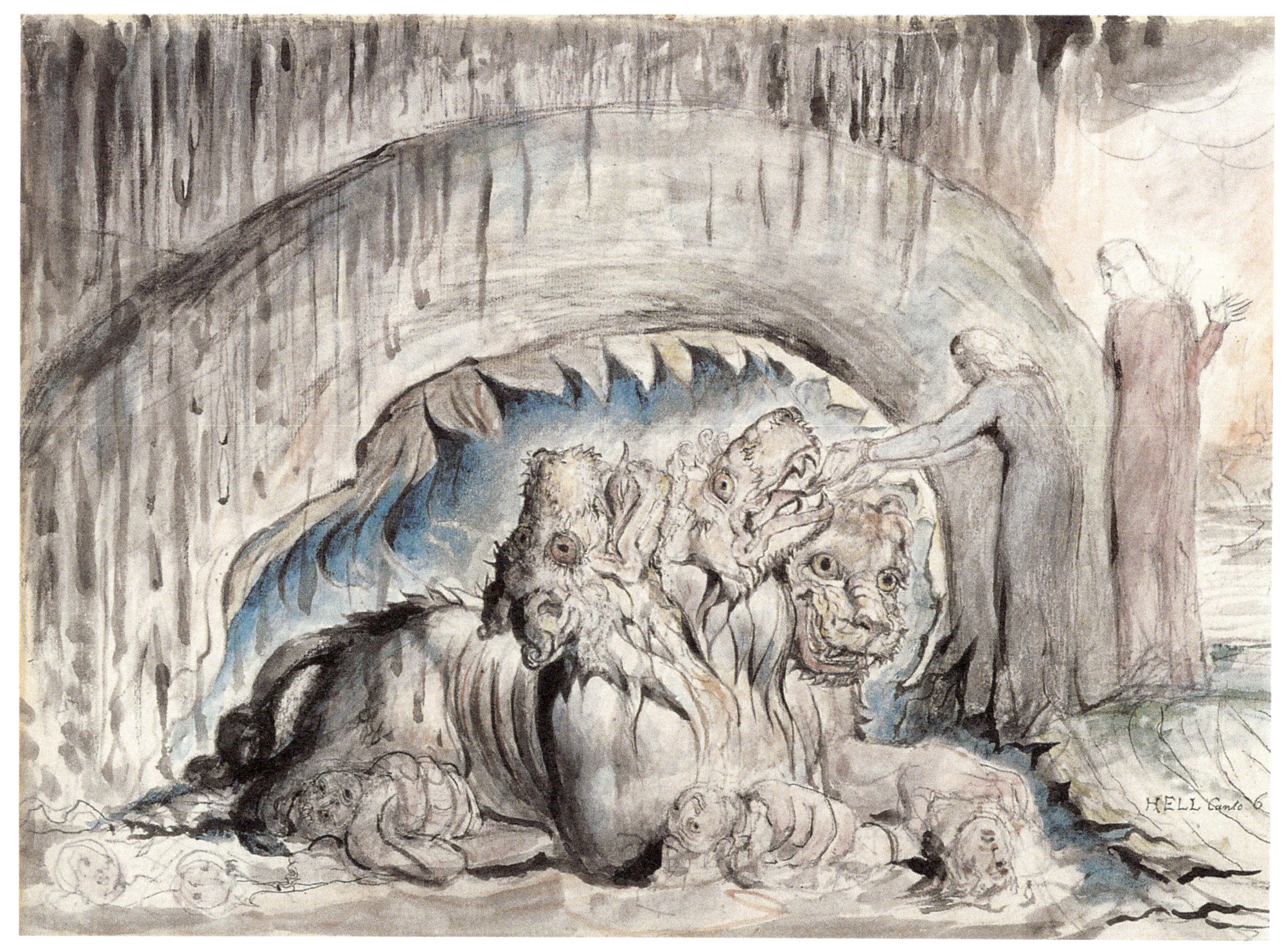

PLATE 13

As Dante looks on, Virgil feeds handfuls of earth to Cerberus.
[*Inferno,* Canto 6, lines 12–35]

PLATE 14

Pluto rules the fourth circle of Hell, where greed is represented by a money bag. [*Inferno,* Canto 7, lines 7–15]

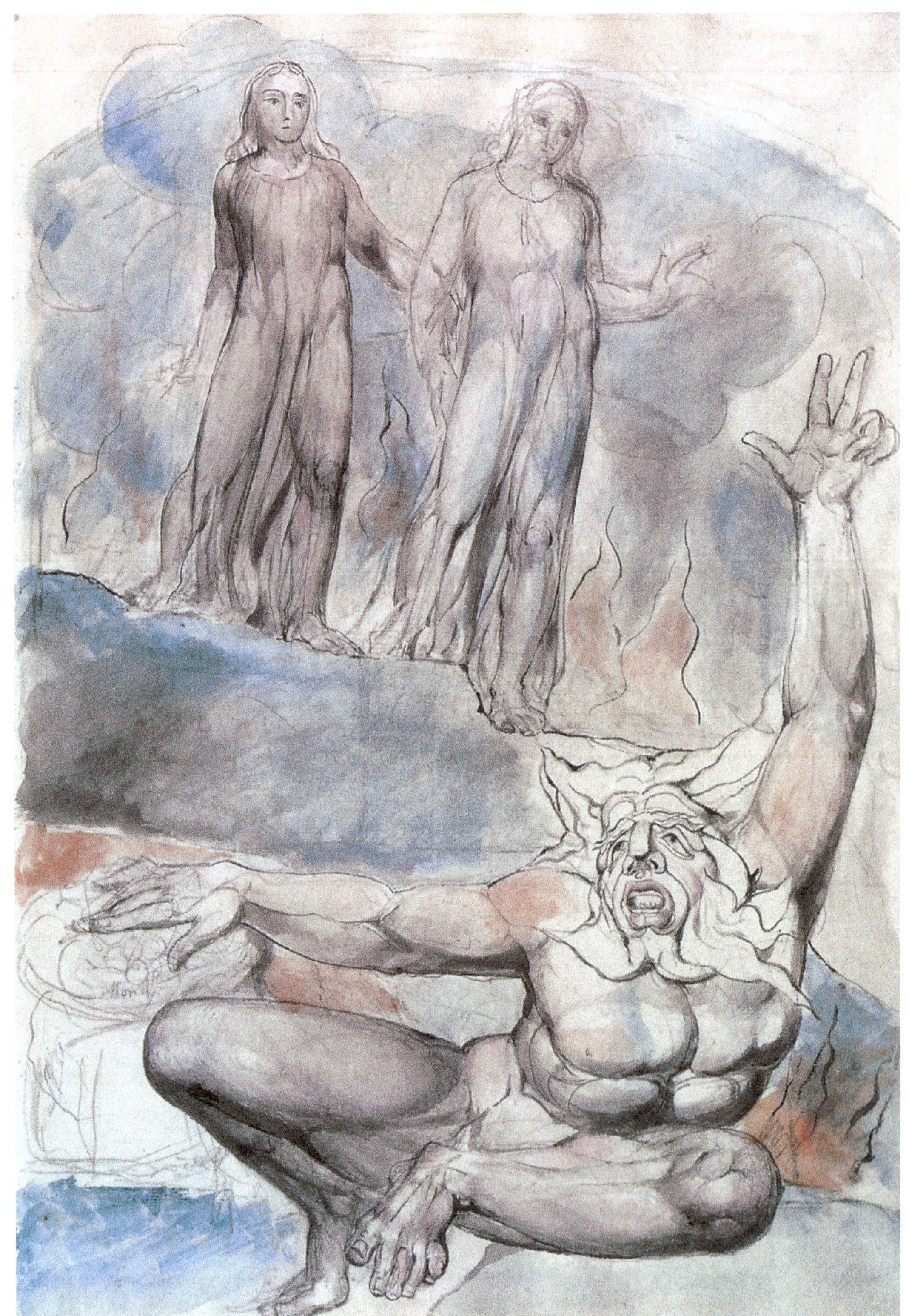

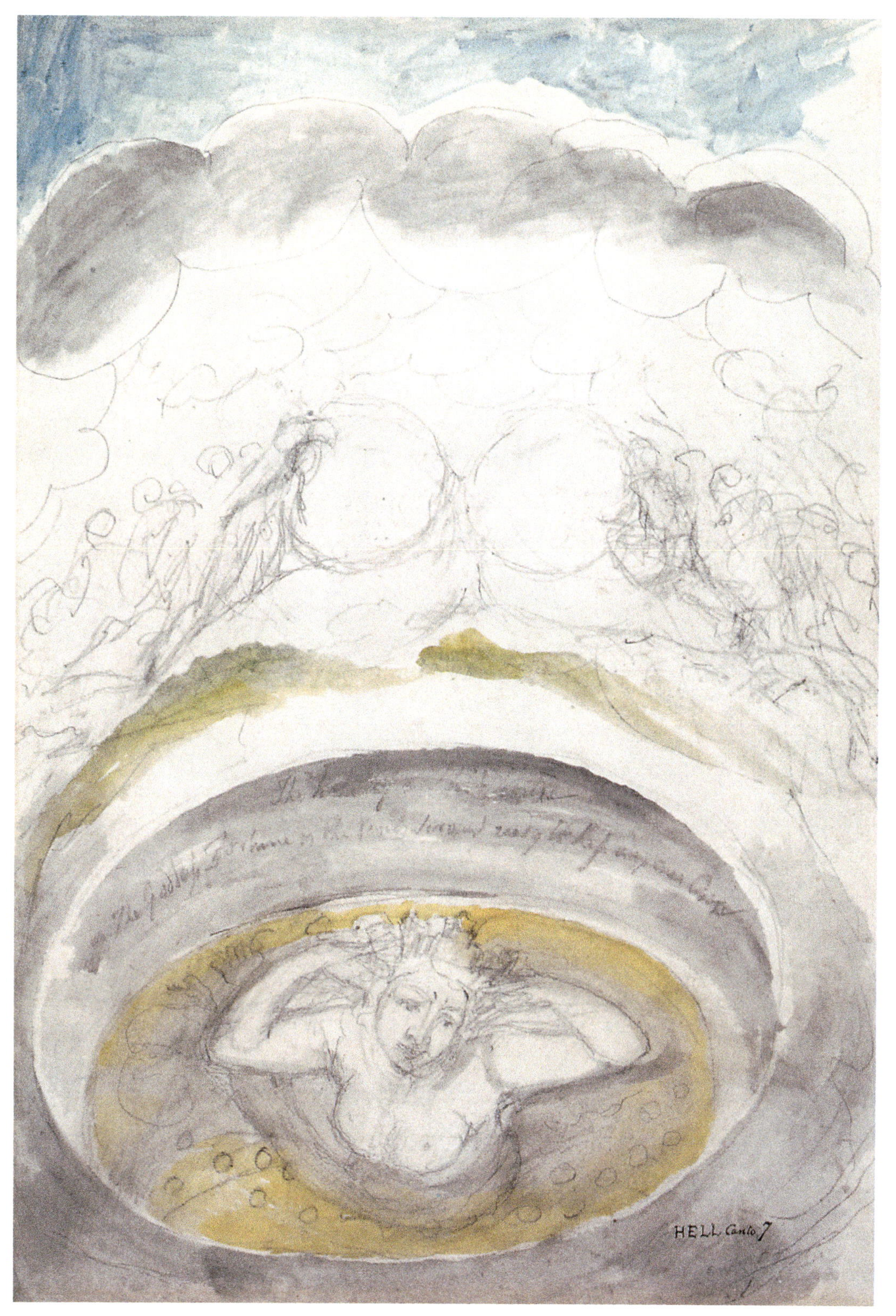

PLATE 15

In the fourth circle, Dante asks Virgil to explain the influence of Fortune on humans. [*Inferno,* Canto 7, lines 22–96]

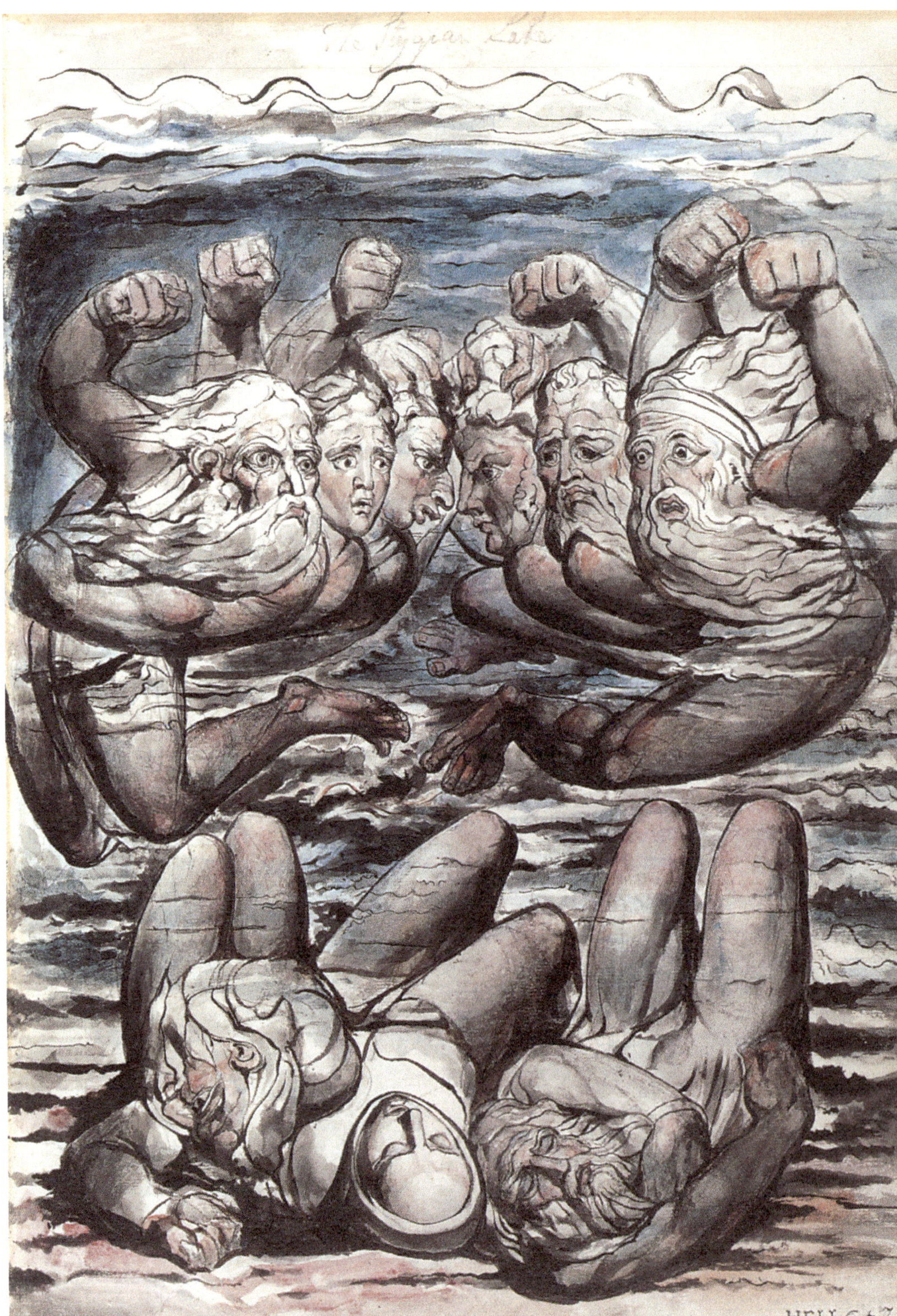

Plate 16

Anger has felled the sinners whom Dante and Virgil observe in the Stygian lake. [*Inferno,* Canto 7, lines 110–127]

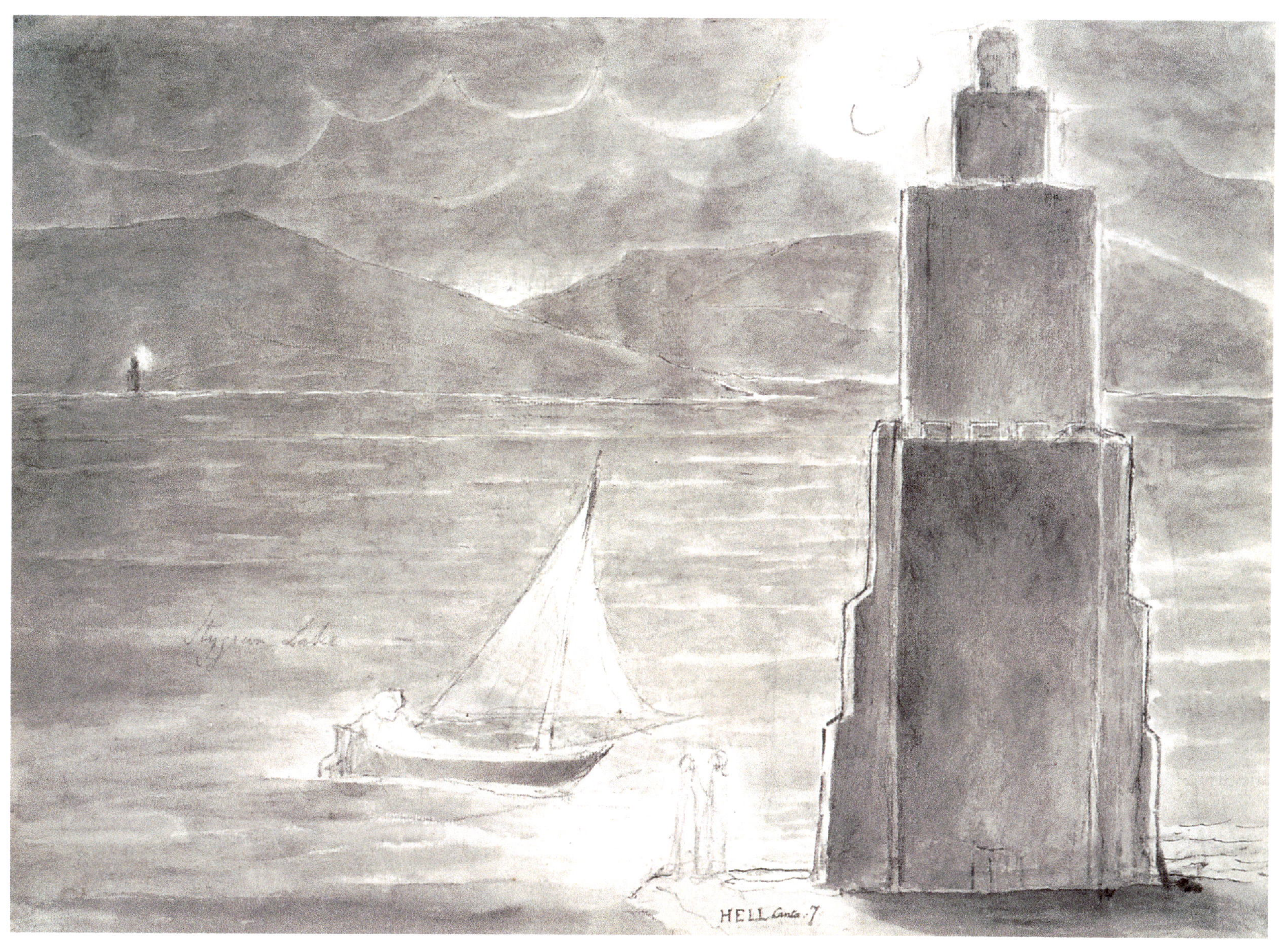

PLATE 17

Dante and Virgil are prepared to cross the Stygian lake with Phlegyas, who will ferry them to the city of Dis.
[*Inferno,* Canto 7, lines 128–134]

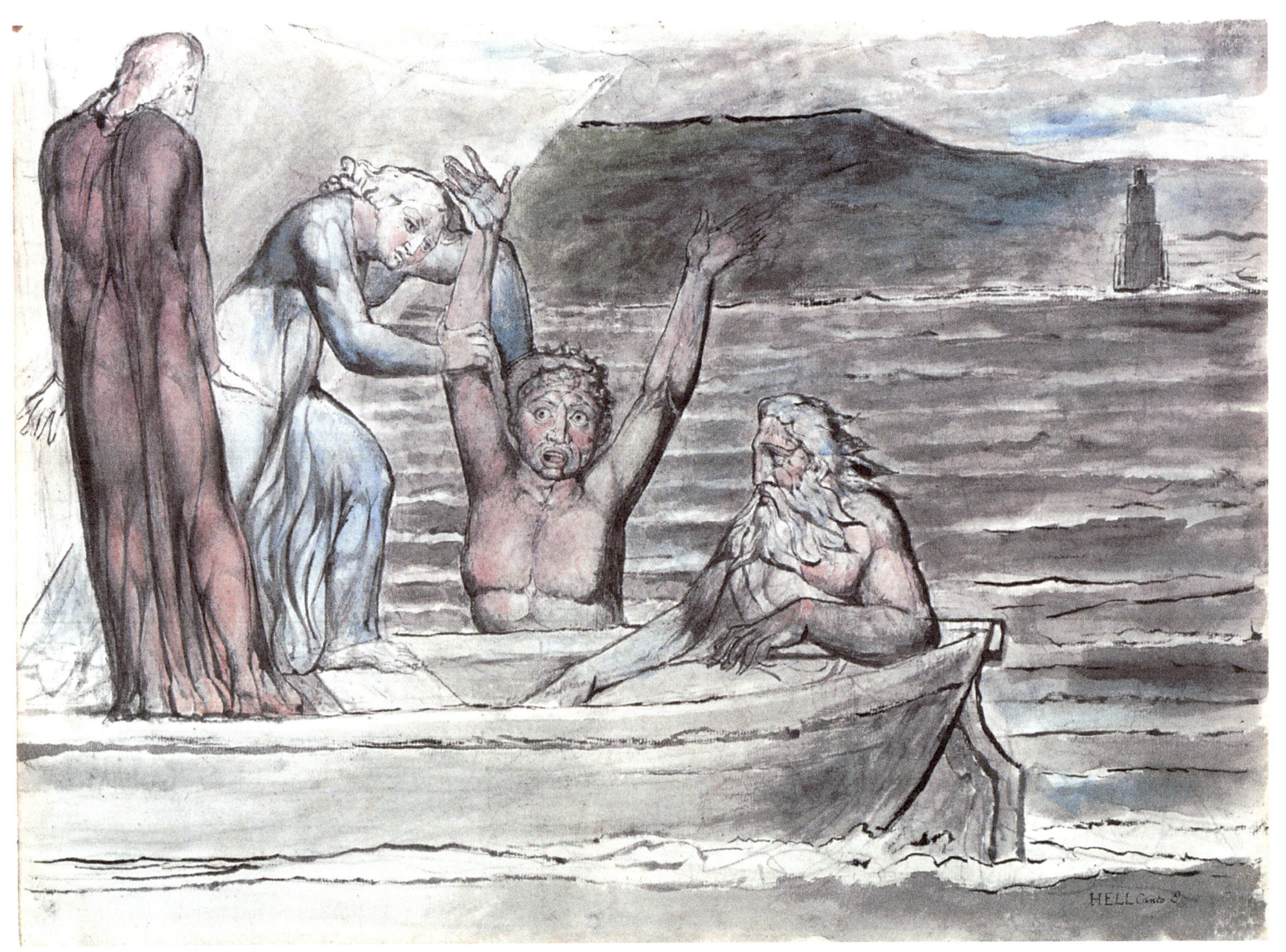

PLATE 18

Virgil forces the arrogant Filippo Argenti back into the Stygian lake.
[*Inferno,* Canto 8, lines 30–64]

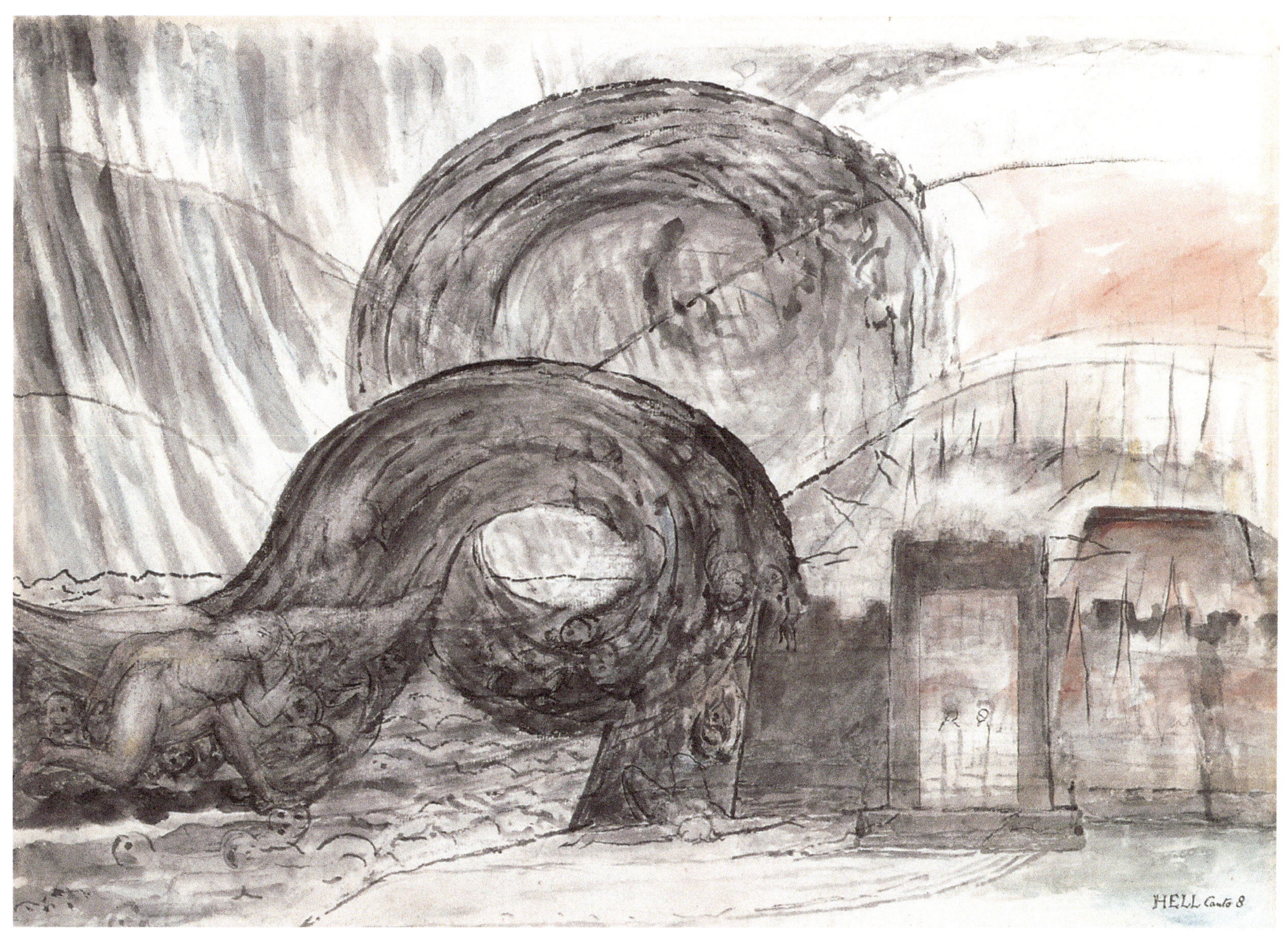

Plate 19

A whirlwind carries damned souls to the city of Dis.
The angel is seen crossing the lake at the left.
[*Inferno,* Canto 8, lines 65–73]

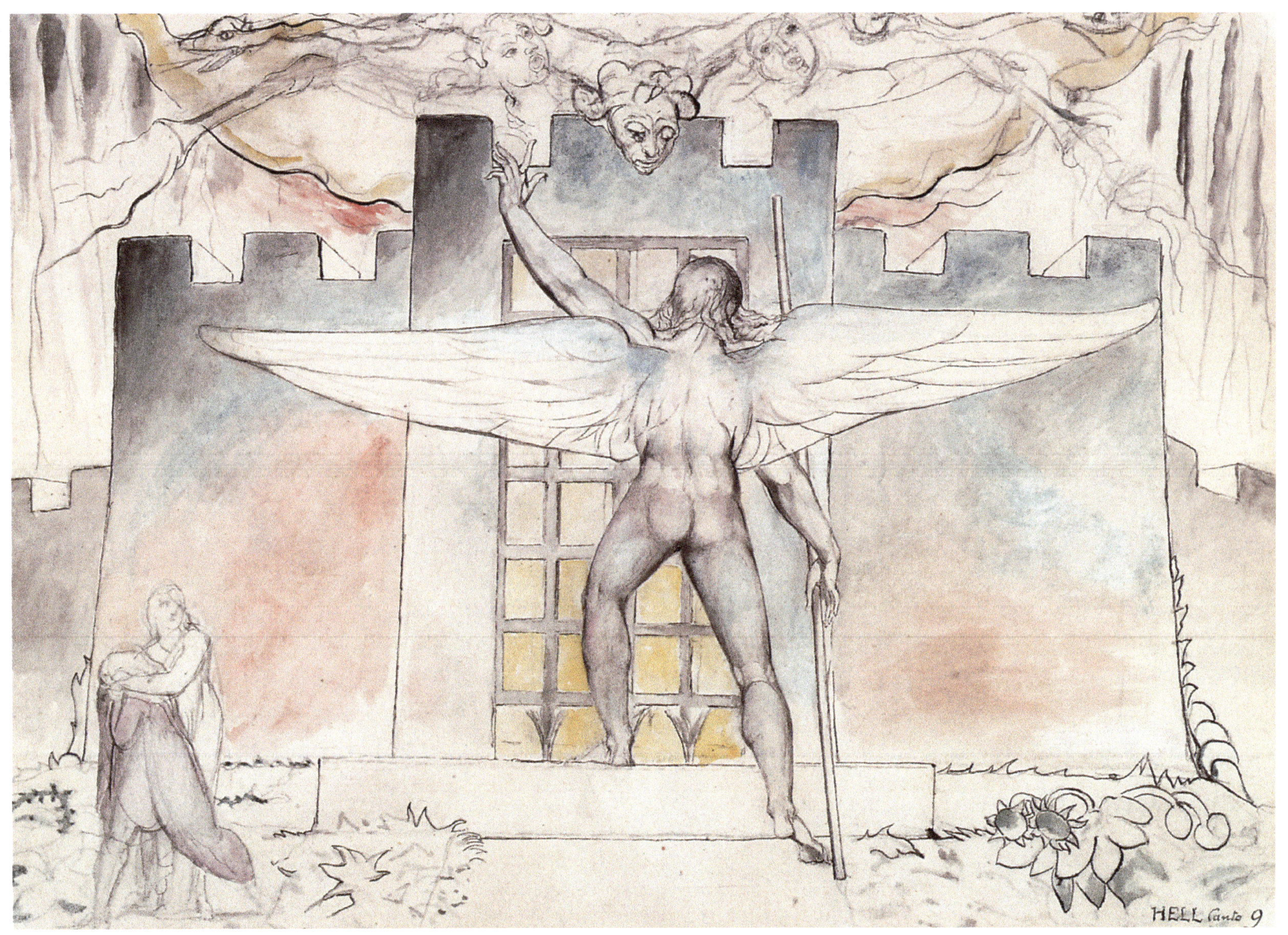

PLATE 20

The angel conquers the gate of Dis—and the three Furies who appear above it—enabling Dante and Virgil to enter.
[*Inferno,* Canto 9, lines 44–64]

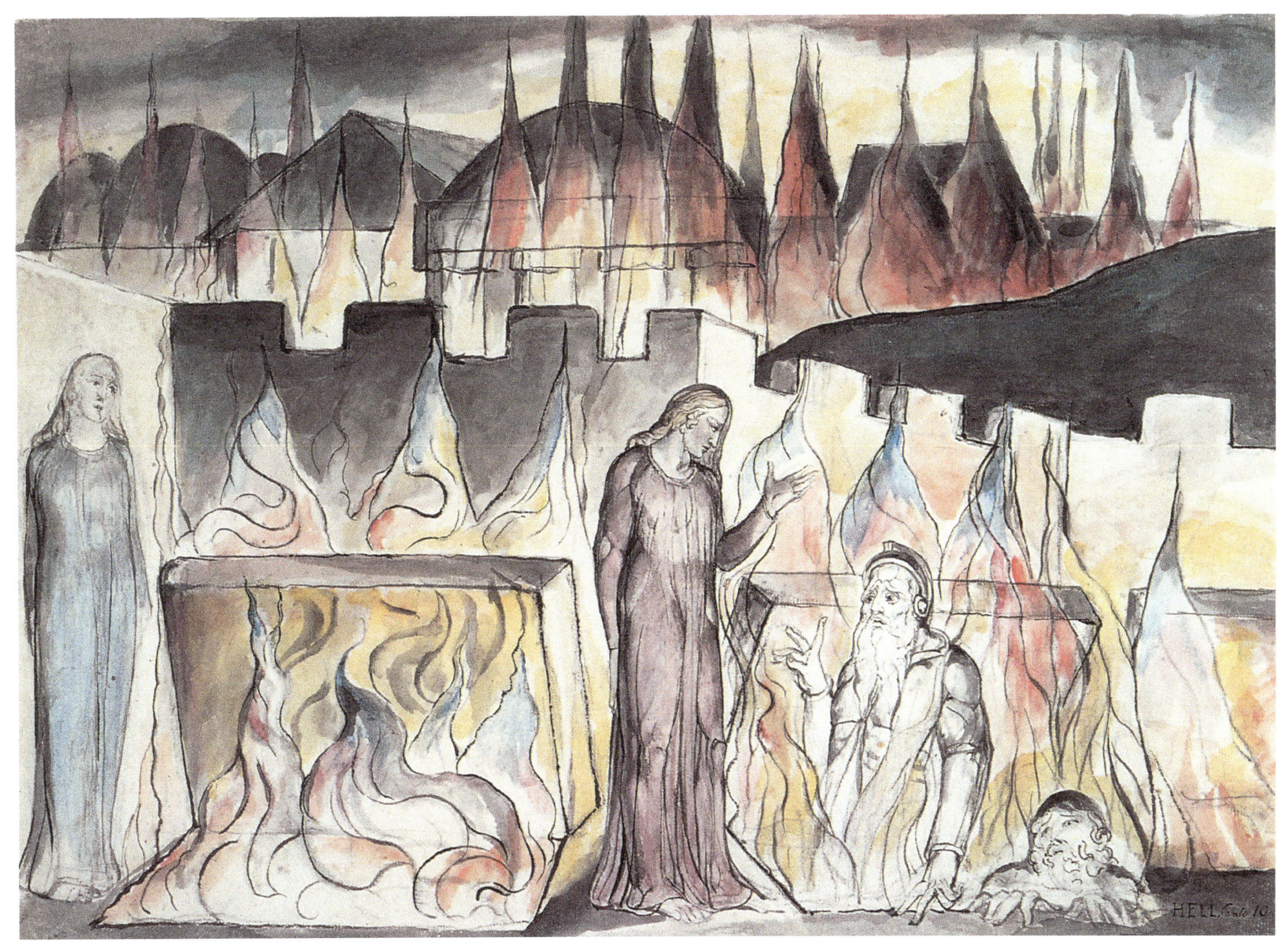

PLATE 21

Dante, surrounded by flames and open tombs,
speaks with Farinata degli Uberti.
[*Inferno,* Canto 10, lines 23–70]

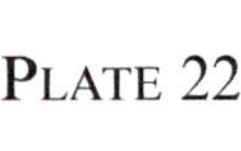

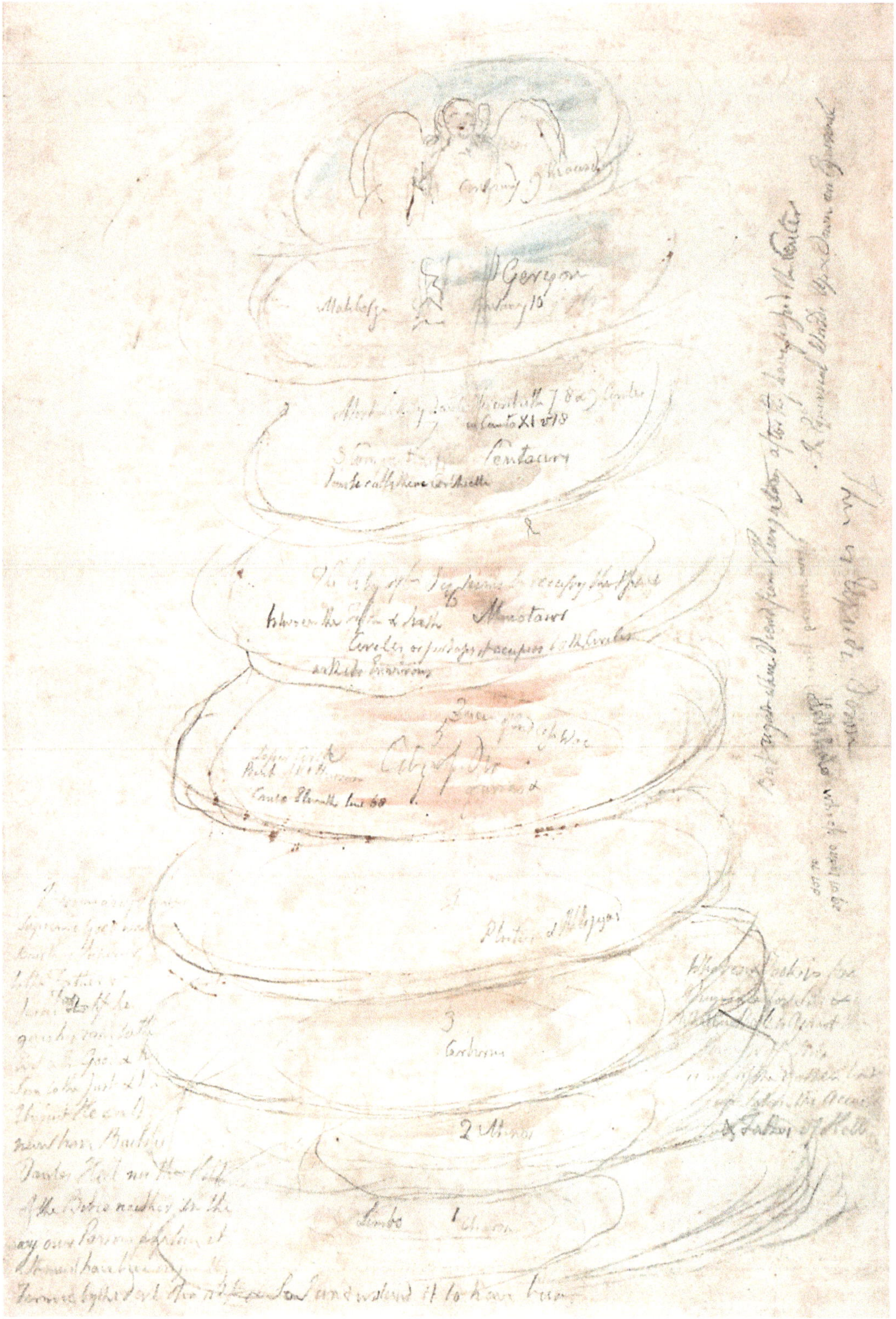

PLATE 22

Blake's roughly drawn diagram depicts the nine circles of Hell. [*Inferno,* Canto 11, lines 1–15]

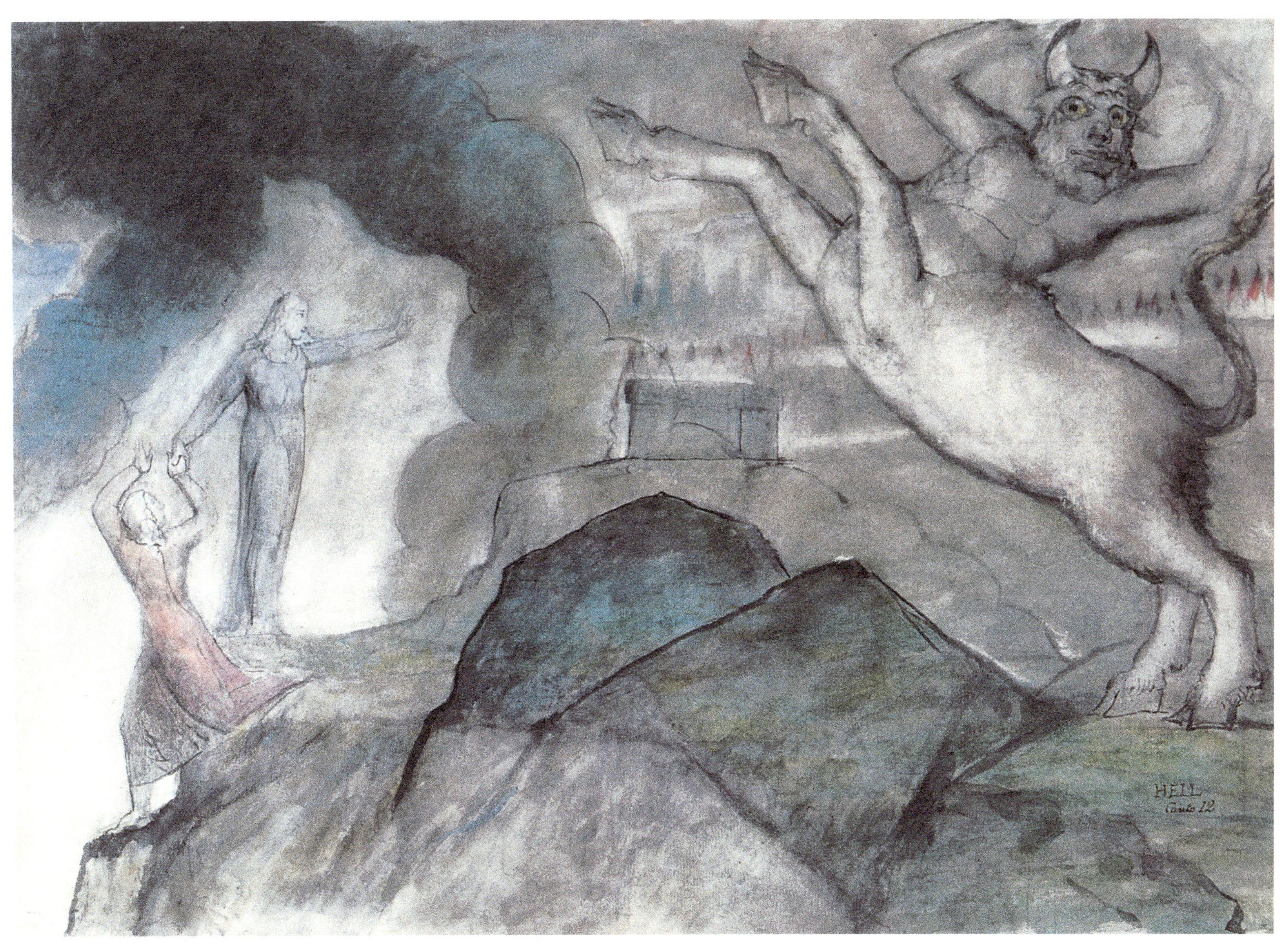

PLATE 23

Dante and Virgil approach the Minotaur, who watches over the souls of the violent in the seventh circle of Hell.
[*Inferno,* Canto 12, lines 12–28]

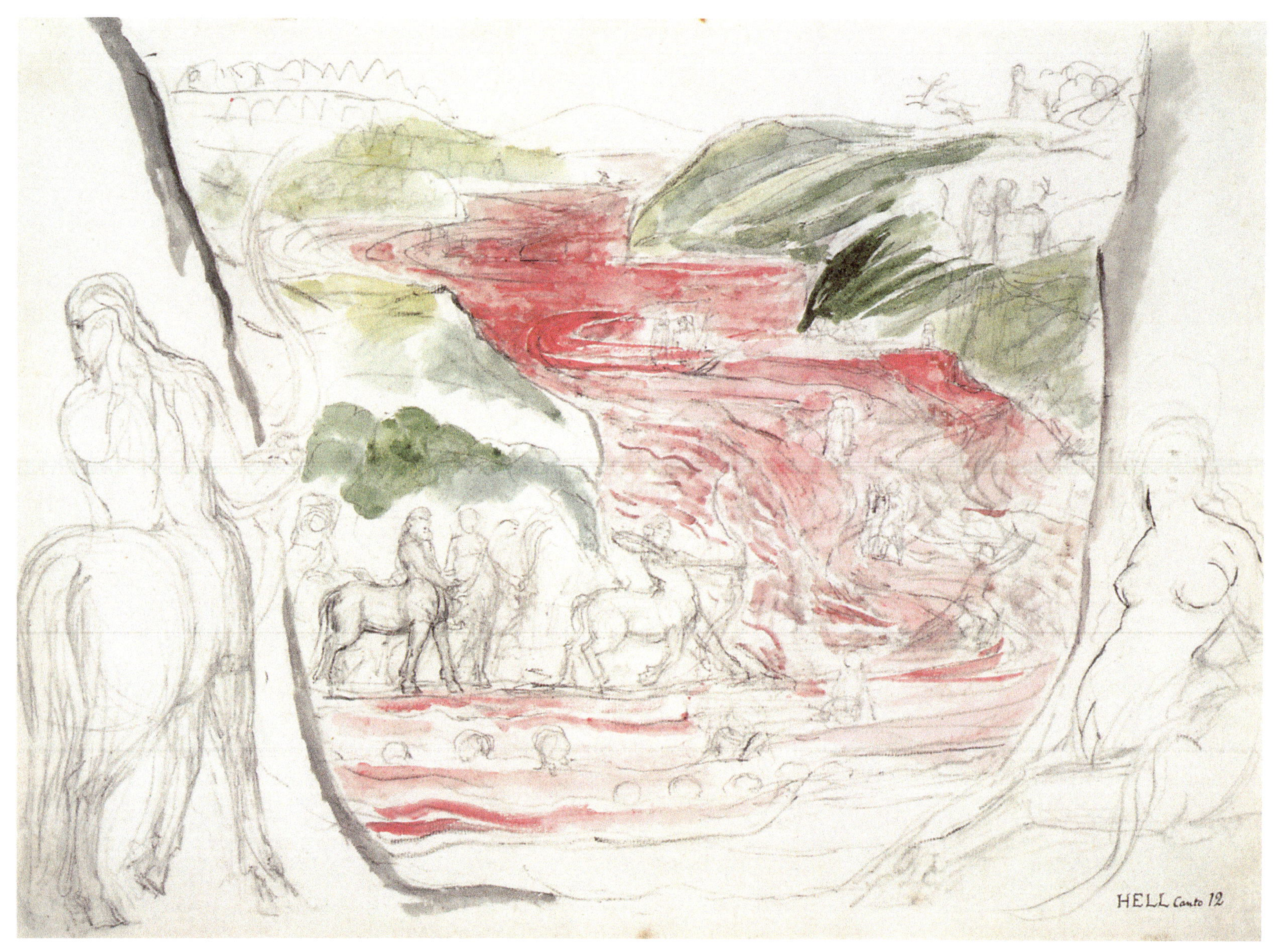

PLATE 24

Two Centaurs, male and female, introduce a scene where the river runs with the blood of the violent. [*Inferno,* Canto 12, lines 44–68]

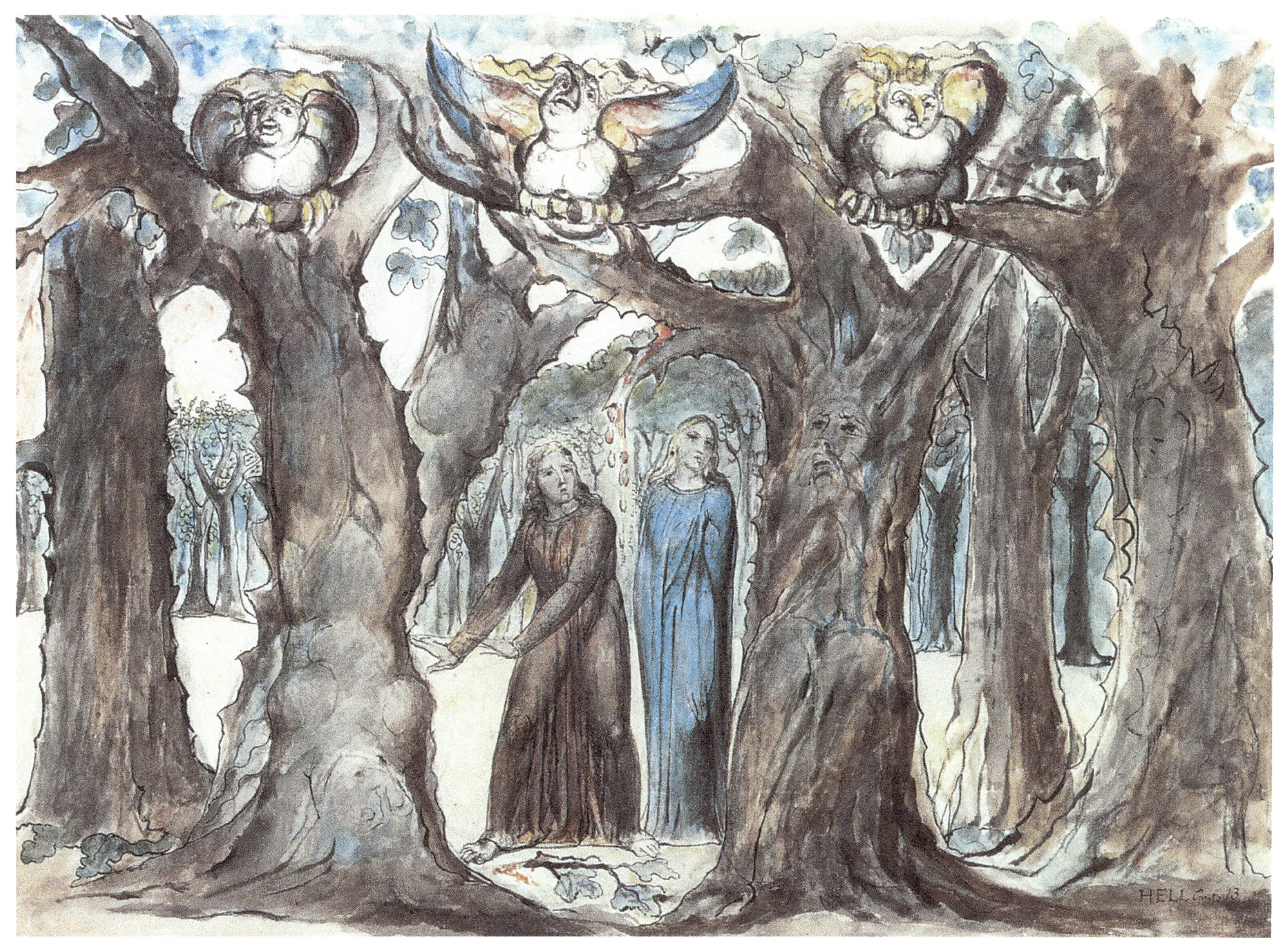

PLATE 25

Harpies roost in trees that once were humans who committed violence against themselves: suicides. [*Inferno,* Canto 13, lines 1–45]

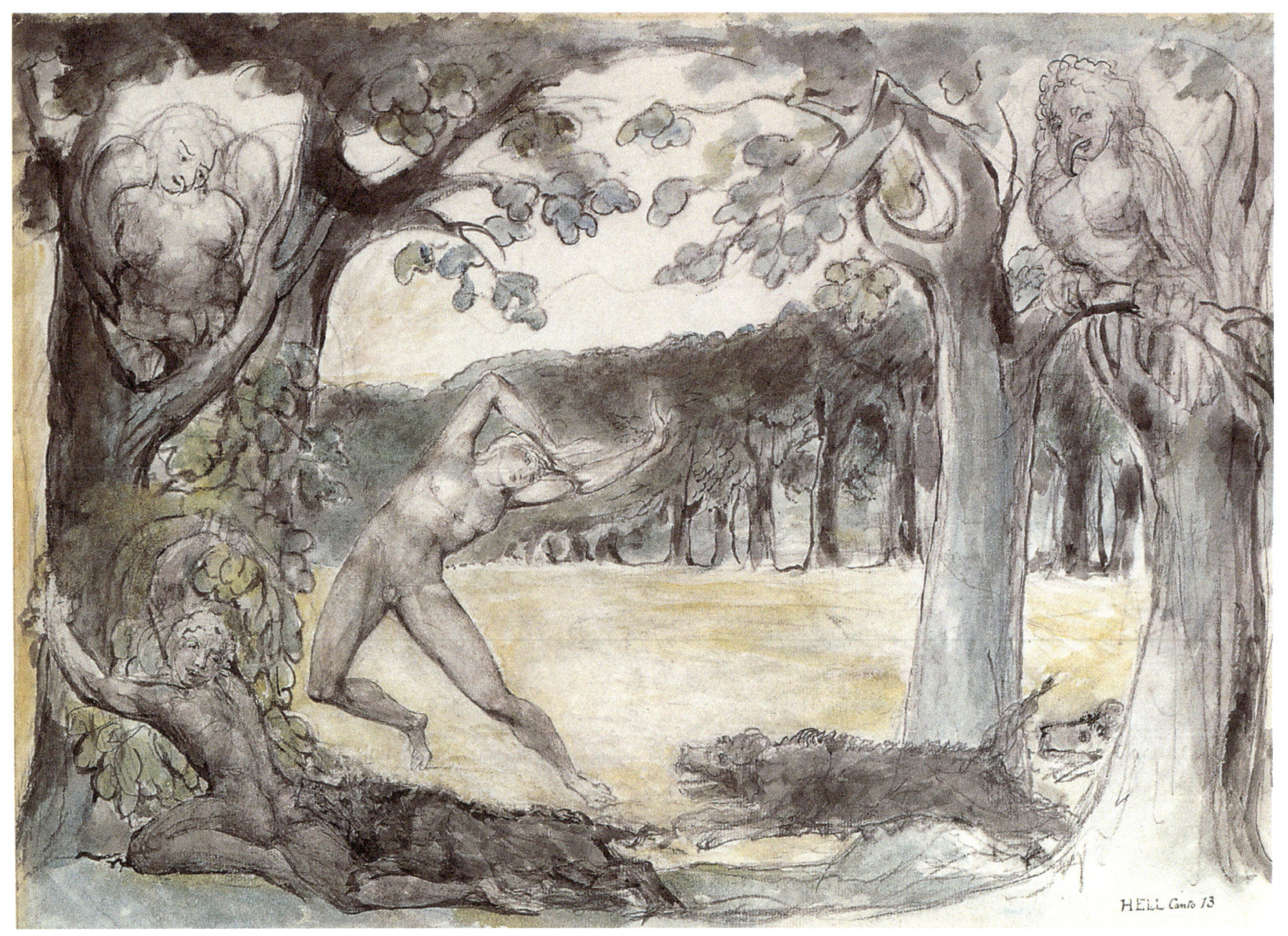

PLATE 26

Lano da Sienna and Giacomo da Sant'Andrea, having wasted their fortunes, are pursued by hell hounds.
[*Inferno,* Canto 13, lines 116–136]

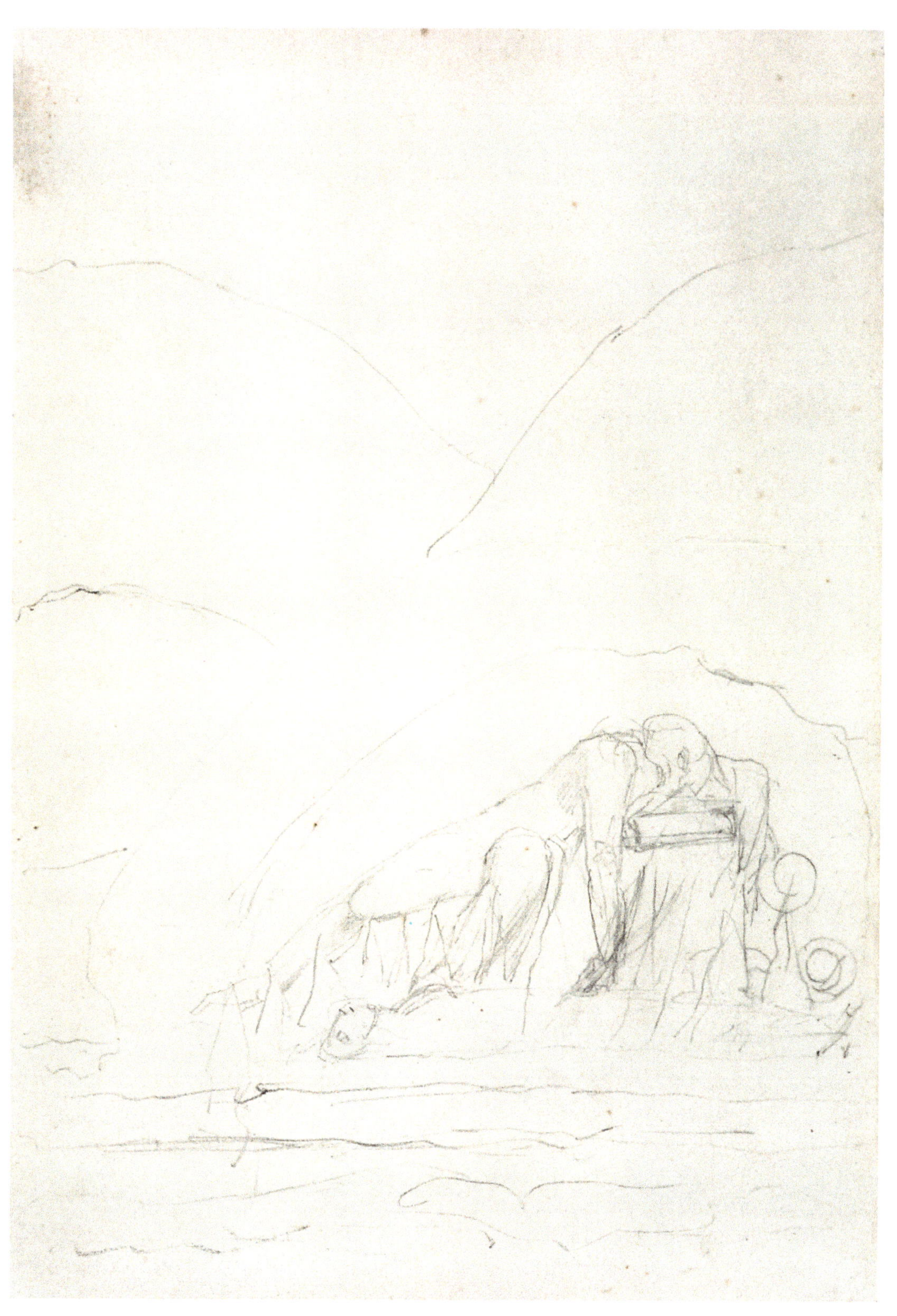

PLATE 27

Blake's sketch of a male figure communicates a weary despair.
[*Inferno,* Canto 14, lines 1–17]

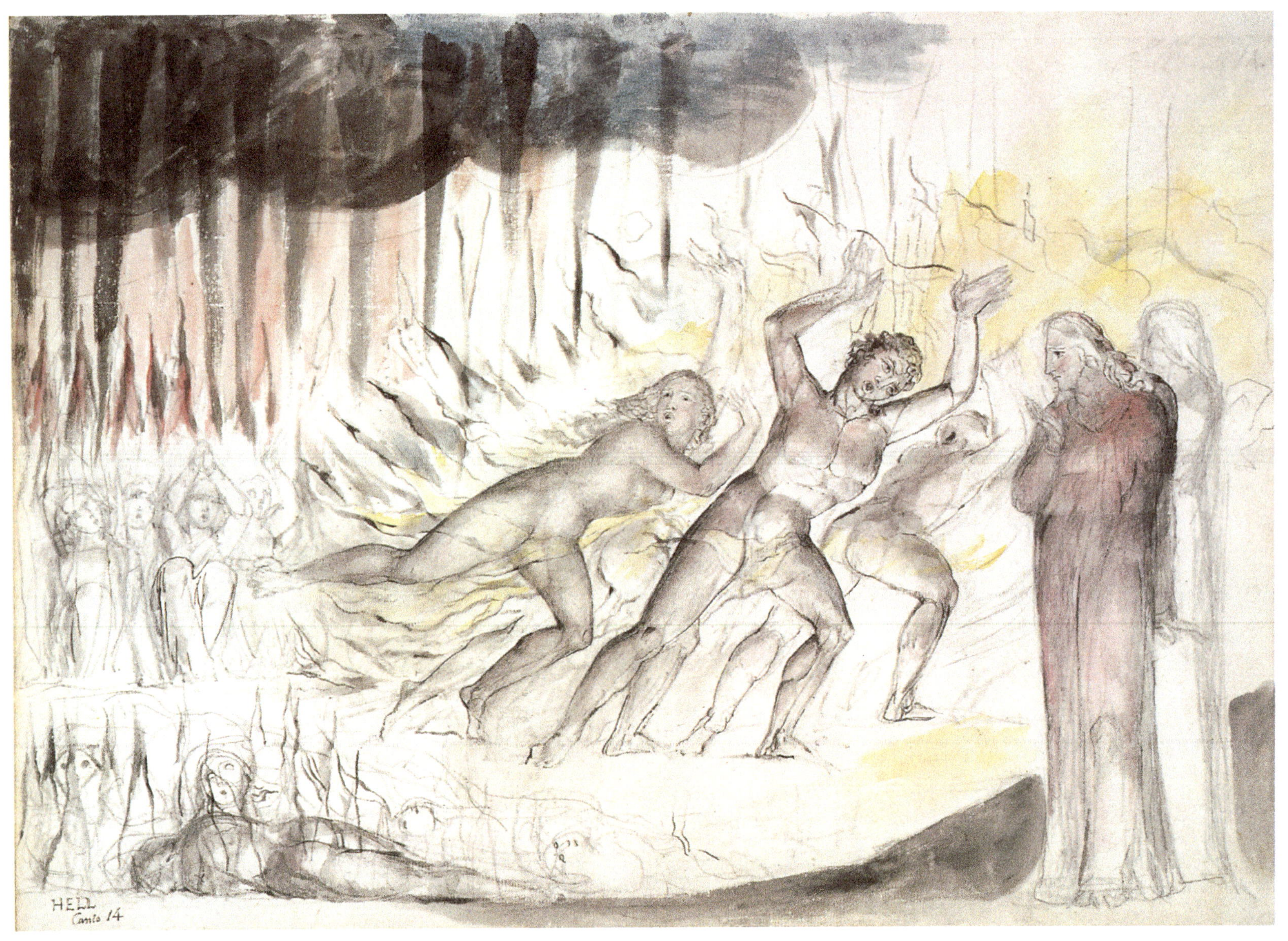

PLATE 28

Under a rain of fire, Dante and Virgil encounter the reclining blasphemers, the sitting usurers, and the pacing sodomites.
[*Inferno,* Canto 14, lines 18–45]

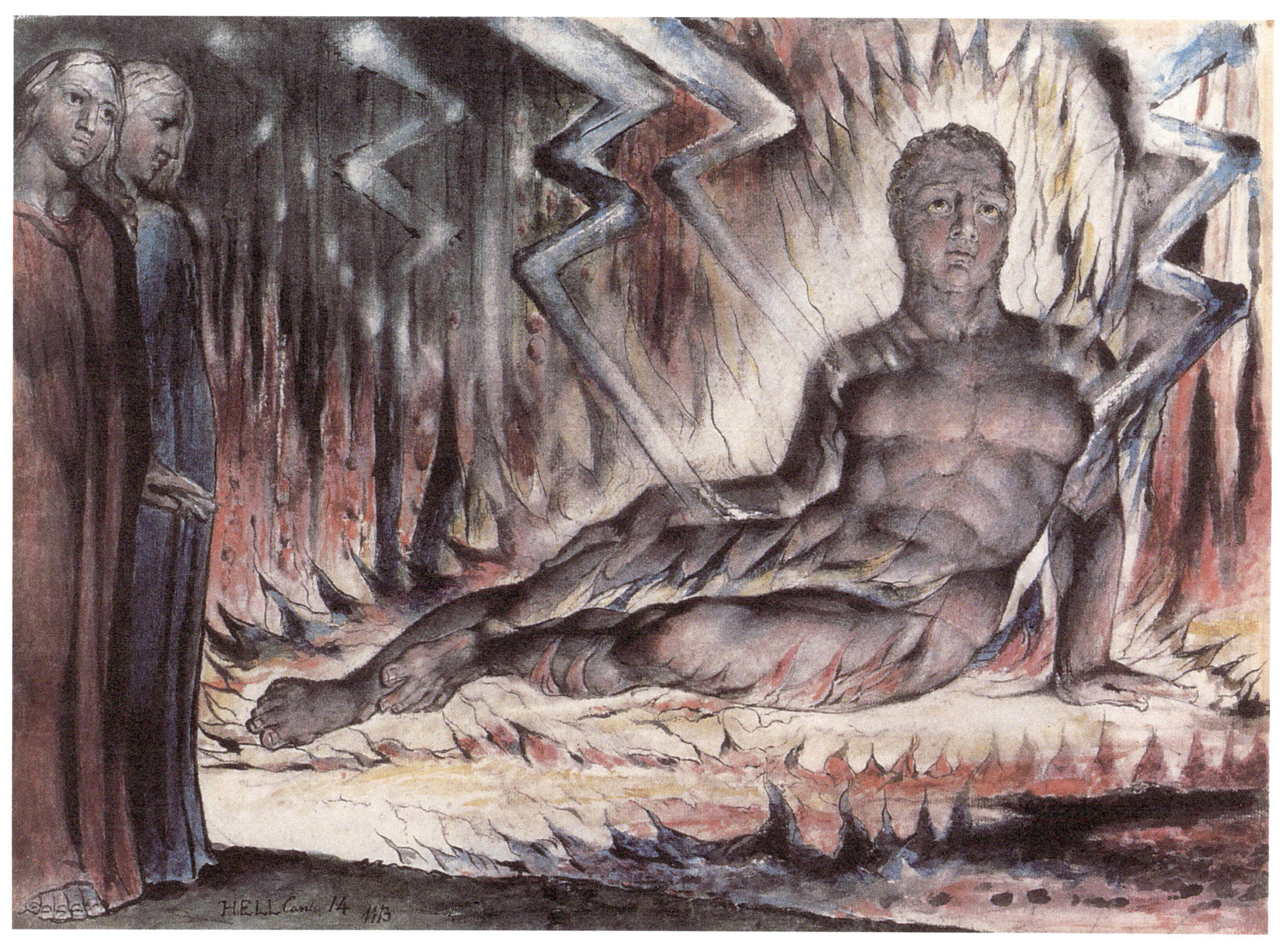

PLATE 29

Dante and Virgil discover the unrepentant Capaneus, whose defiance of Zeus led to his being struck down by lightning bolts.
[*Inferno,* Canto 14, lines 58–68]

PLATE 30

Representing power, this imposing figure is a reference to the concept of empire in the Bible's *Book of Daniel.*
[*Inferno,* Canto 14, lines 96–115]

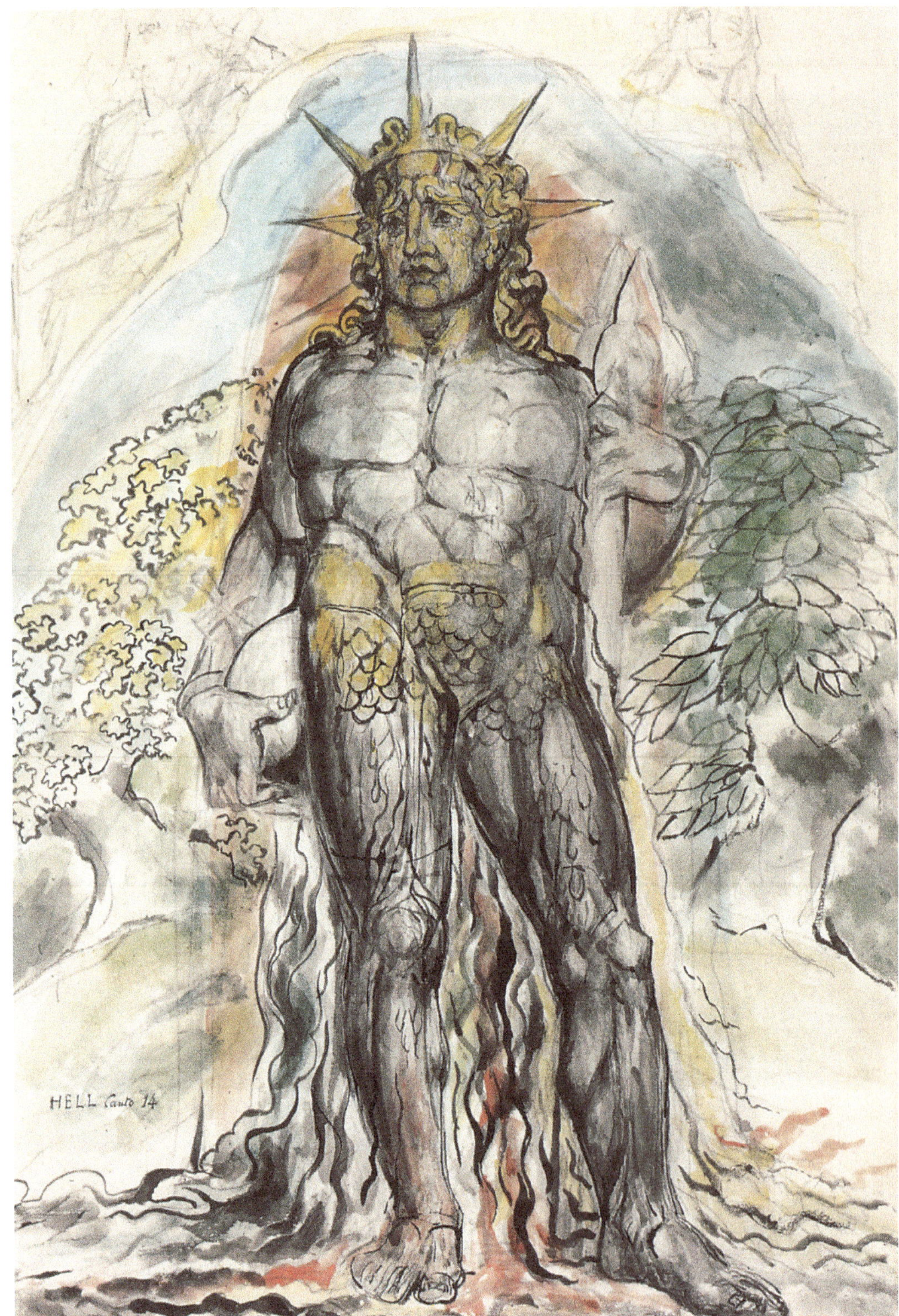

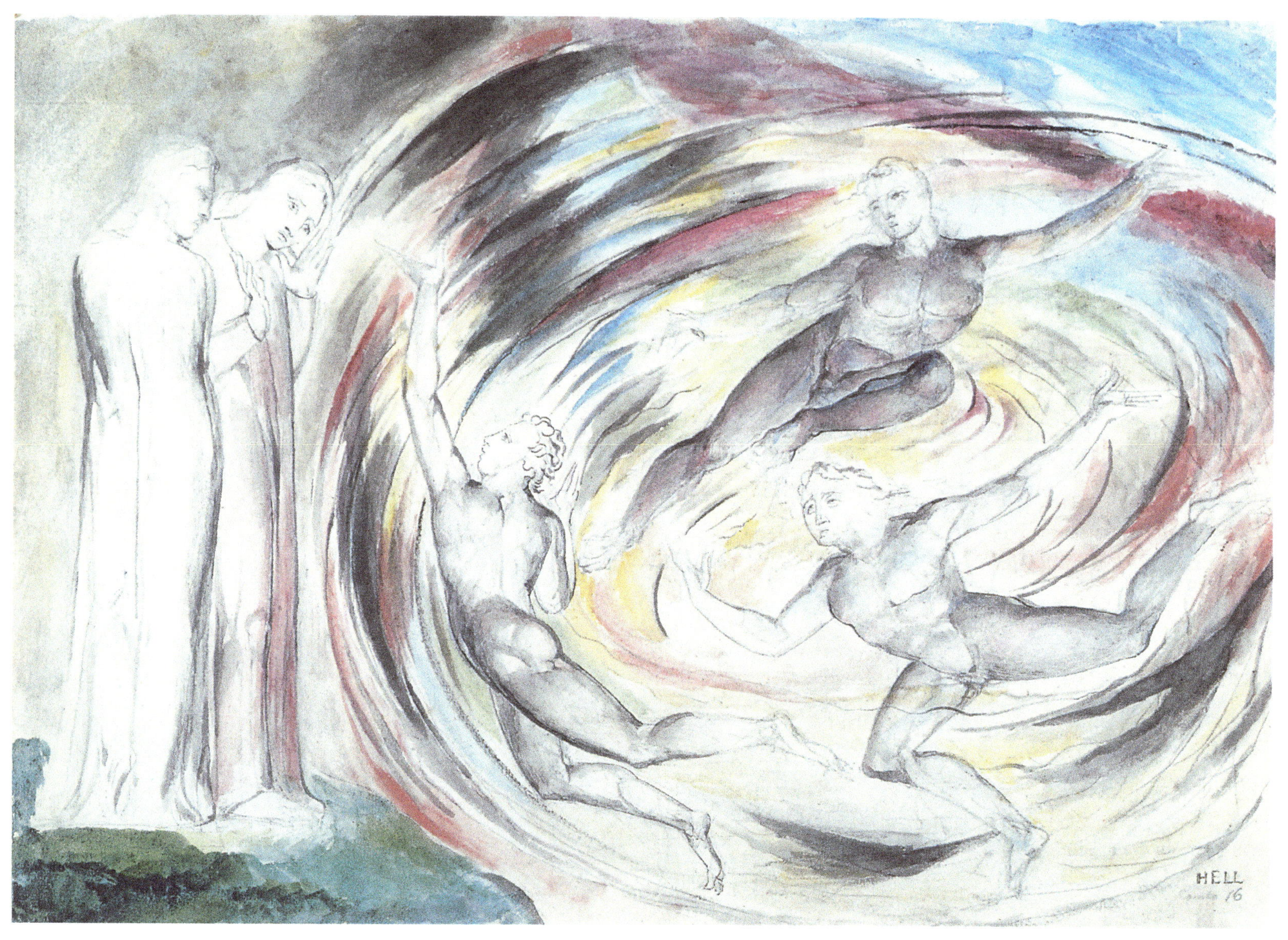

PLATE 31

Dante and Virgil behold the figures of three Florentines, whirling in a "restless wheel."
[*Inferno,* Canto 16, lines 45–85]

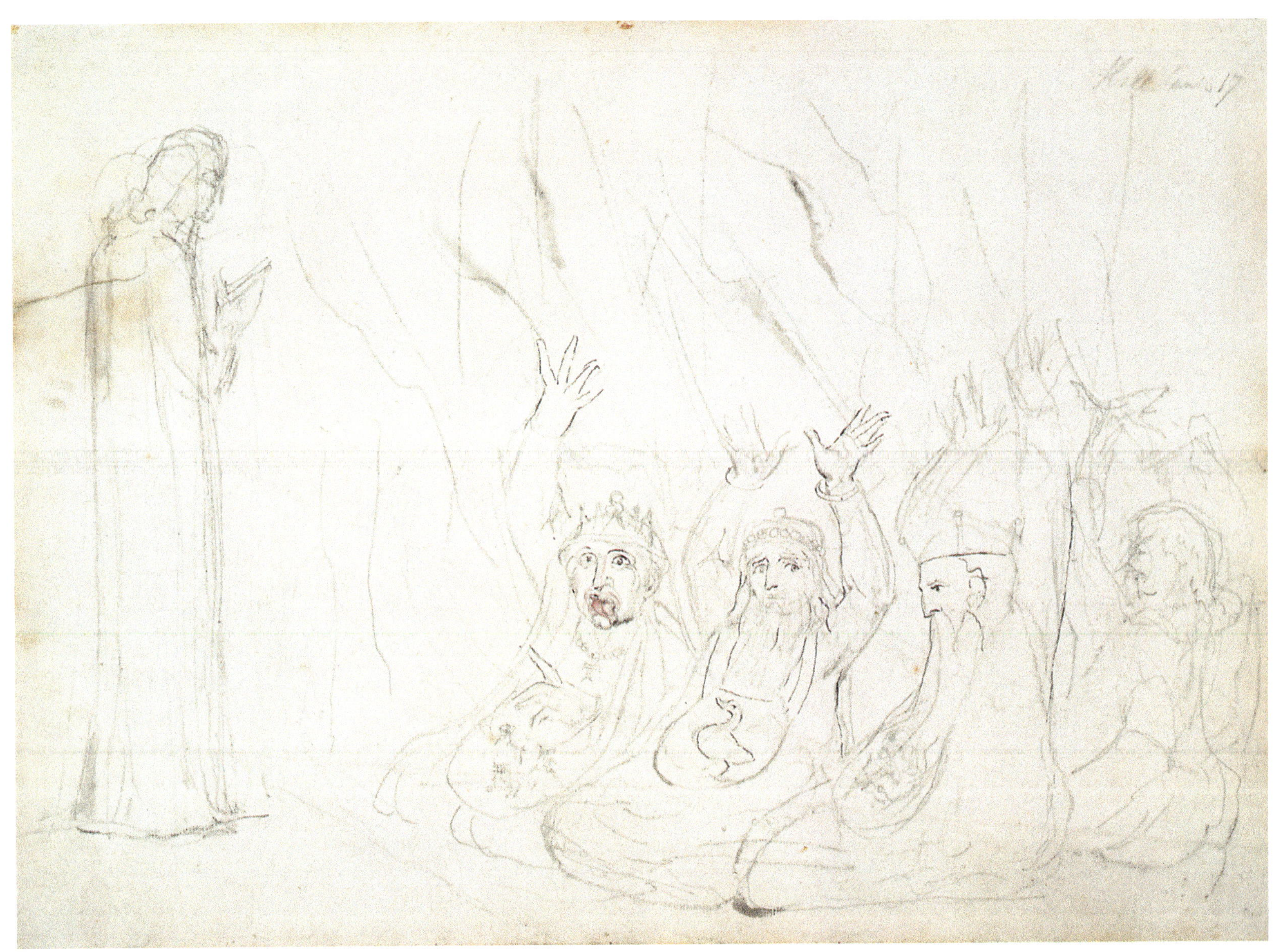

PLATE 32

Usurers are depicted, all representing families of Florence and Padua.
[*Inferno,* Canto 17, lines 34–55]

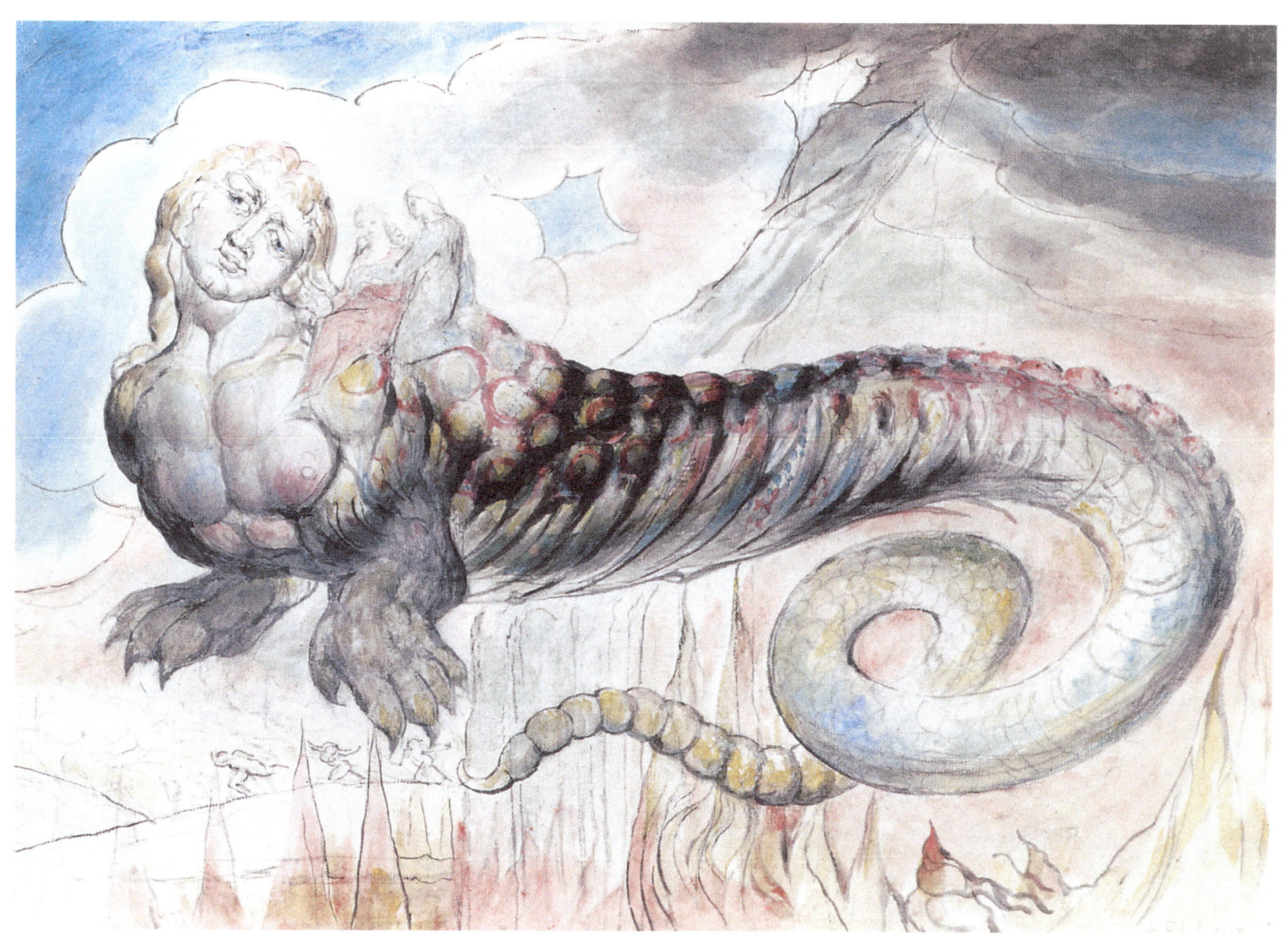

PLATE 33

Dante and Virgil descend into Hell, carried on the back of the serpent Geryon.
[*Inferno,* Canto 17, lines 72–77]

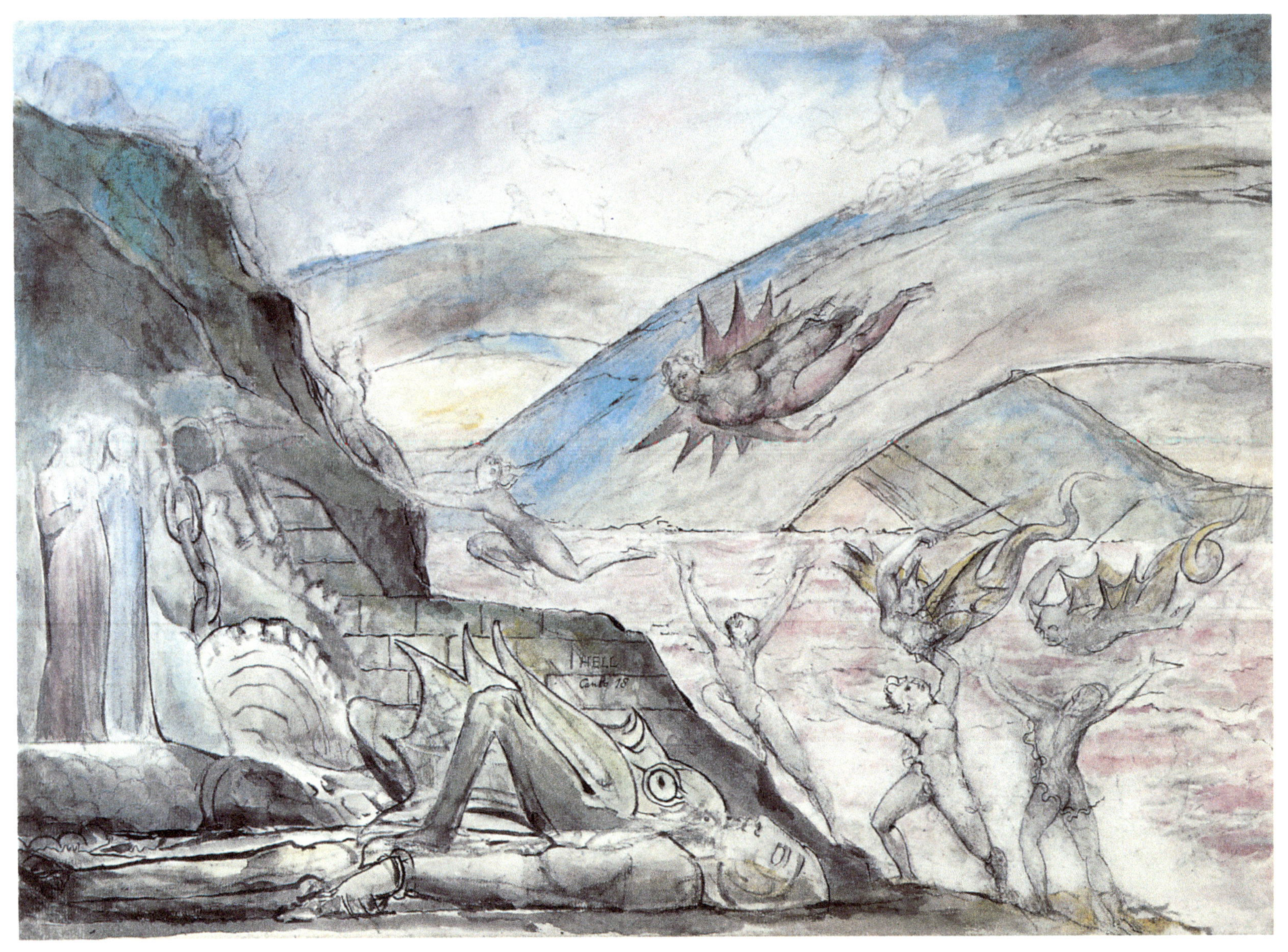

PLATE 34

In the eighth circle of Hell, naked seducers are tormented by horned demons.
[*Inferno,* Canto 18, lines 23–100]

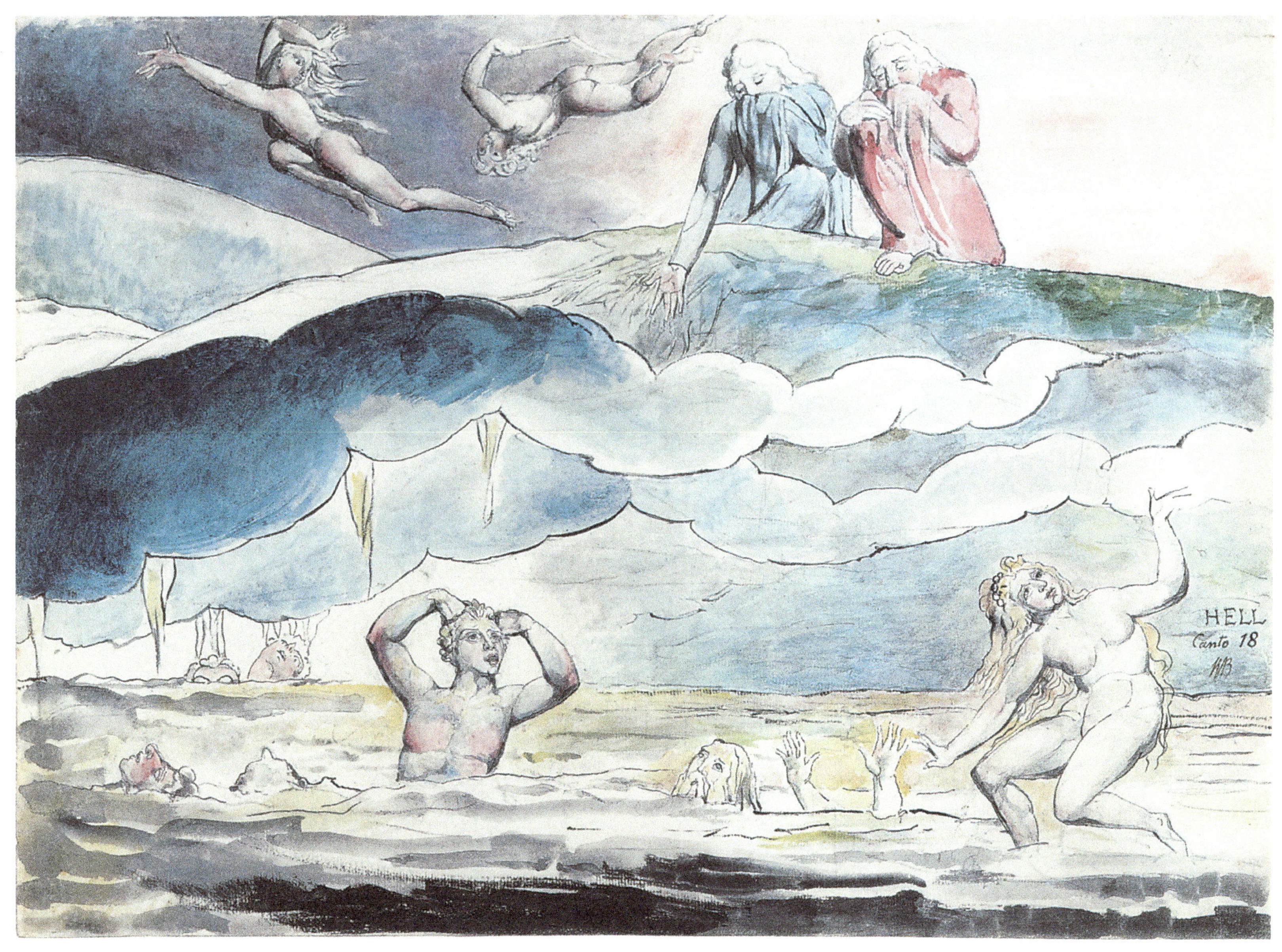

Plate 35

Dante and Virgil, in the eighth circle, witness flatterers mired in a ditch of dung.
[*Inferno,* Canto 18, lines 101–133]

Plate 36

Clergy guilty of simony are punished in a vat of fire.
[*Inferno,* Canto 19, lines 42 120]

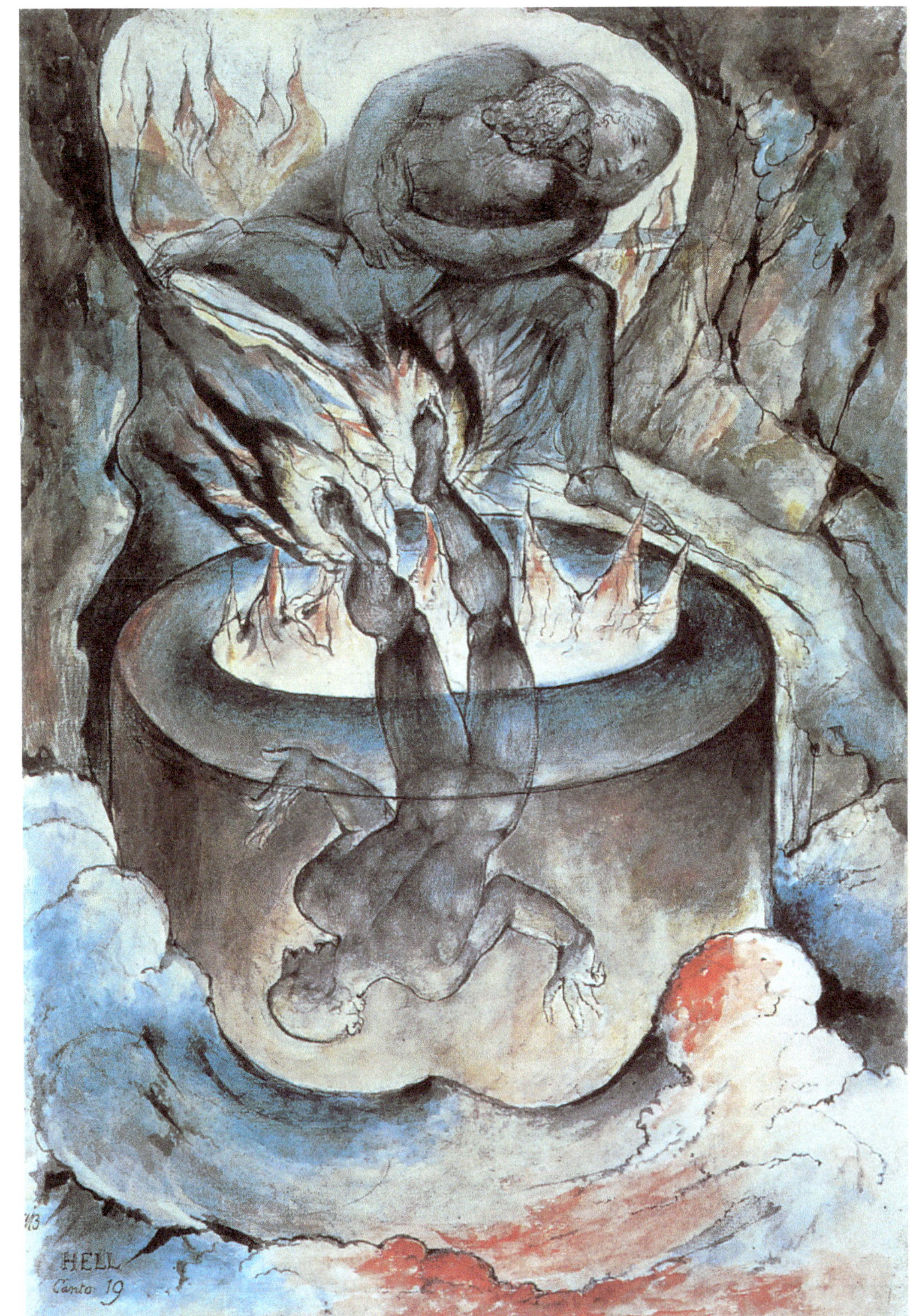

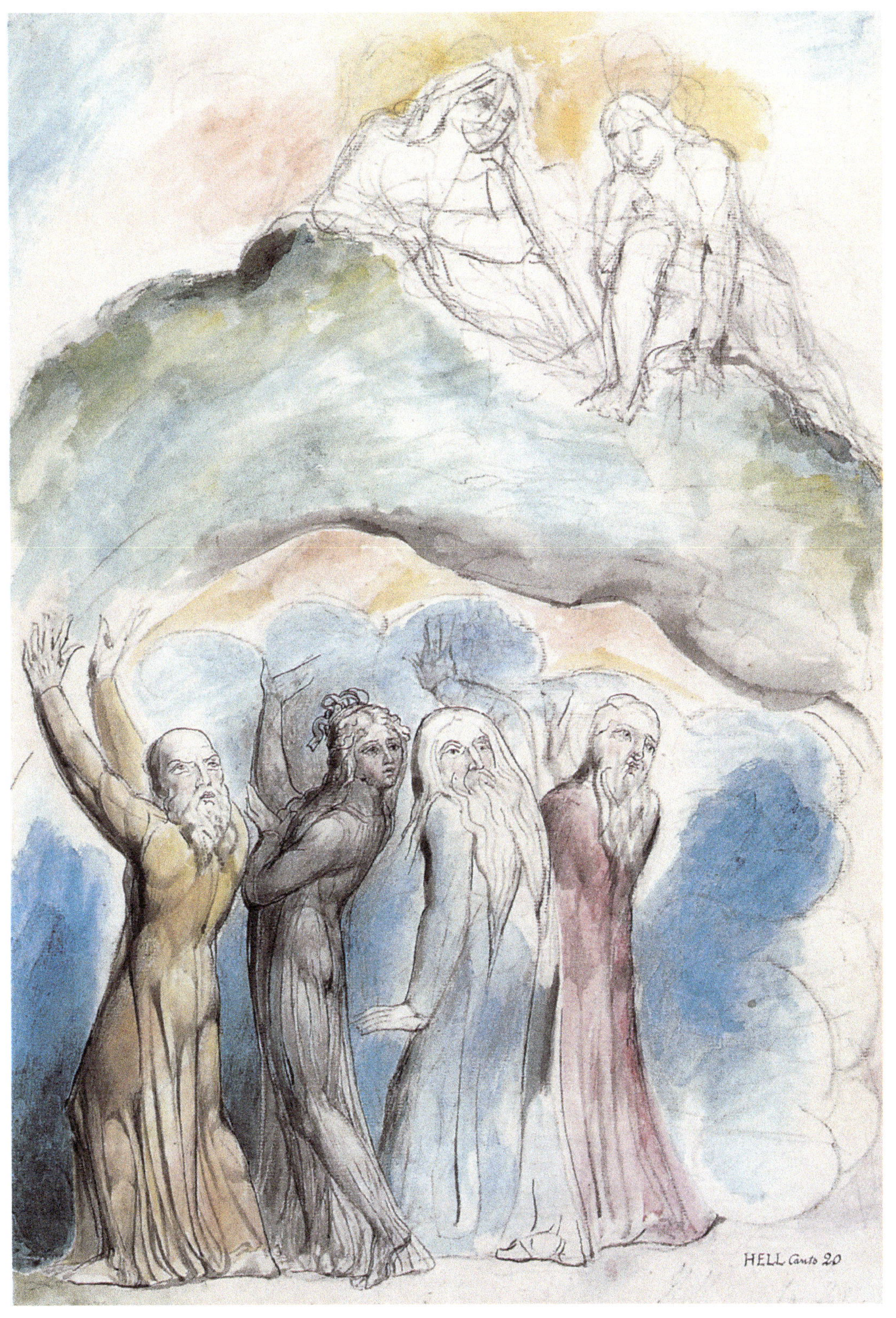

Plate 37

The punishment of necromancers, including Manto, the daughter of Tiresias, is to have their heads turned from front to back. [*Inferno,* Canto 20, lines 4–115]

PLATE 38

Dante and Virgil view a lake of pitch, into which those who exploit their public offices are hurled.
[*Inferno,* Canto 21, lines 28–38]

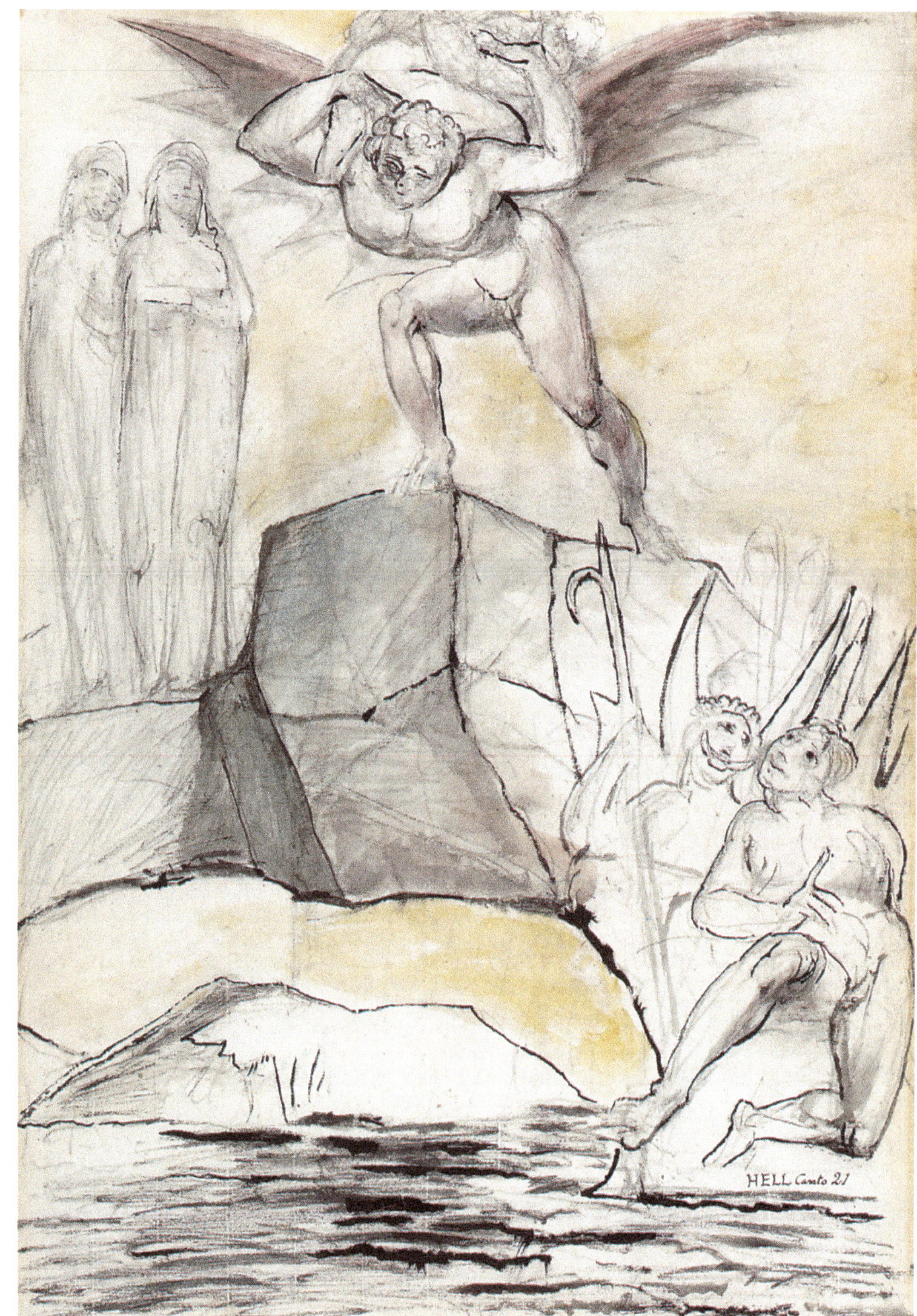

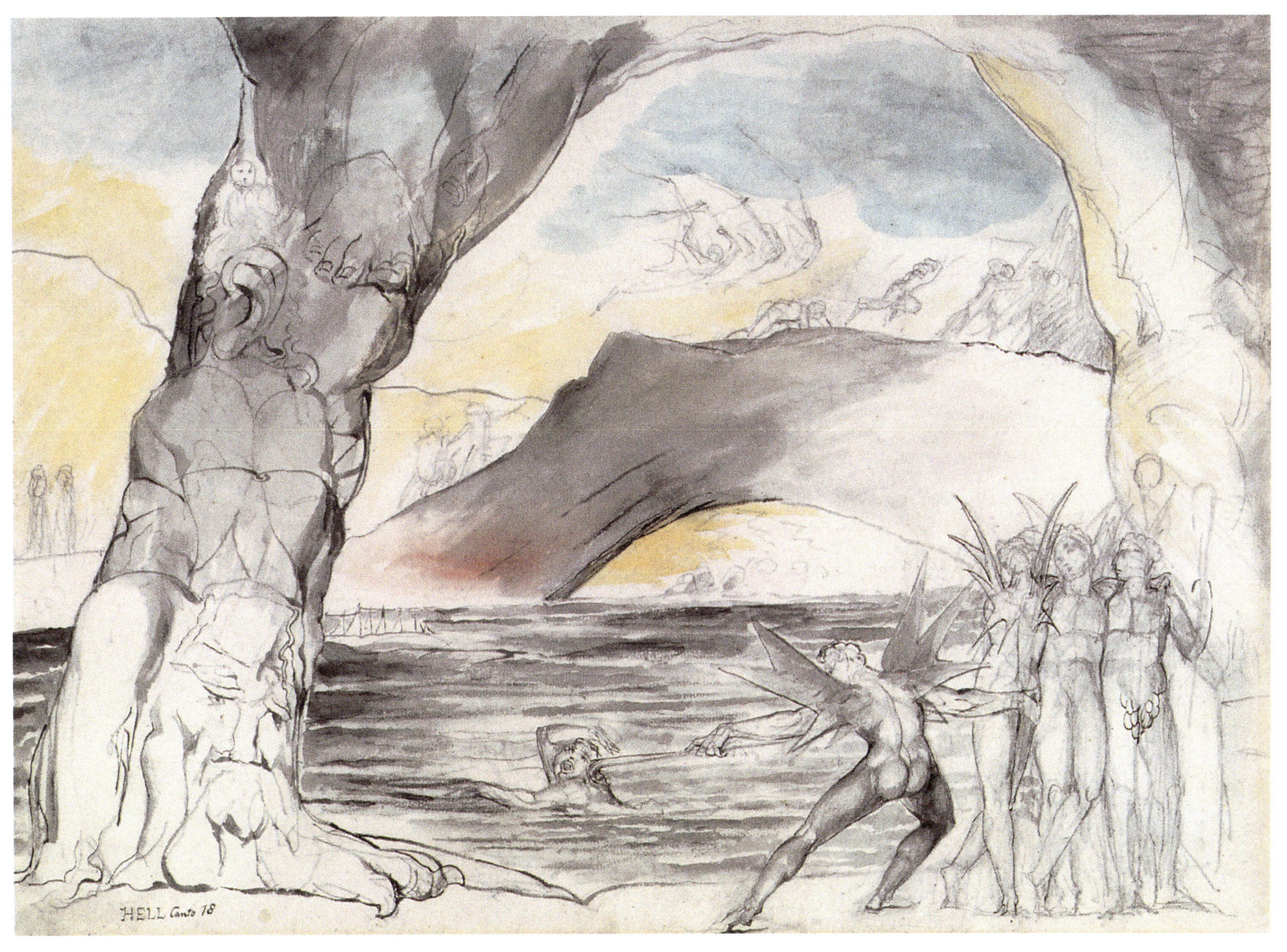

PLATE 39

Beneath a bridge made of human fragments, devils torment a corrupt public official.
[*Inferno,* Canto 21, lines 46–56]

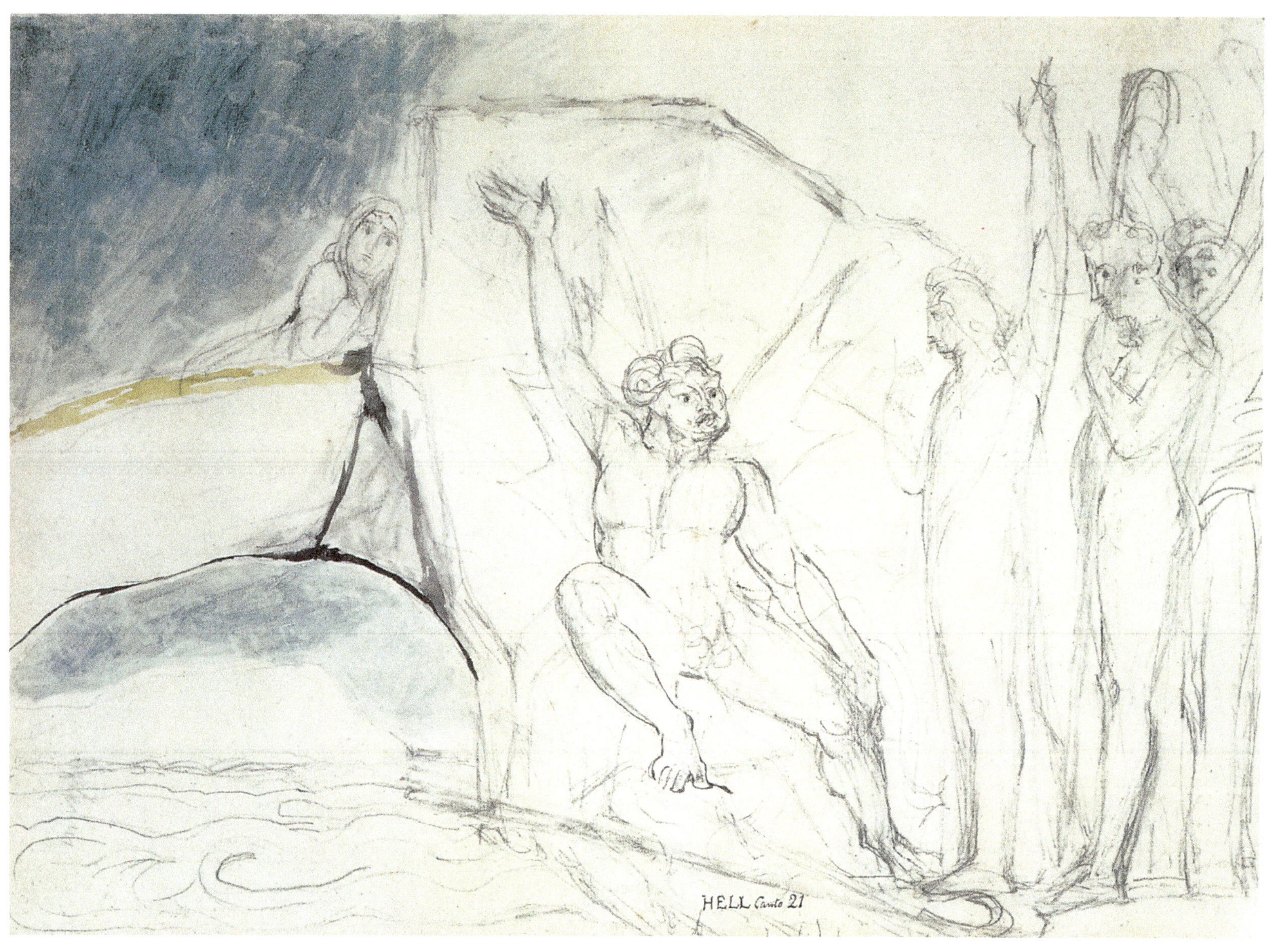

PLATE 40

While Dante listens, Virgil proclaims that he and his companion to the underworld enjoy divine protection.
[*Inferno,* Canto 21, lines 73–88]

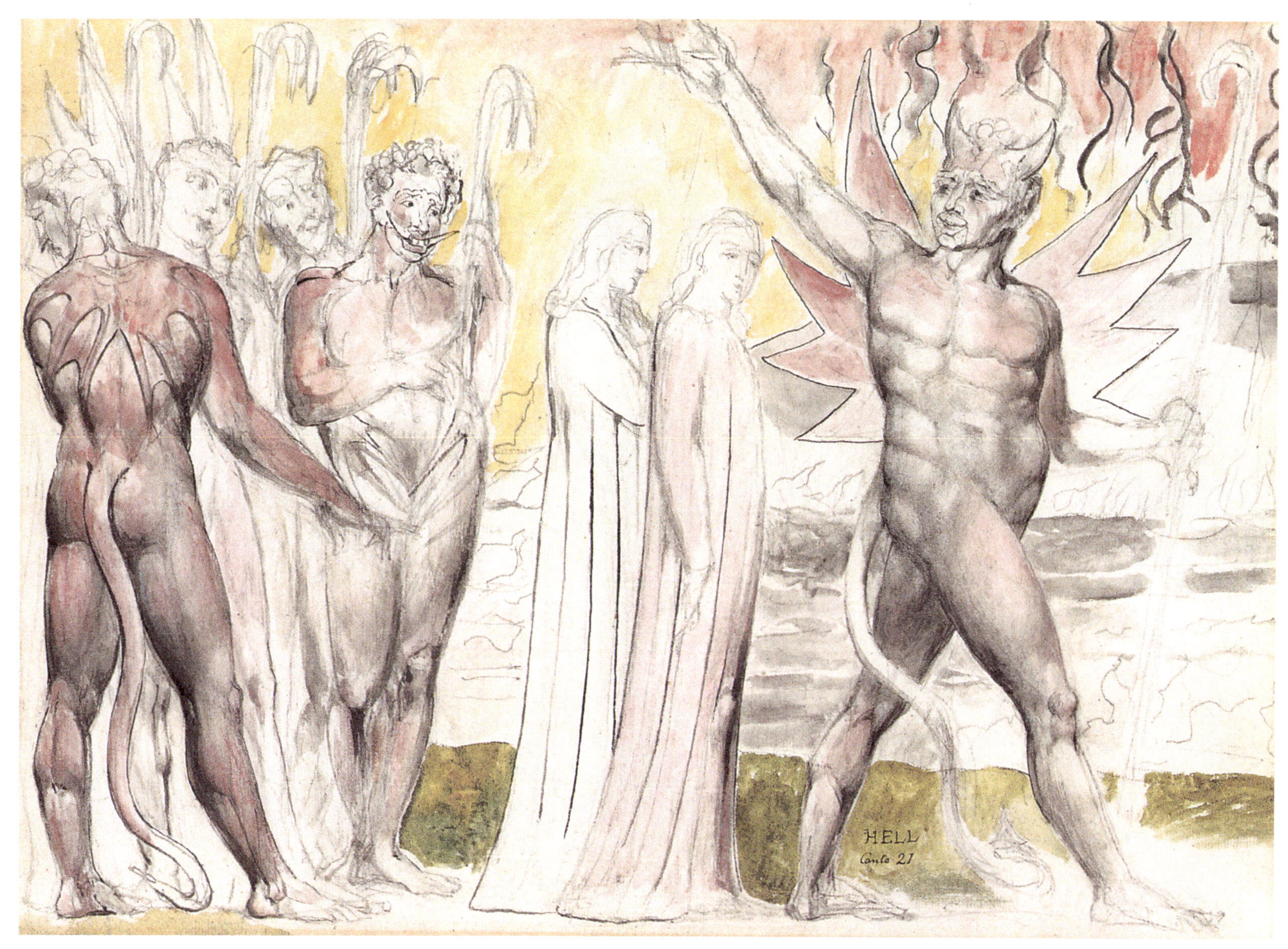

PLATE 41

A cohort of devils provide an escort for Dante and Virgil.
[*Inferno,* Canto 21, lines 118–124]

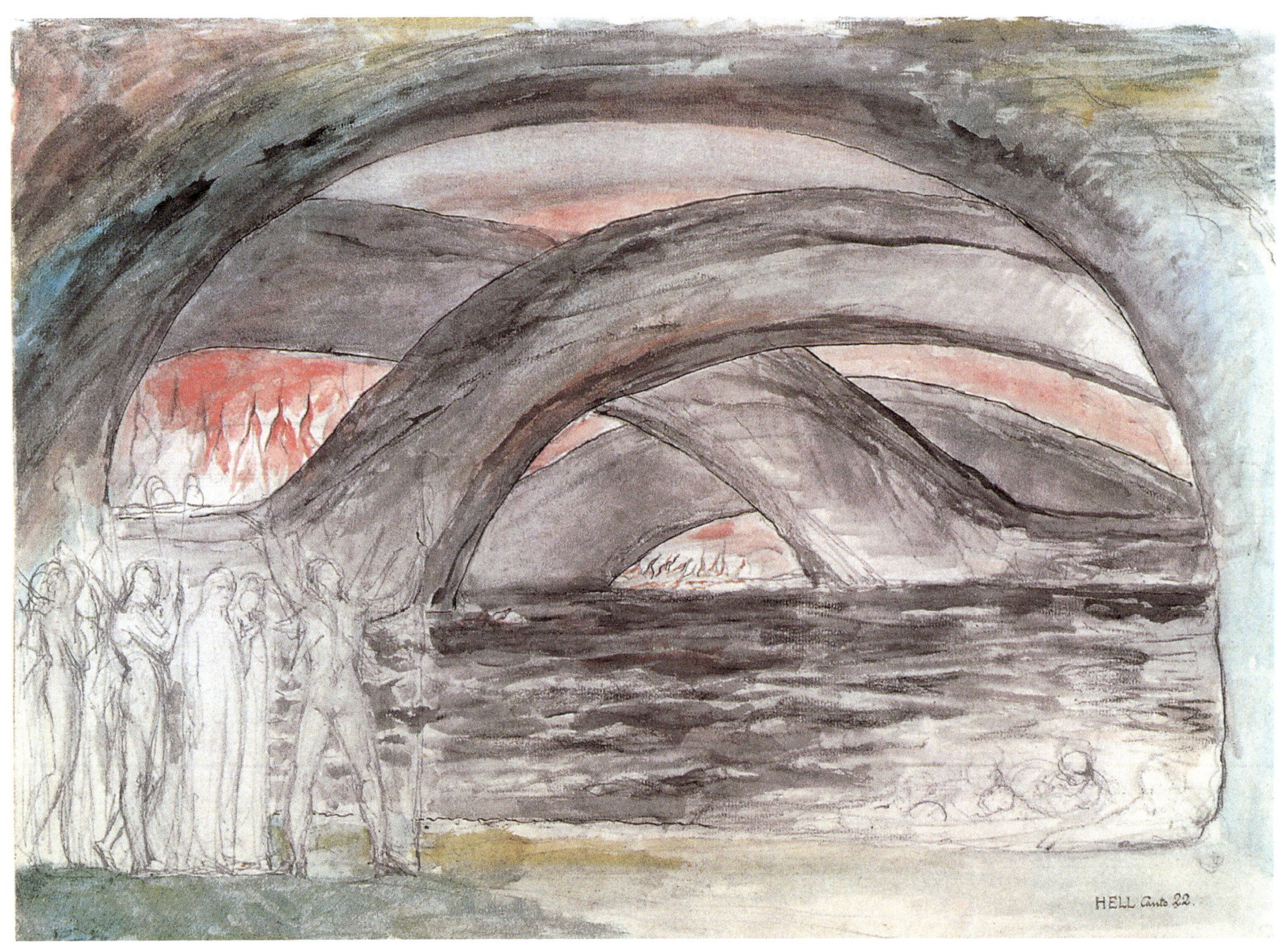

PLATE 42

Dante, Virgil, and their demonic escort behold the lake of burning pitch.
[*Inferno,* Canto 22, lines 1–26]

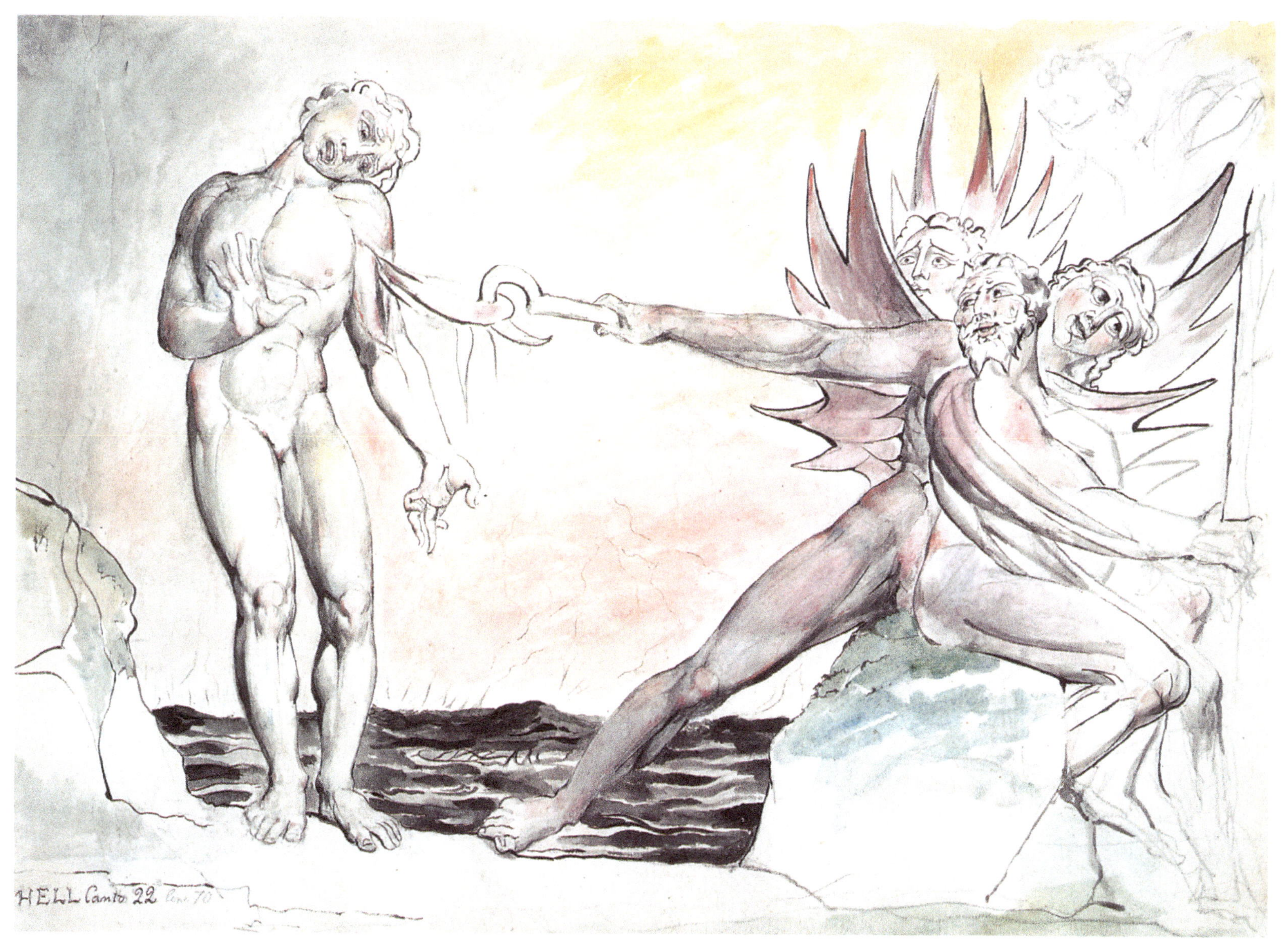

PLATE 43

A corrupt public servant, Ciampolo, is attacked by the devil Libicocco.
[*Inferno,* Canto 22, lines 43–72]

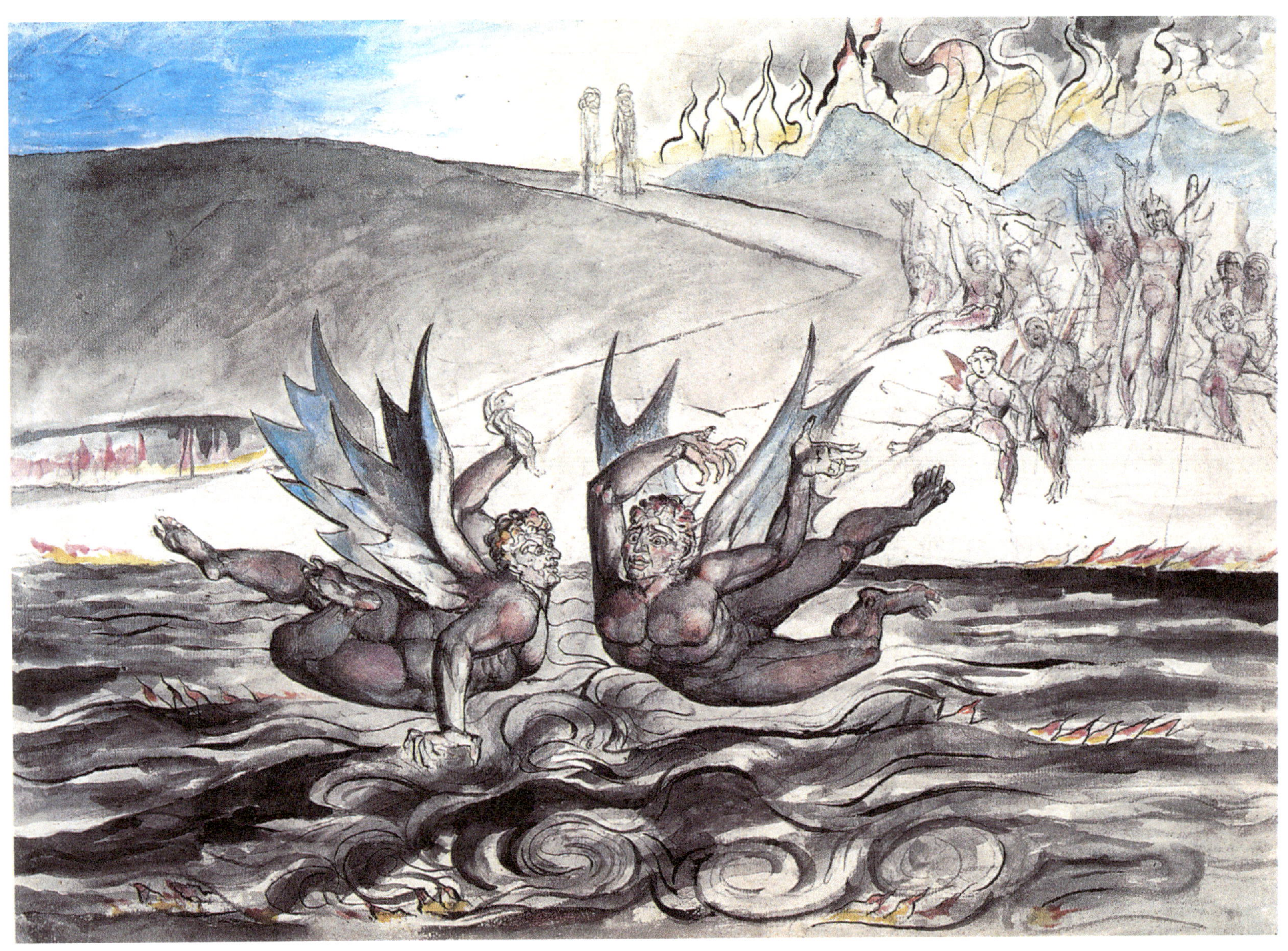

PLATE 44

Dante and Virgil exit, as a pair of devils engage in battle.
[*Inferno,* Canto 22, lines 125–148]

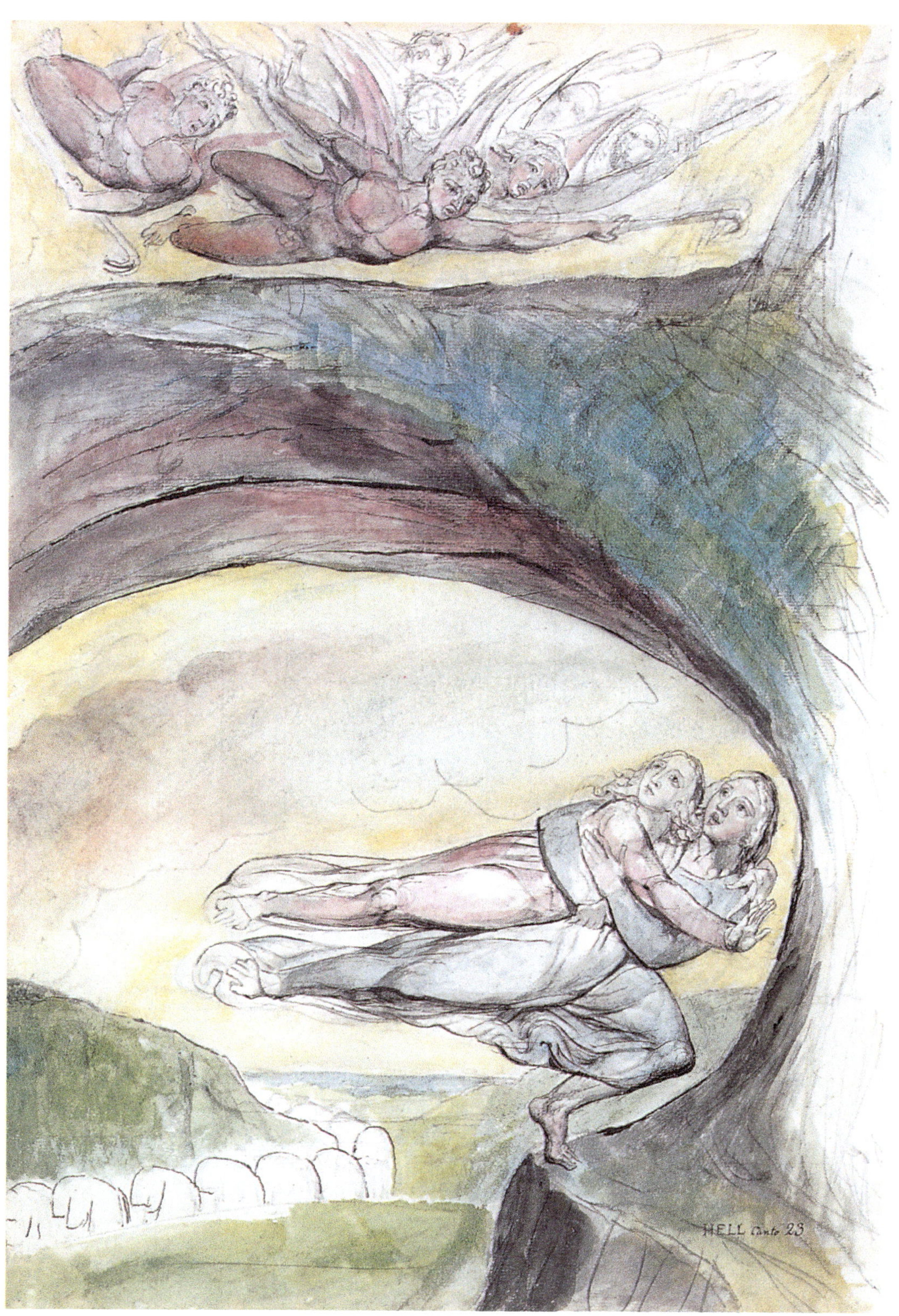

PLATE 45

As the devils pursue them, Dante and Virgil escape to a gulf inhabited by hypocrites. [*Inferno,* Canto 23, lines 36–52]

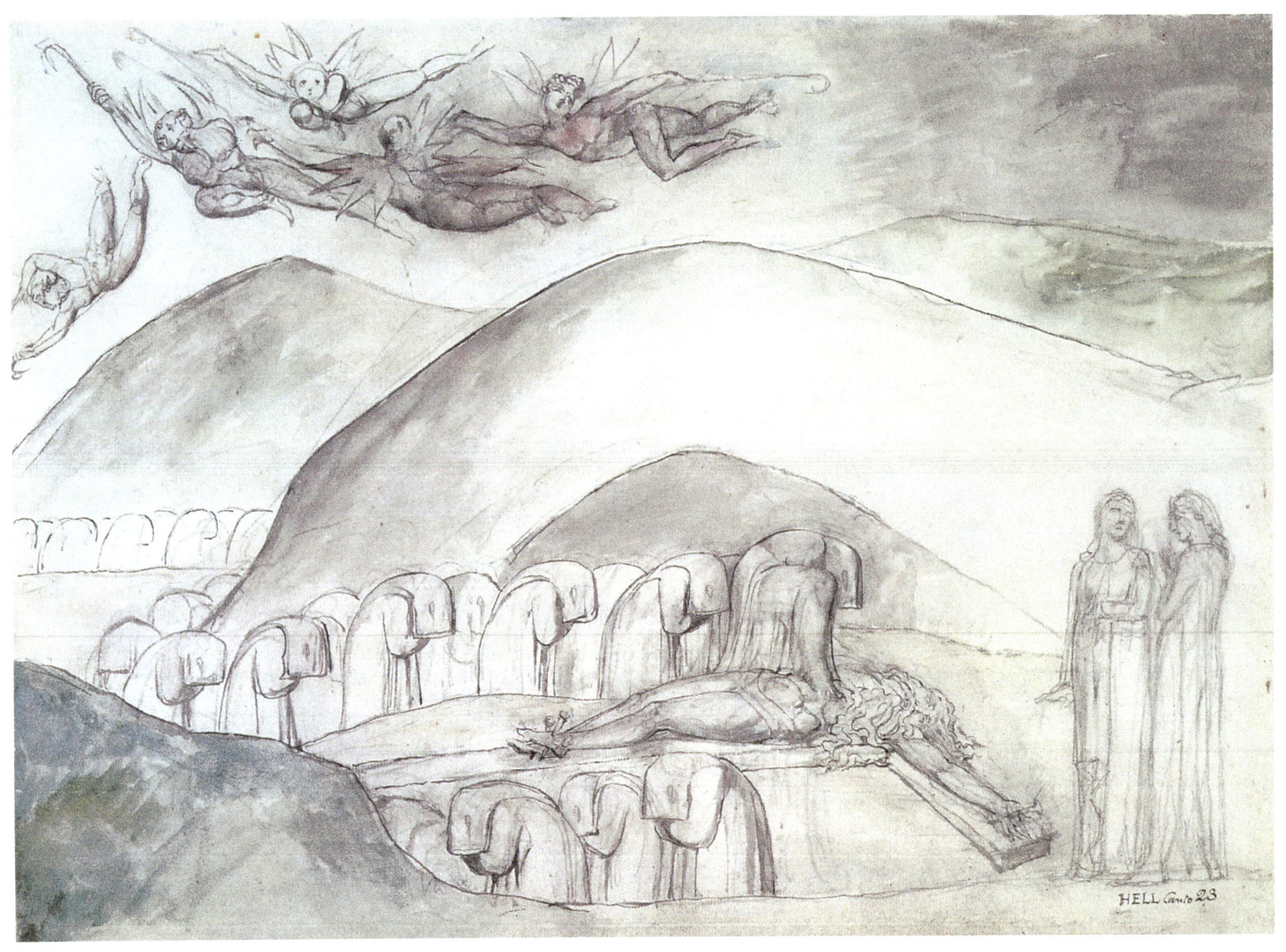

PLATE 46

The hypocrites, including the crucified Caiaphas, are depicted beneath the flight of devils.
[*Inferno,* Canto 23, lines 58–142]

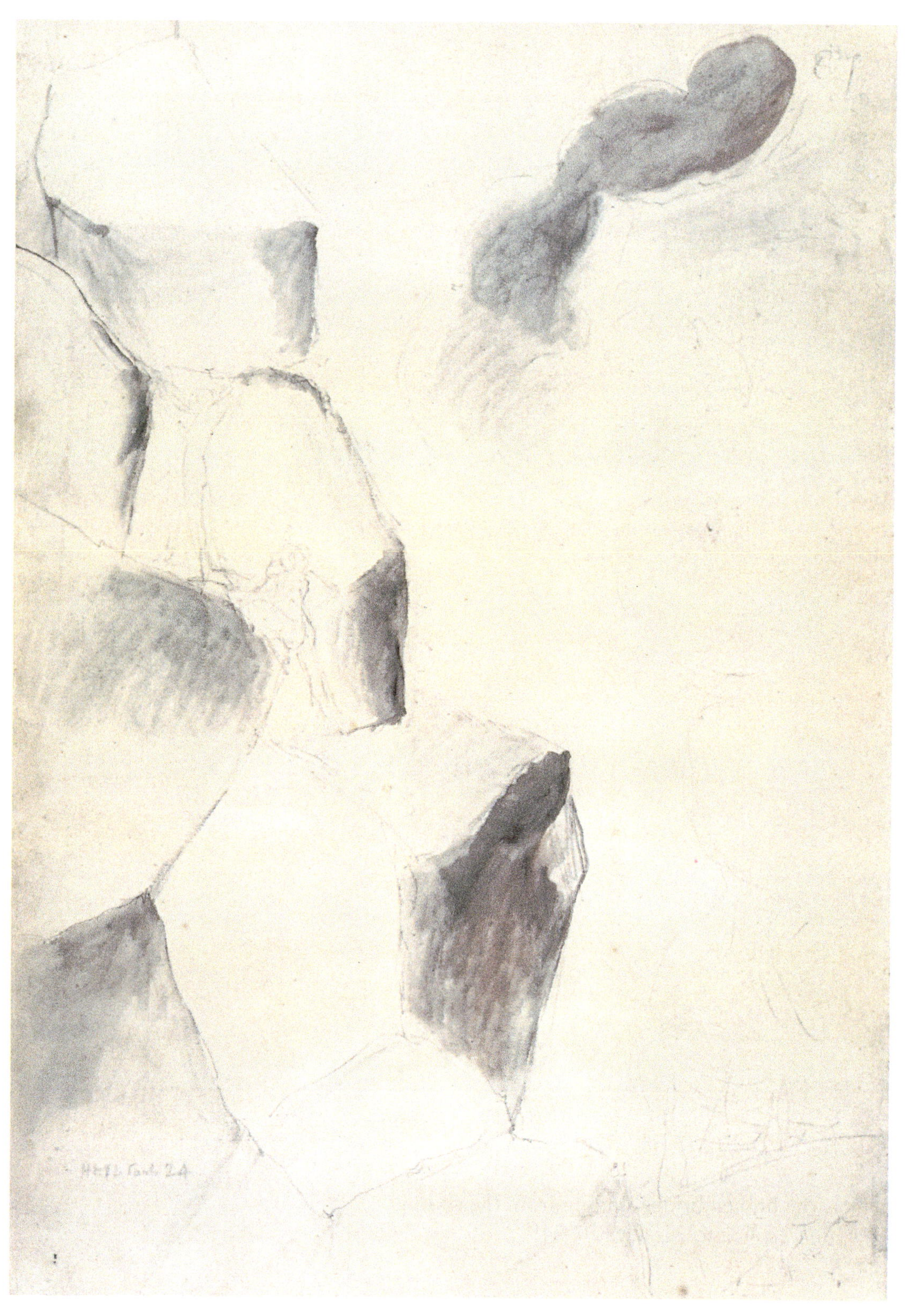

PLATE 47

Huge boulders provide a passageway out of the sixth gulf.
[*Inferno,* Canto 24, lines 20–34]

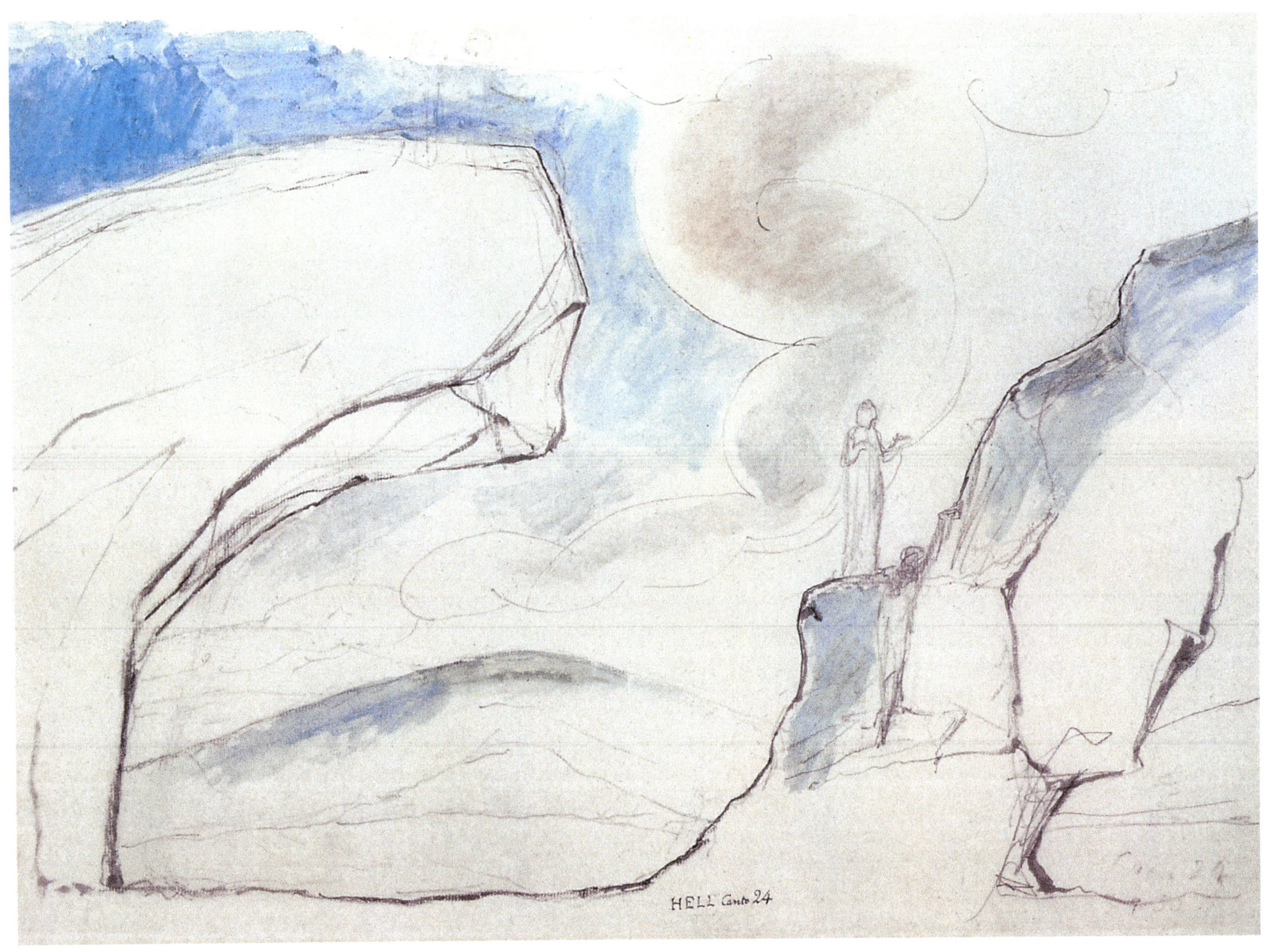

PLATE 48

This sketch depicts the broken bridge leading from the sixth gulf.
[*Inferno,* Canto 24, lines 20–34]

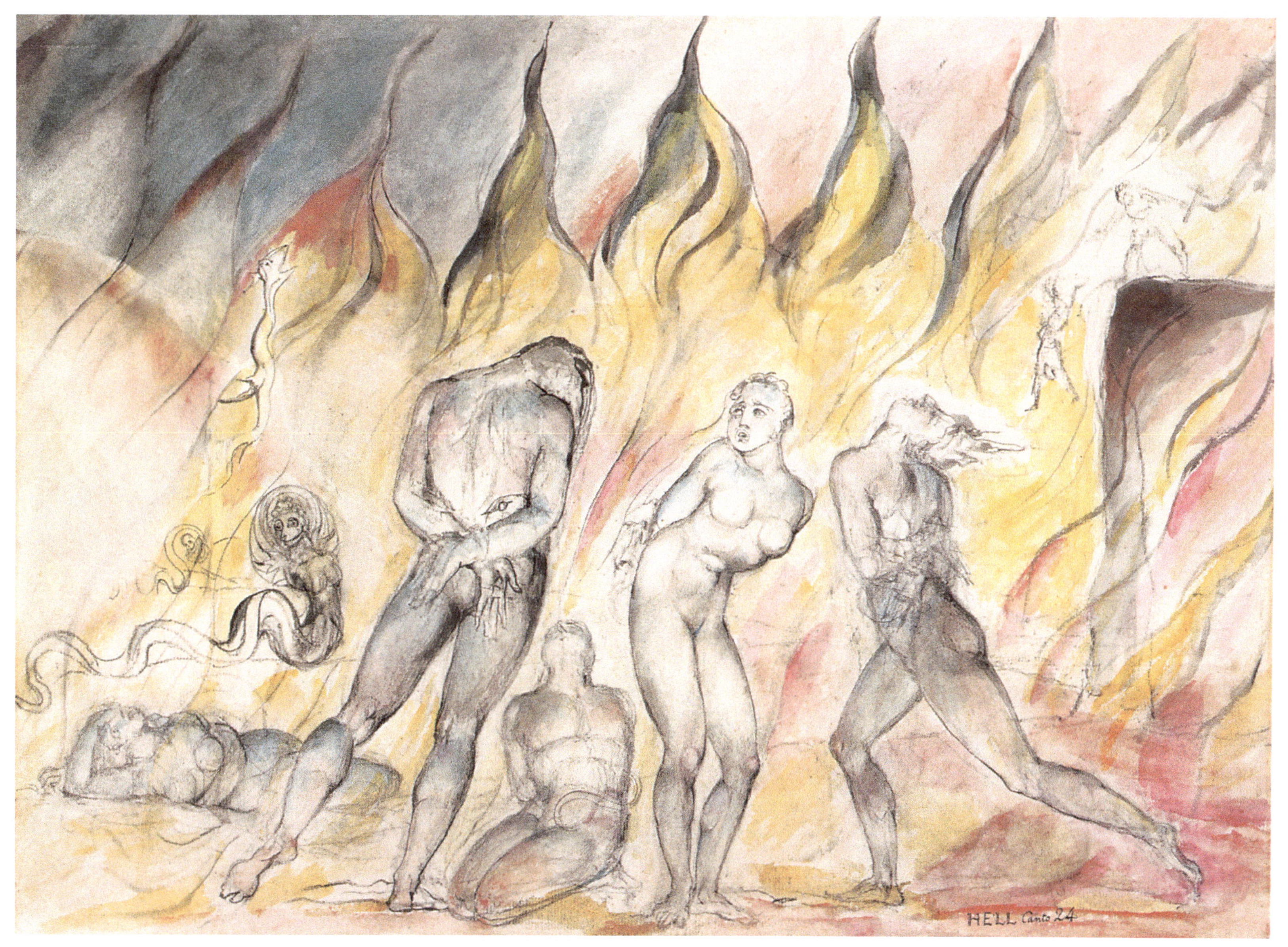

PLATE 49

Five thieves—possibly representing the five senses—are tormented by serpents.
[*Inferno,* Canto 24, lines 88–100]

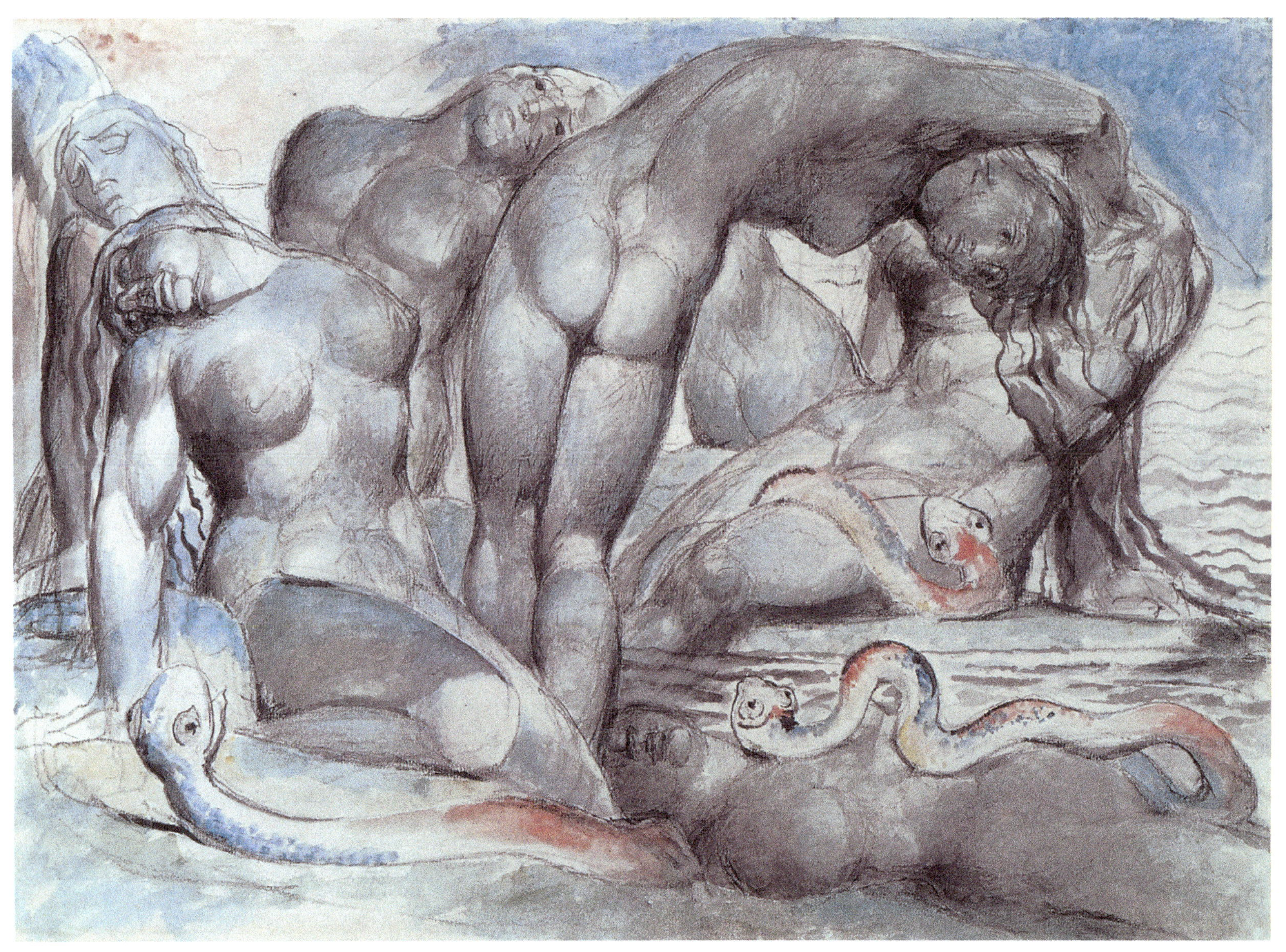

PLATE 50

The serpents attack the five thieves.
[*Inferno,* Canto 24, lines 88–100]

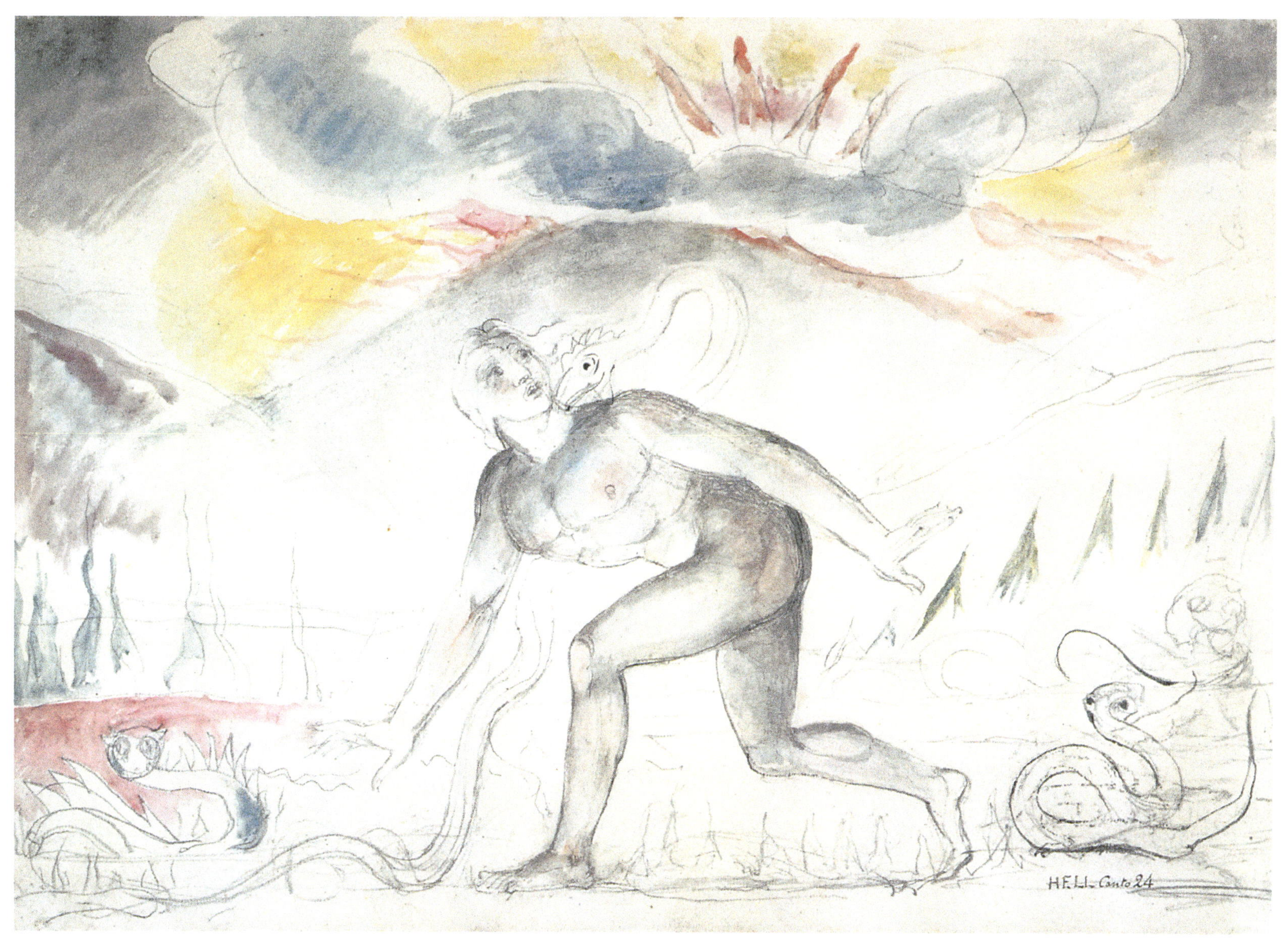

PLATE 51

The thief Vanni Fucci, bitten by the serpent, has been condemned to perpetual punishment. [*Inferno,* Canto 24, lines 95–124]

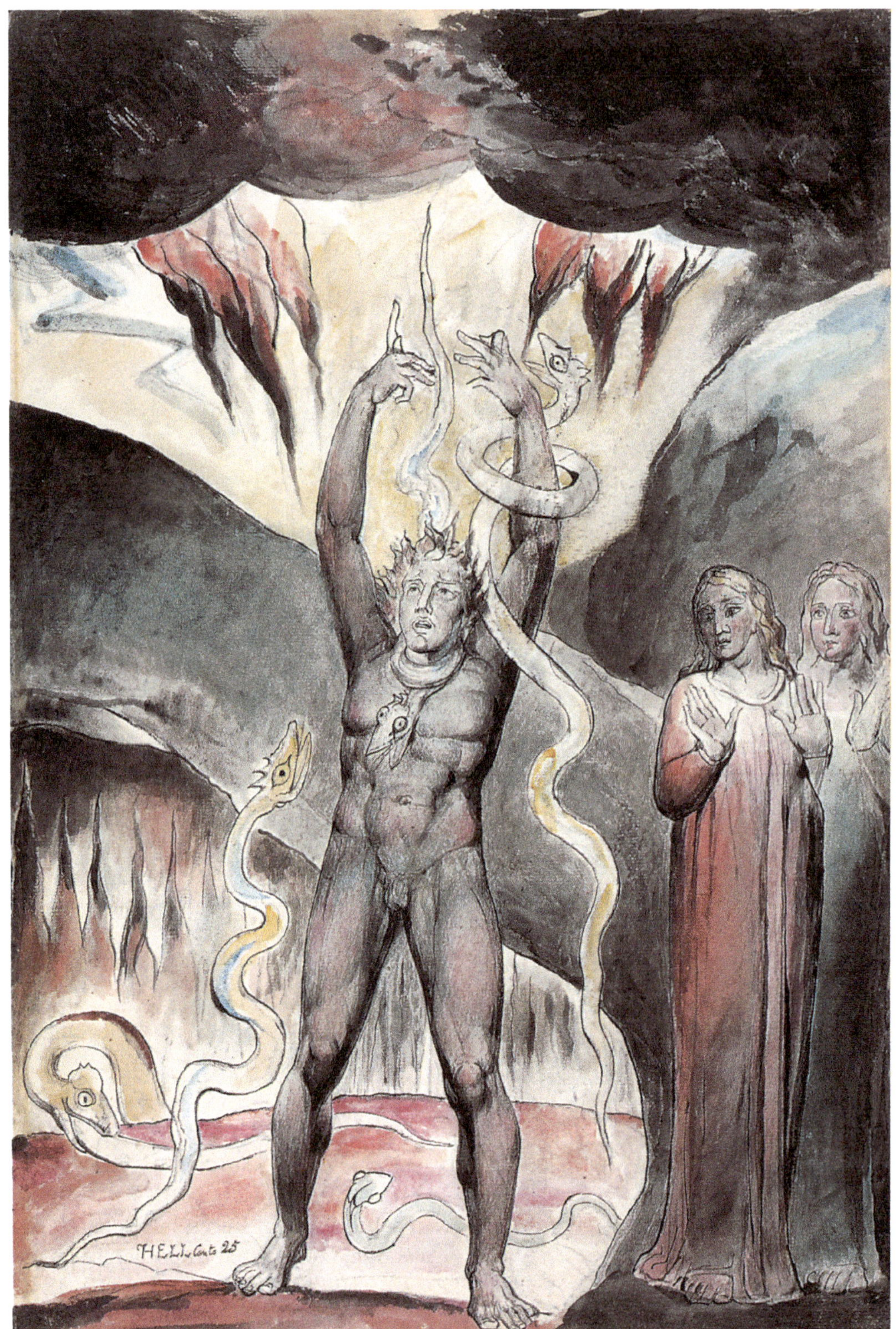

PLATE 52

The defiant Vanni Fucci makes a vulgar gesture toward the gods. [*Inferno,* Canto 25, lines 1–10]

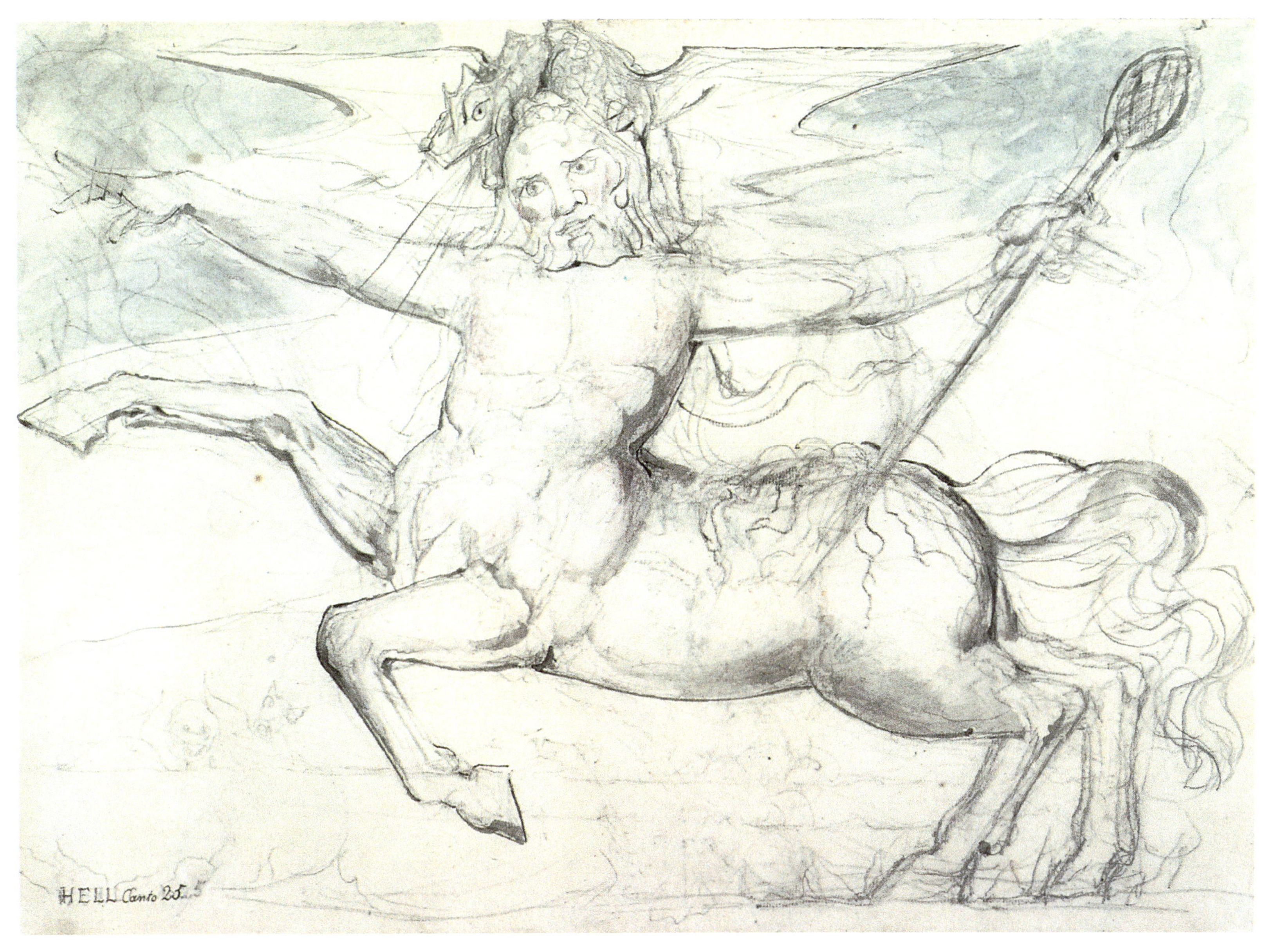

PLATE 53

The hideous monster Cacus, a centaur, prepares to pursue Vanni Fucci.
[*Inferno,* Canto 25, lines 12–33]

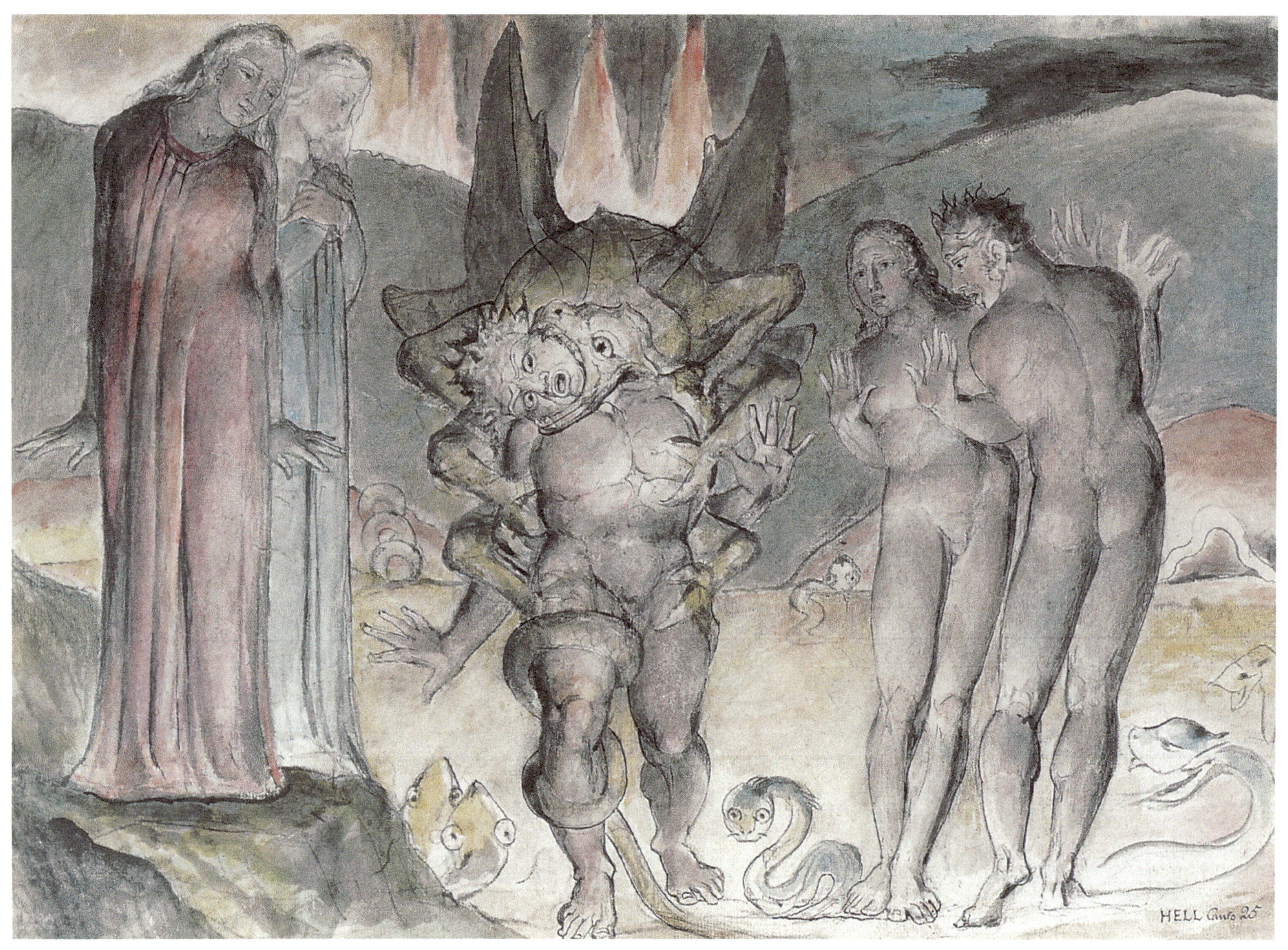

PLATE 54

The six-footed serpent Cianfa de' Donati swallows Agnello Brunelleschi, a Florentine.
[*Inferno,* Canto 25, lines 38–62]

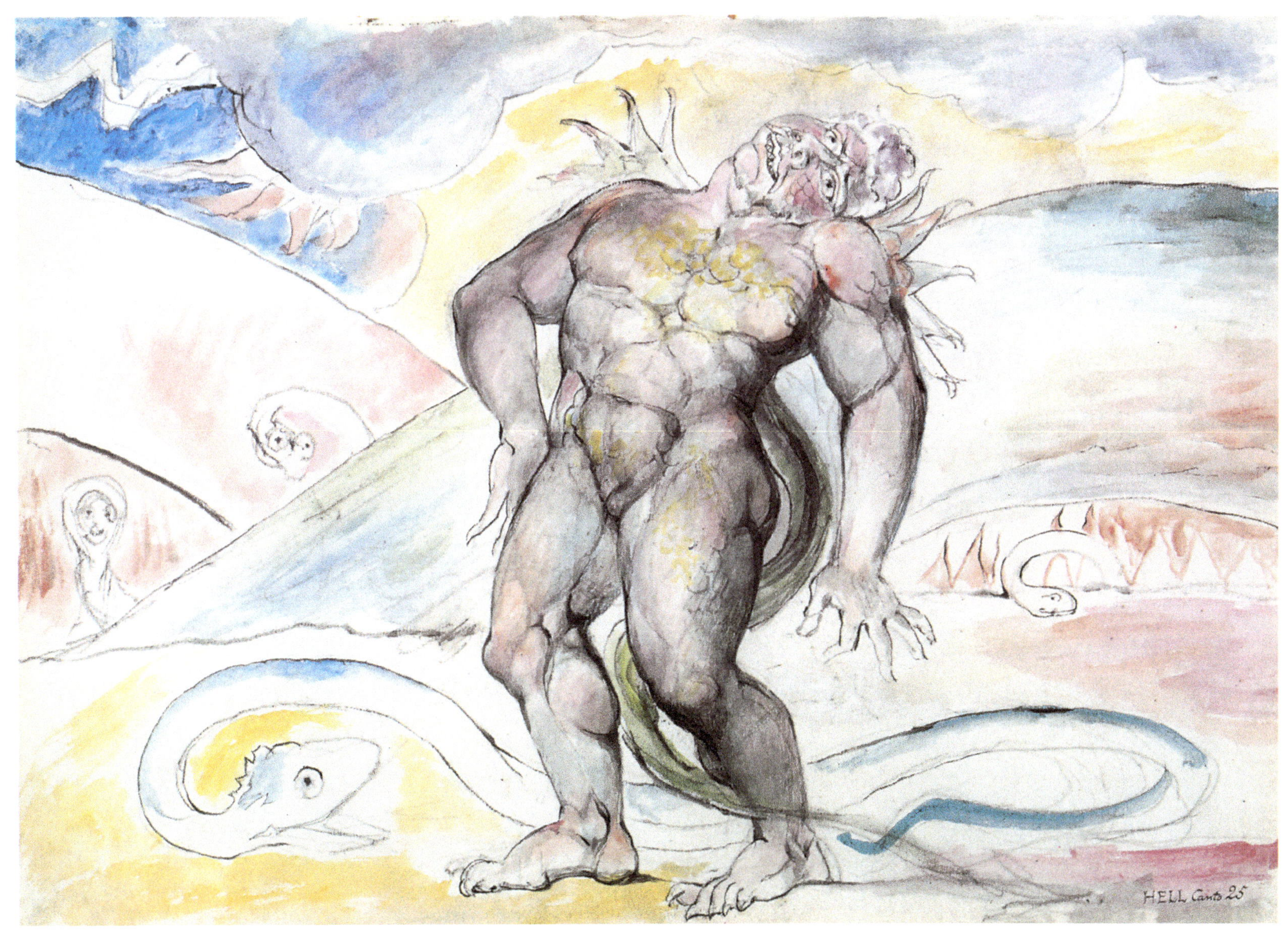

PLATE 55

Agnello Brunelleschi is depicted in the throes of his transformation back into human form, but retaining elements of the serpent that swallowed him.
[*Inferno,* Canto 25, lines 60–70]

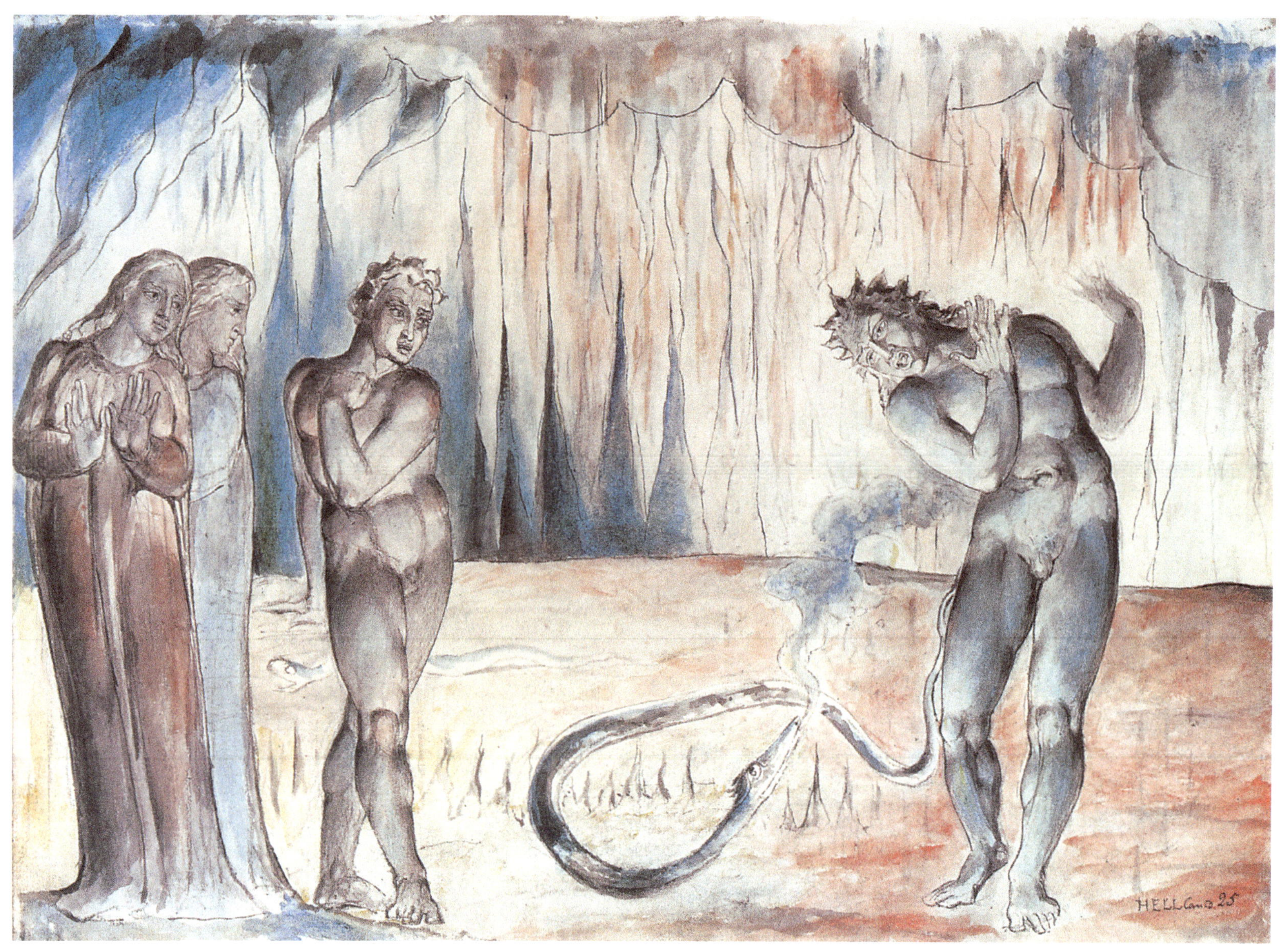

PLATE 56

Buoso de' Donati and the serpent that attacks him (Guercio de' Cavalcanti) will be transformed into serpent and man.
[*Inferno,* Canto 25, lines 94–105]

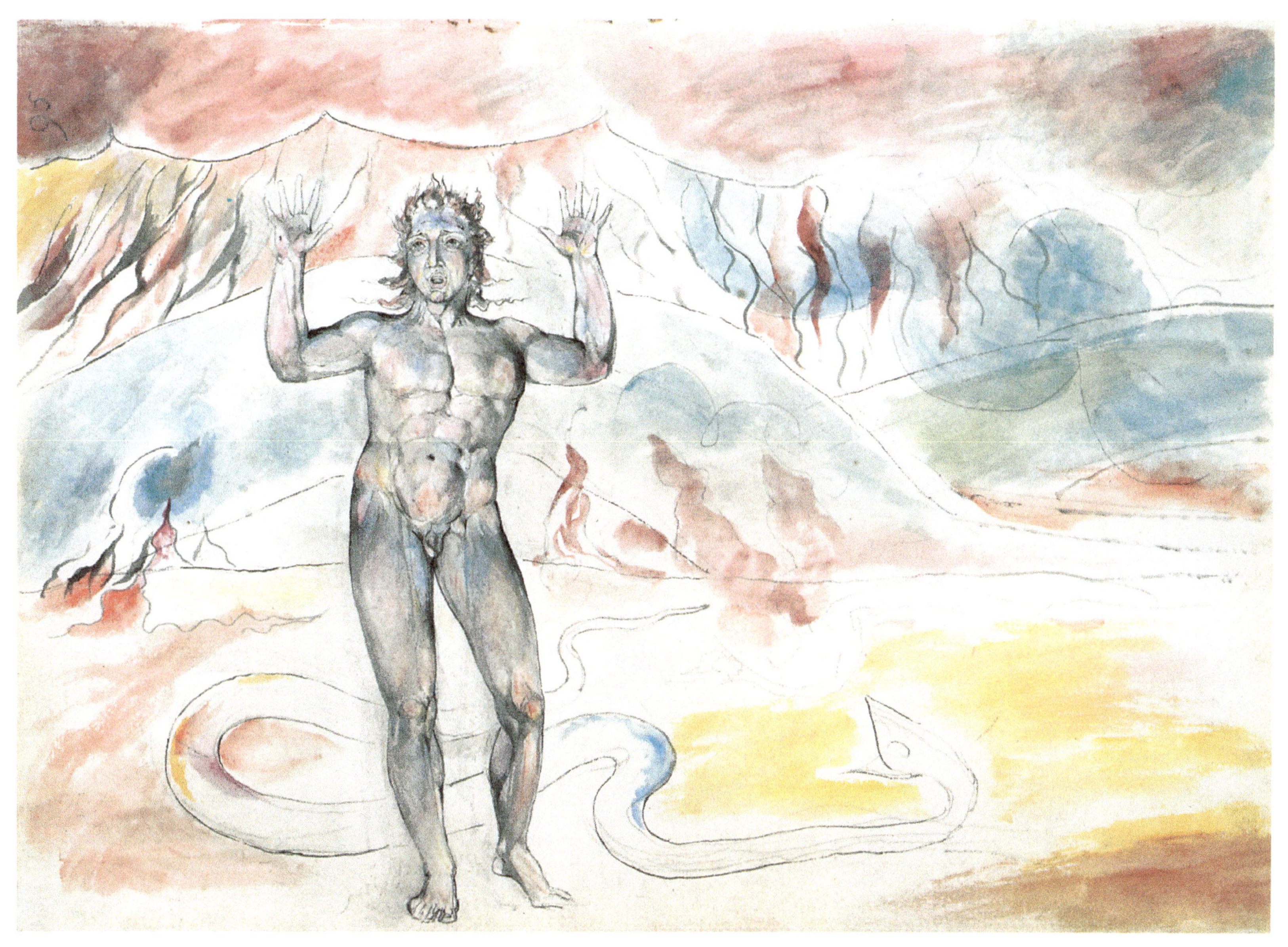

PLATE 57

The final transformation: Donati from man to serpent, and Cavalcanti from serpent to man.
[*Inferno,* Canto 25, lines 106–131]

PLATE 58

Ulysses and Diomedes, engulfed in flames, are tormented for their roles in the Trojan War. [*Inferno,* Canto 26, lines 44–71]

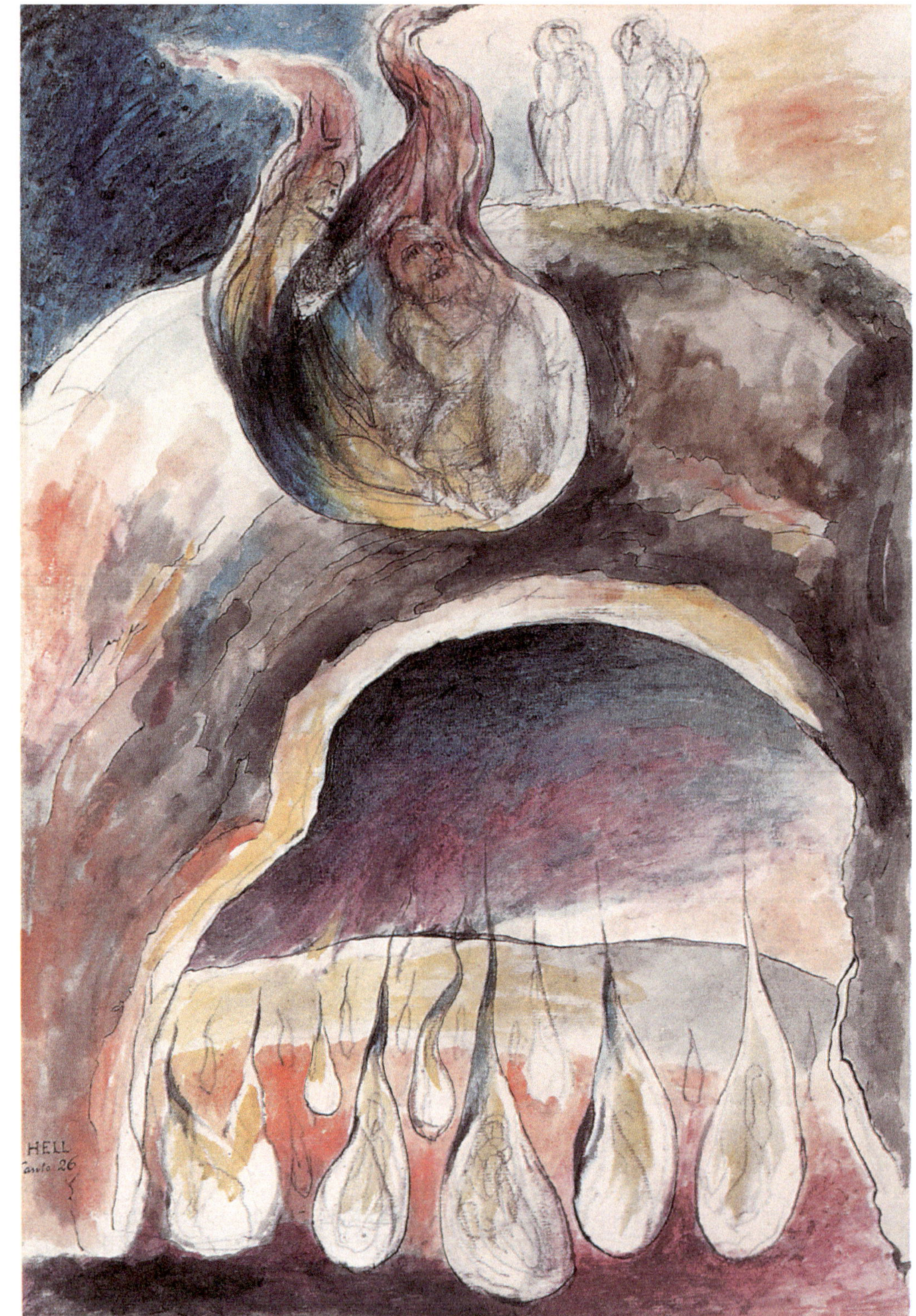

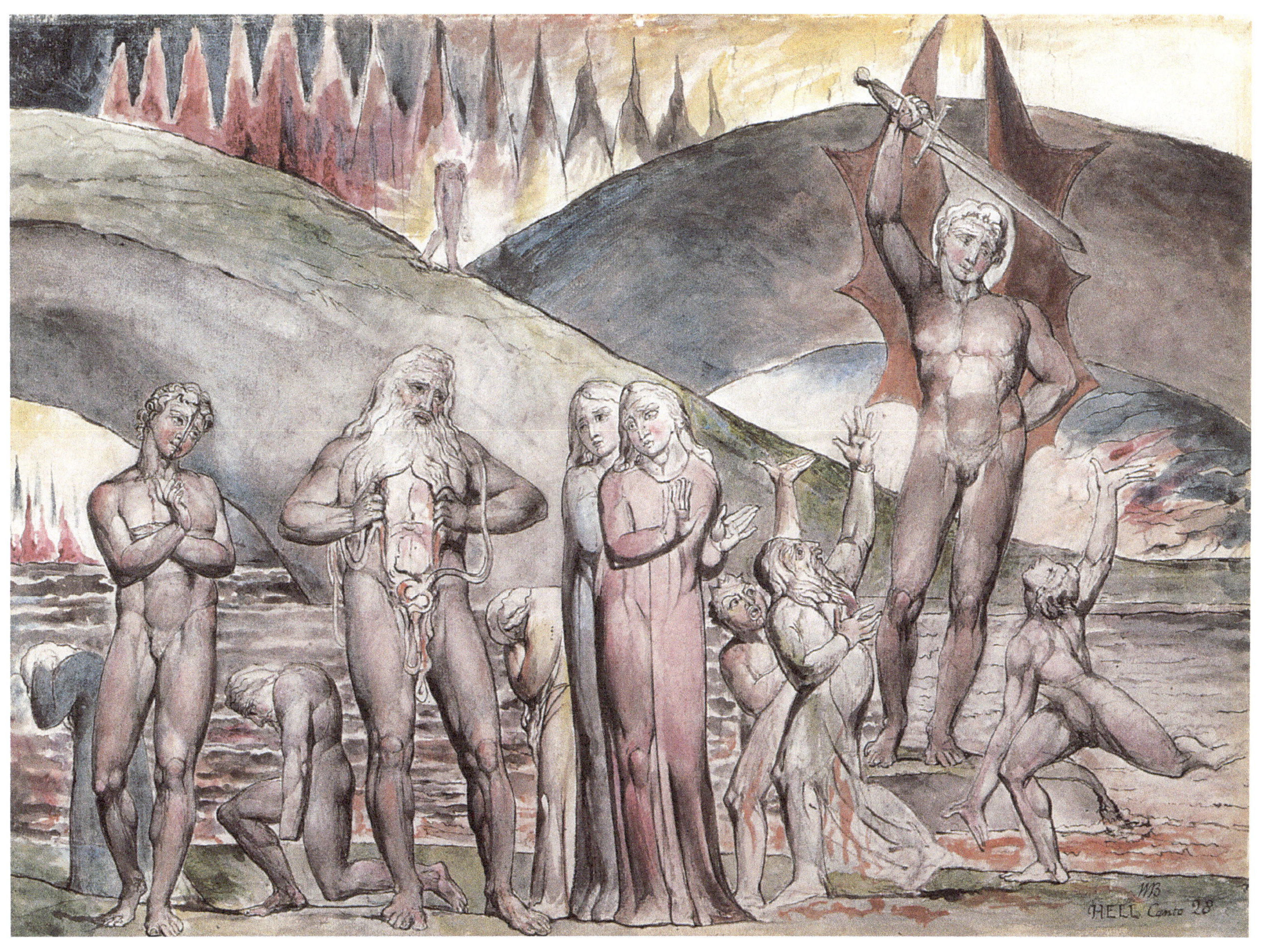

PLATE 59

Schismatics and heretics—those whose beliefs cause divisions and dissent within organized religion—are themselves split apart. The angel to the right reopens their wounds as they heal. [*Inferno,* Canto 28, lines 20–48]

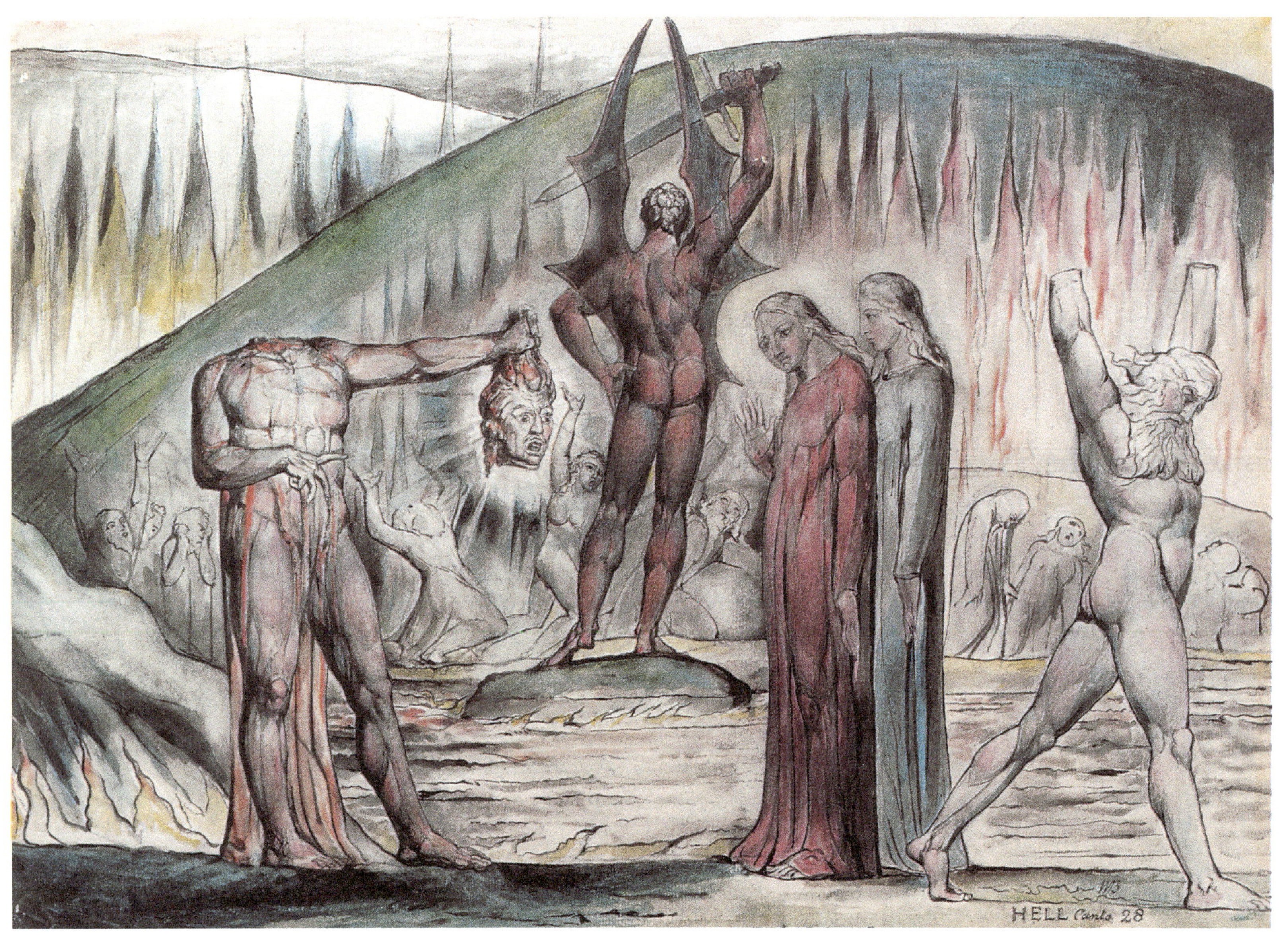

PLATE 60

Further punishment of schismatics—whose actions led to murder and war— is depicted.
[*Inferno,* Canto 28, lines 98–138]

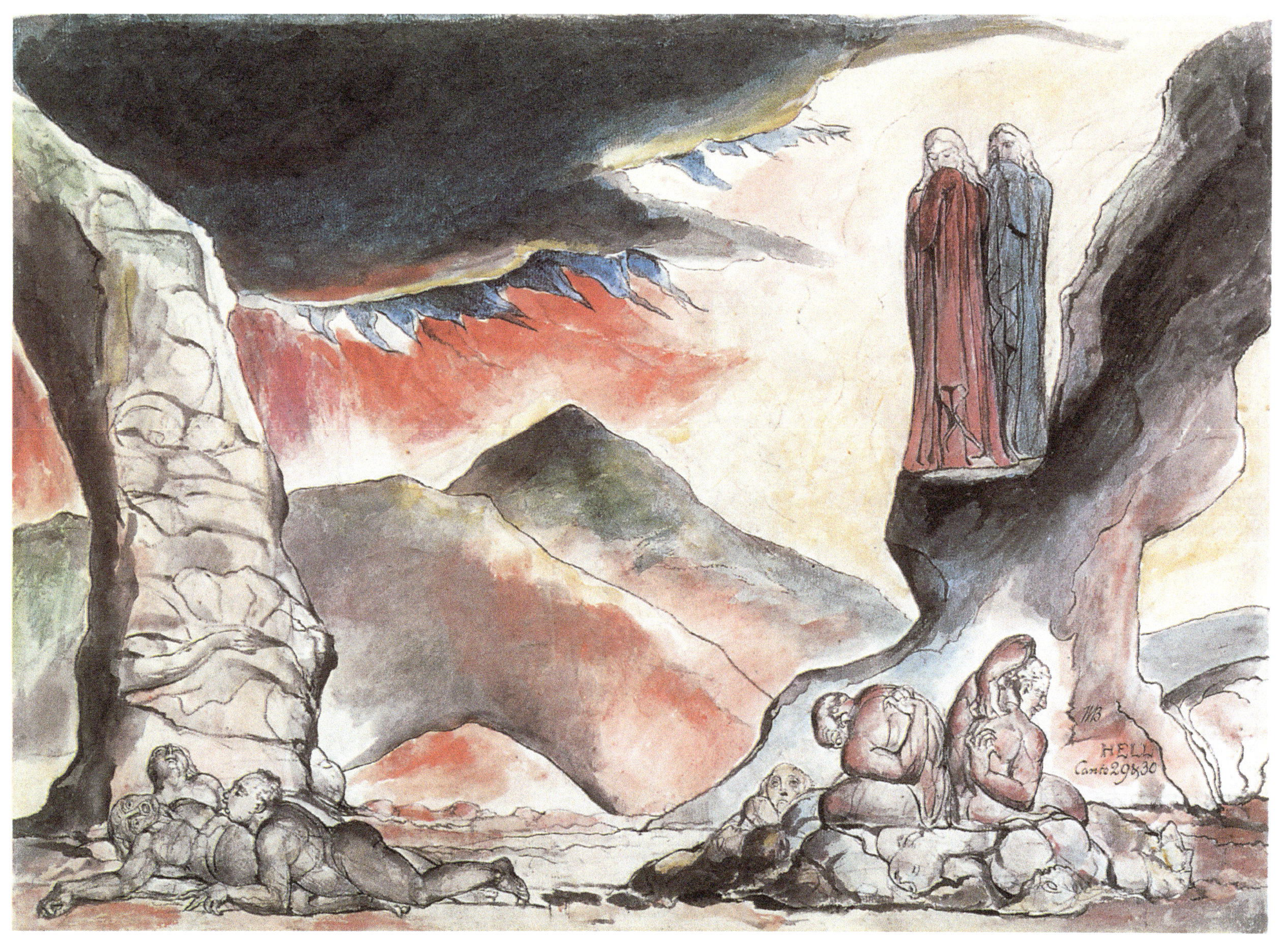

PLATE 61

Dante and Virgil, approaching the tenth gulf, witness the torment of forgers and alchemists.
[*Inferno,* Canto 29, lines 72–118]

PLATE 62

Those who have taken the shapes of others, including a thief of a dead person's identity, are tossed into flames.
[*Inferno,* Canto 30, lines 33–48]

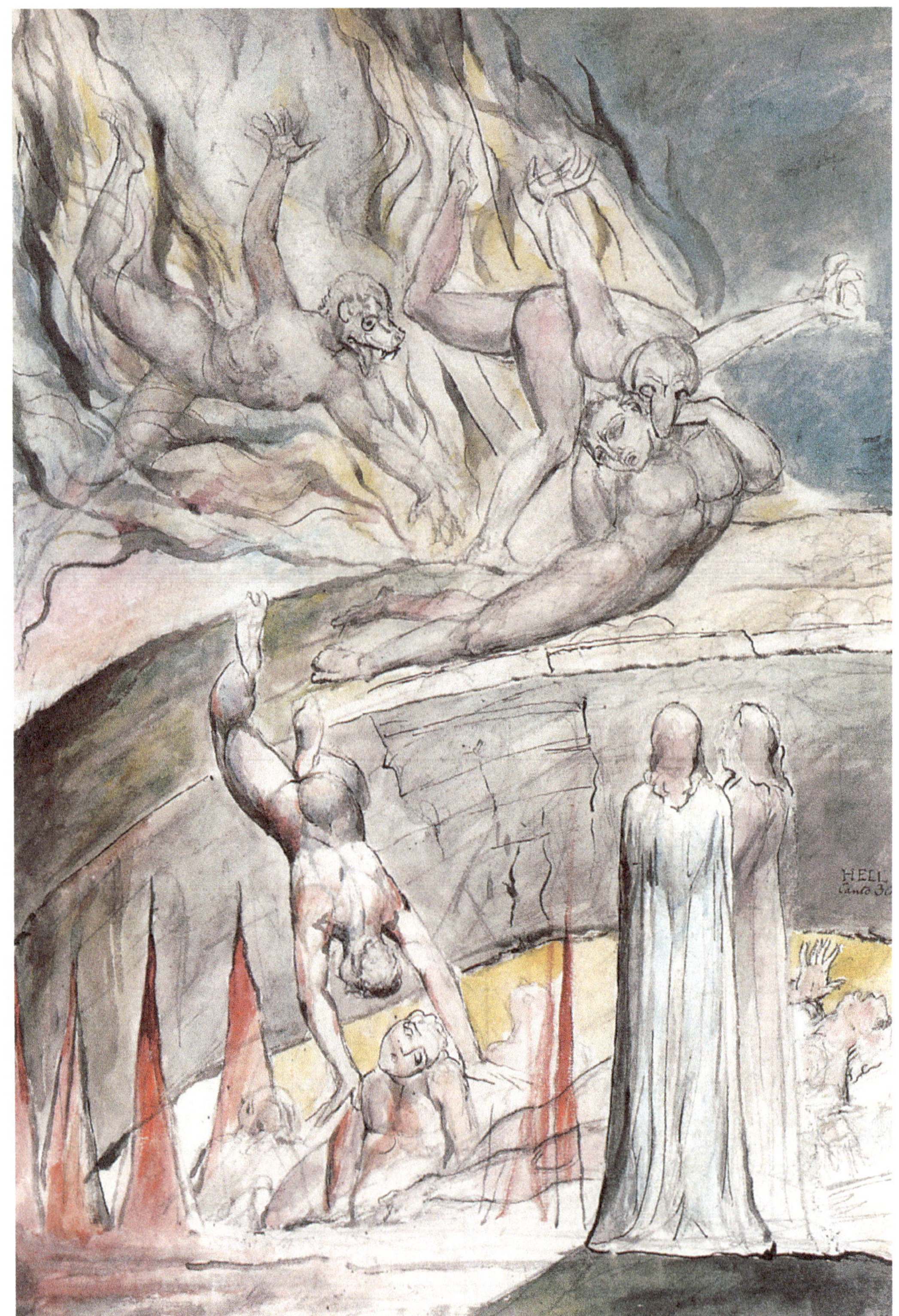

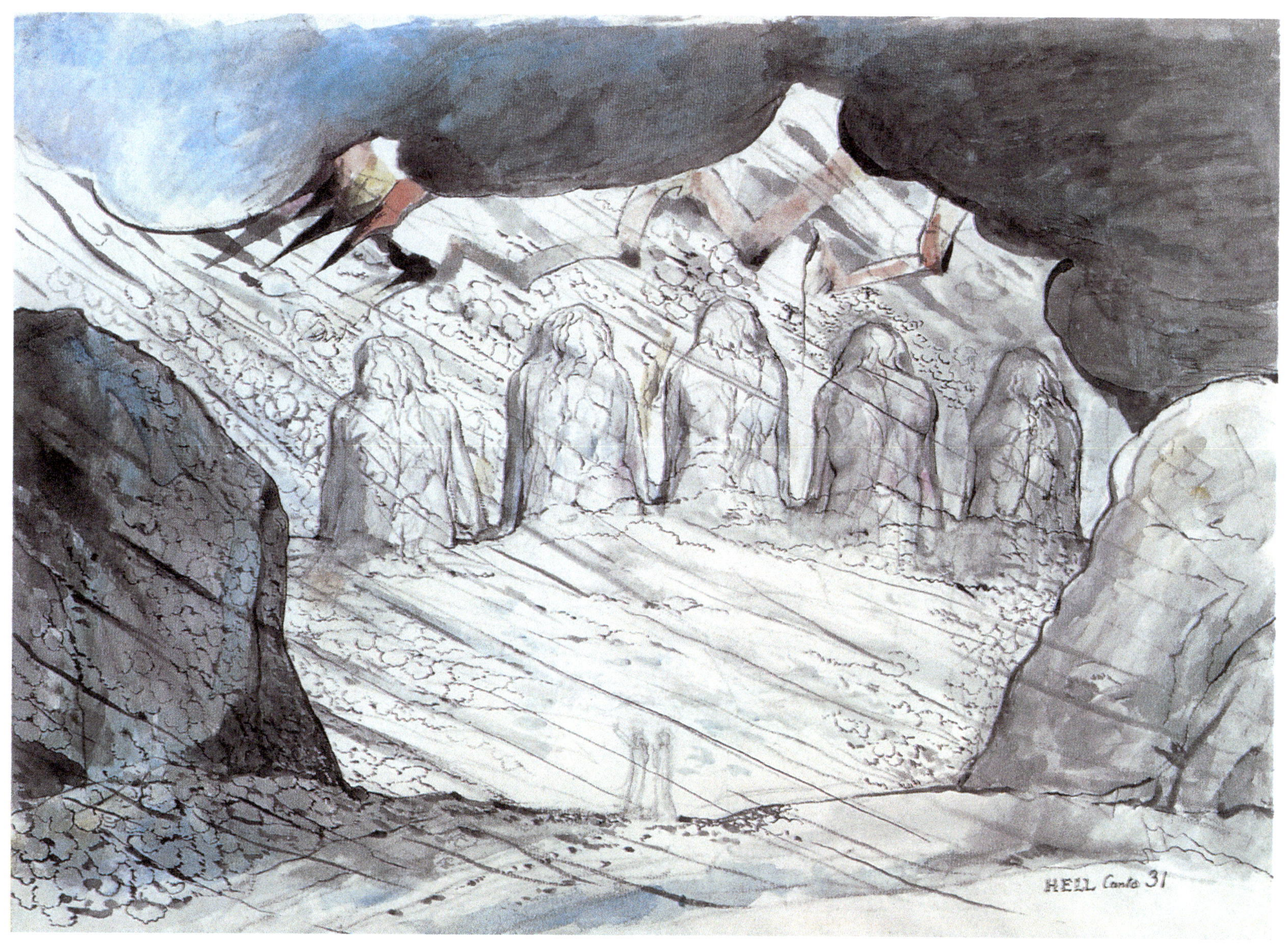

PLATE 63

Five giants—appearing to the poets as organic forms in the landscape—
perhaps are representatives of the five senses.
[*Inferno,* Canto 31, lines 17–43]

PLATE 64

Nimrod, in building Babel, destroyed the ability of the human race to speak with a single language. [*Inferno,* Canto 31, lines 53–74]

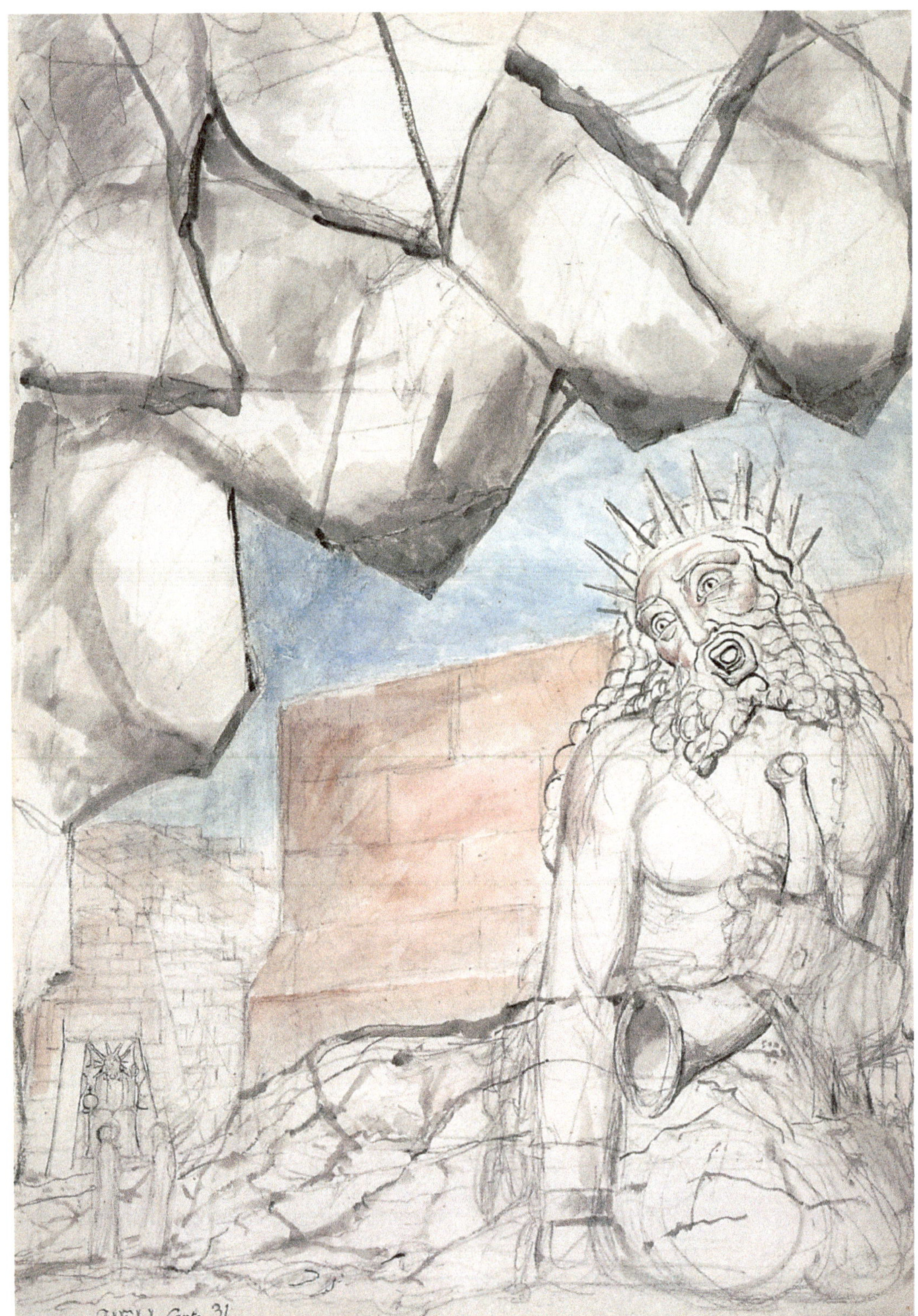

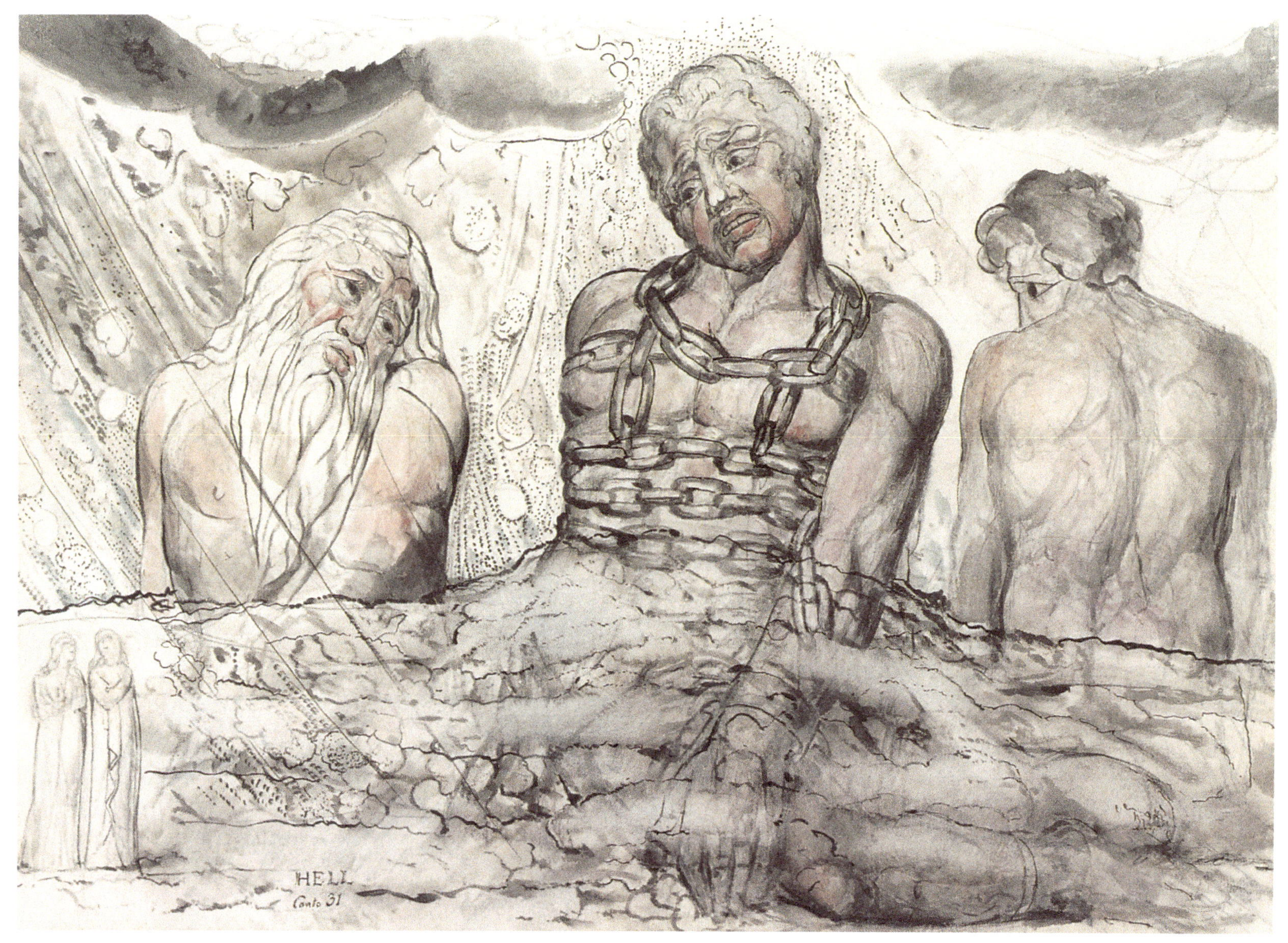

PLATE 65

Neptune's rebellious son, Ephialtes, and two other giants, are immobilized, their arms buried.
[*Inferno,* Canto 31, lines 75–105]

PLATE 66

Neptune's son Anteus lost his powers when airborne, thus leading to his defeat by Hercules. [*Inferno,* Canto 31, lines 103–134]

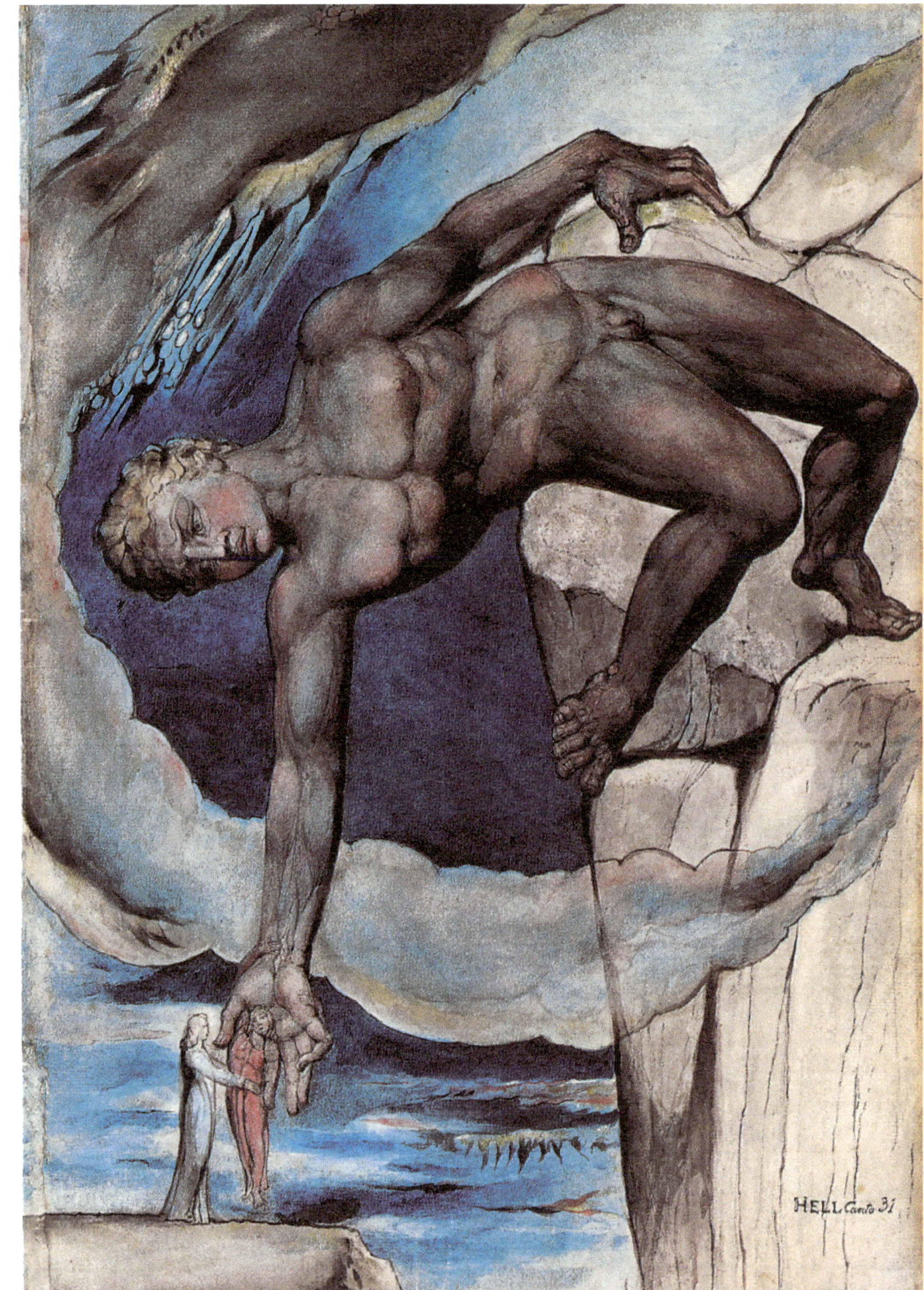

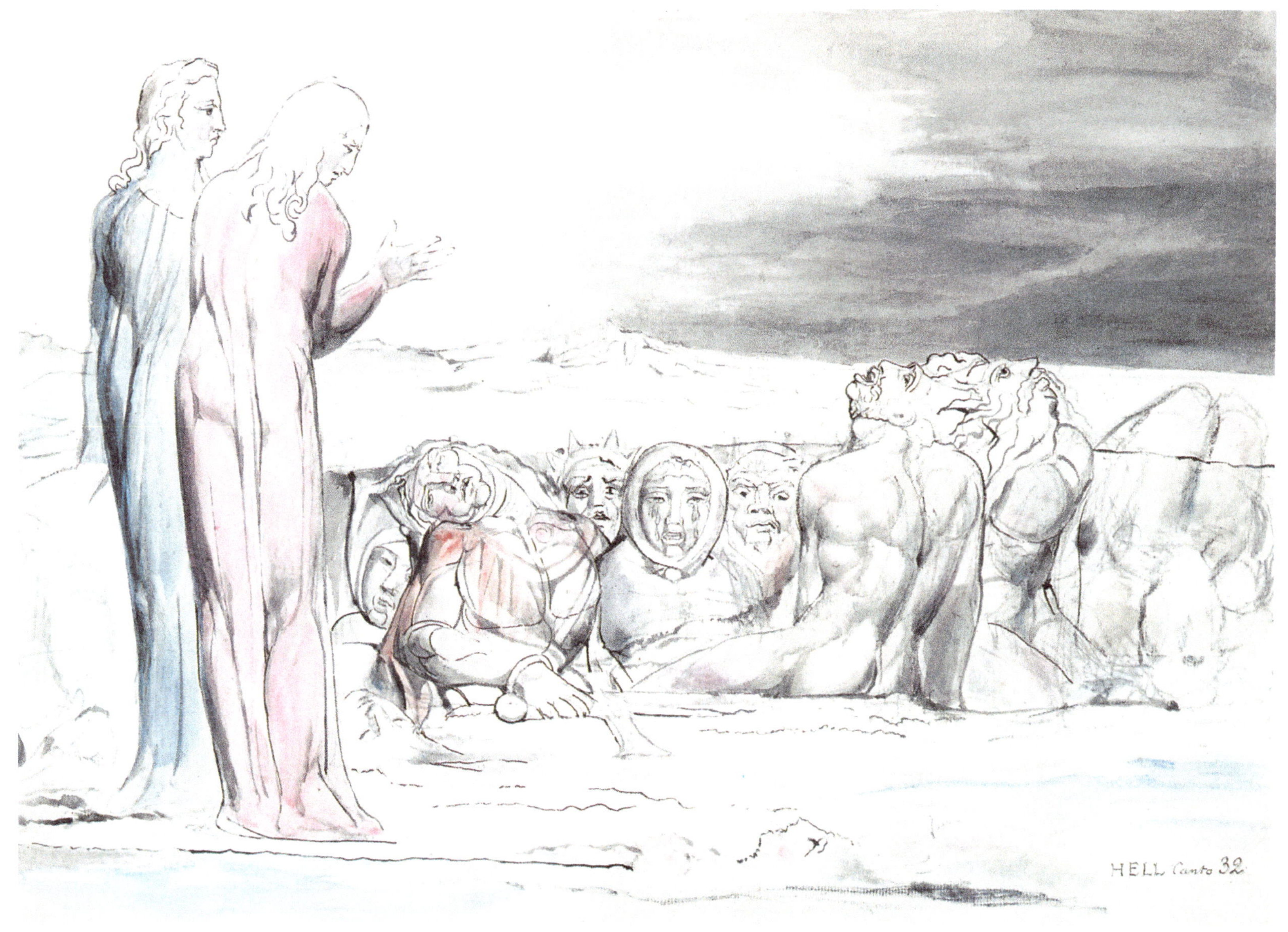

PLATE 67

At the frozen lake, the poets find the Alberti brothers, whose bodies have been fused together as punishment for their crime of murdering each other.
[*Inferno,* Canto 32, lines 22–64]

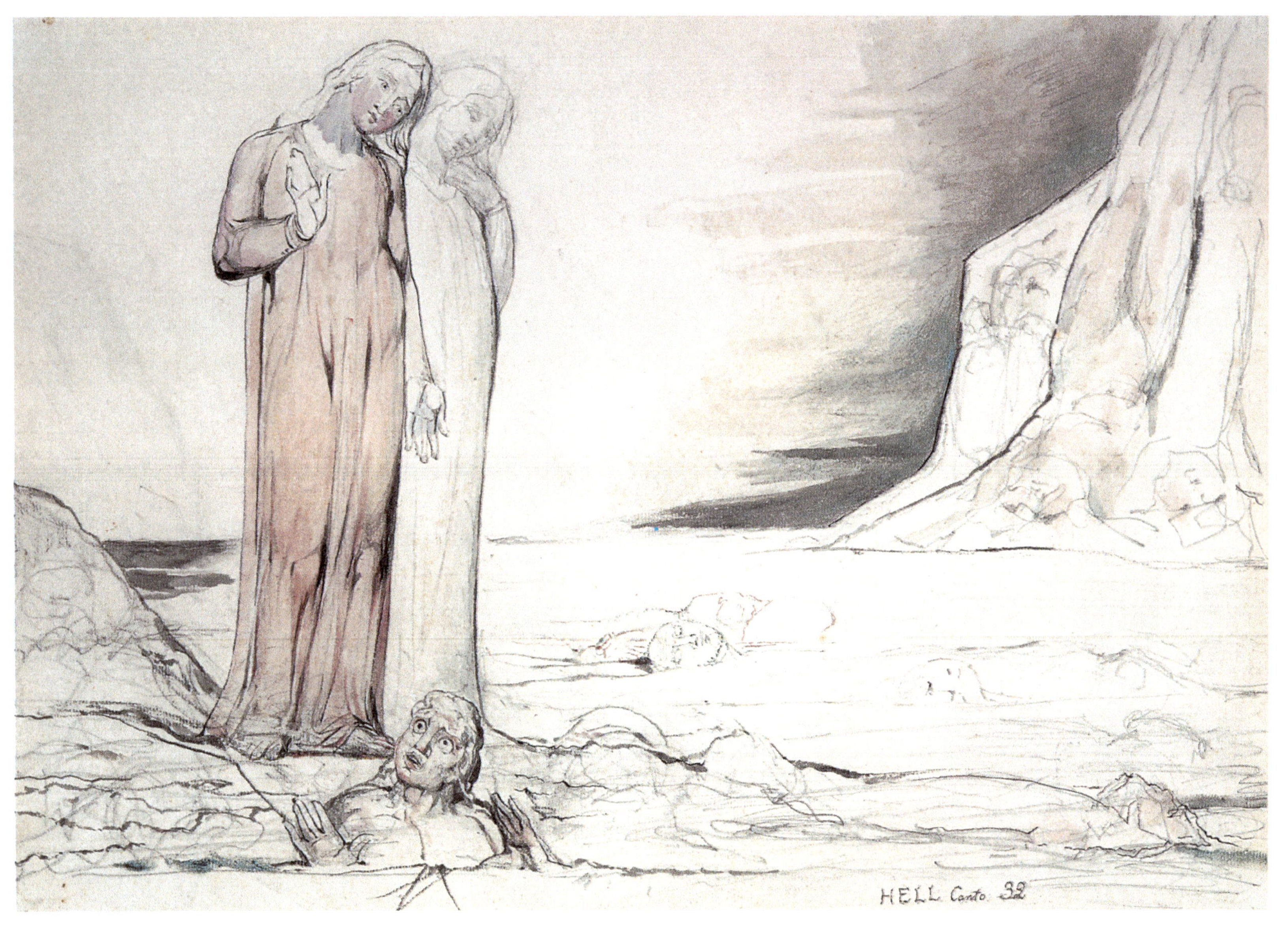

PLATE 68

The protruding frozen head and shoulders belong to Bocca degli Abbati, the Florentine traitor.
[*Inferno* Canto 32, lines 77–89]

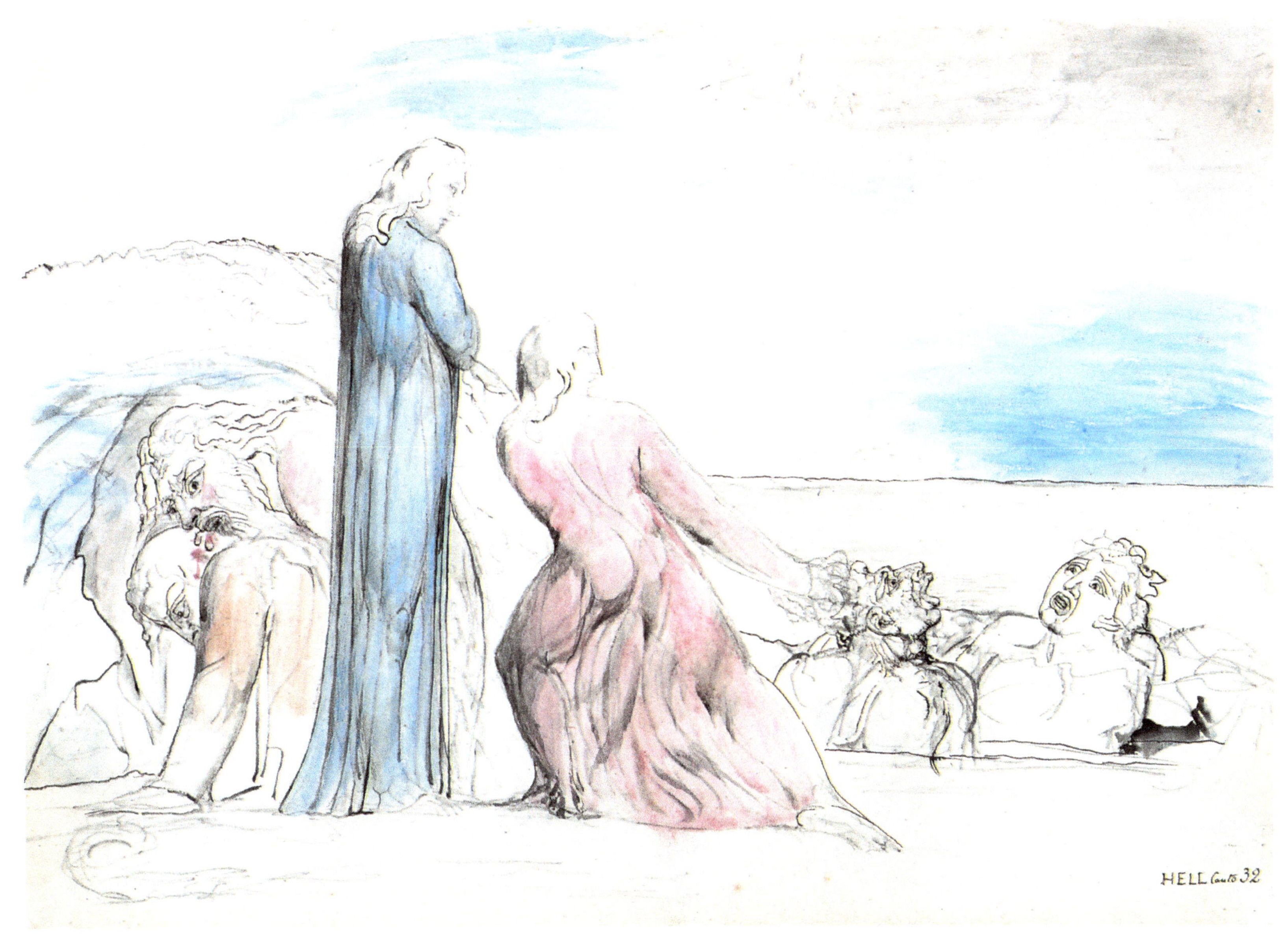

PLATE 69

As Dante attempts to drag Bocca degli Abbati from the frozen lake, Count Ugolino, at the left, gnaws into a nearby head.
[*Inferno* Canto 32, lines 97–137]

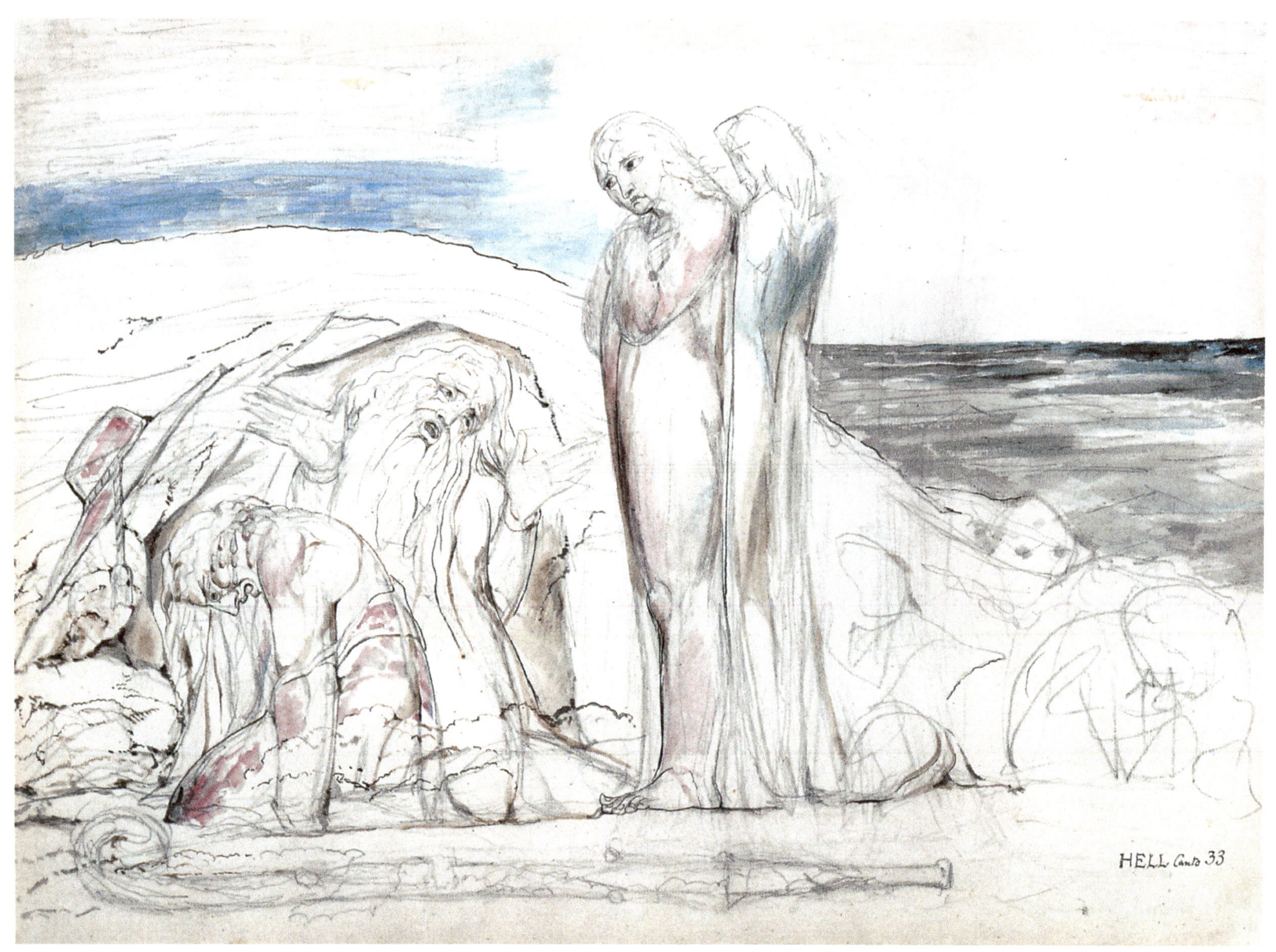

PLATE 70

The tyrant Count Ugolino relates to the poets how he and his family were held captive by the Archbishop Ruggieri in the tower of Pisa.
[*Inferno* Canto 33, lines 1–93]

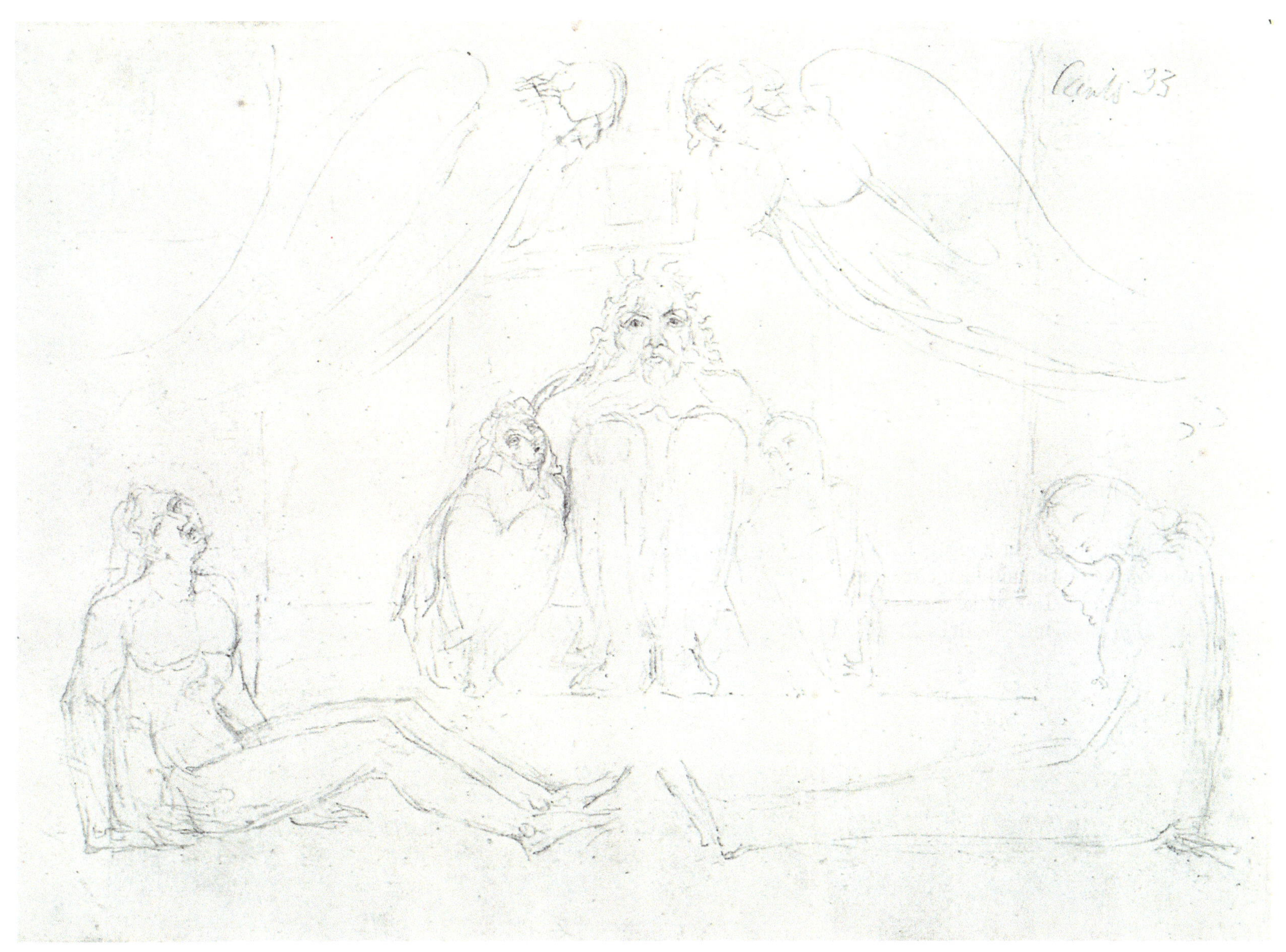

PLATE 71

Count Ugolino's imprisonment in the tower—where his children and grandchildren starved to death—is depicted in this scene.
[*Inferno* Canto 33, lines 13–93]

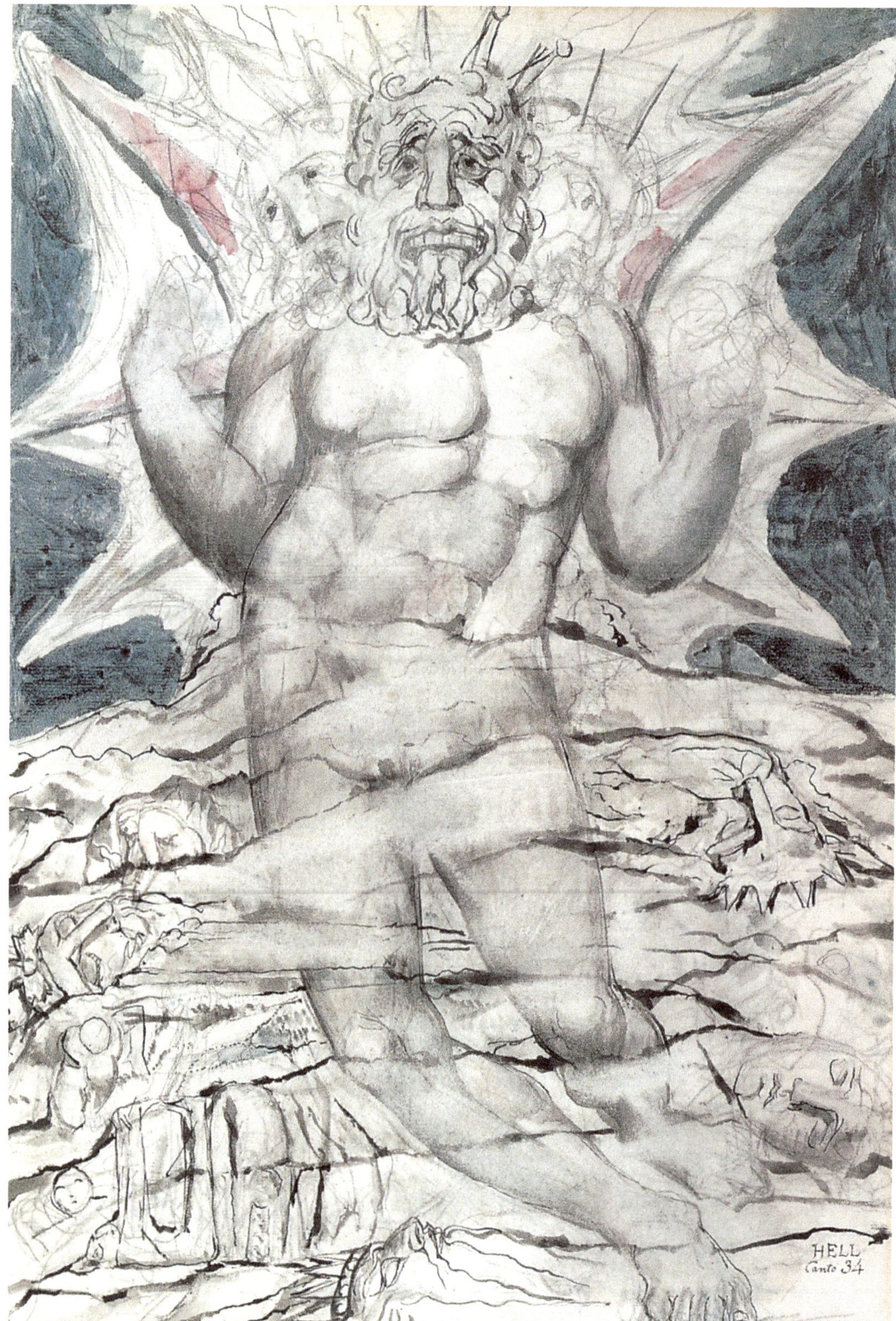

PLATE 72

The terrible figure of Lucifer appears in the final section of the ninth, and last, circle of Hell. Virgil and Dante make their exit. [*Inferno* Canto 34, lines 22–64]

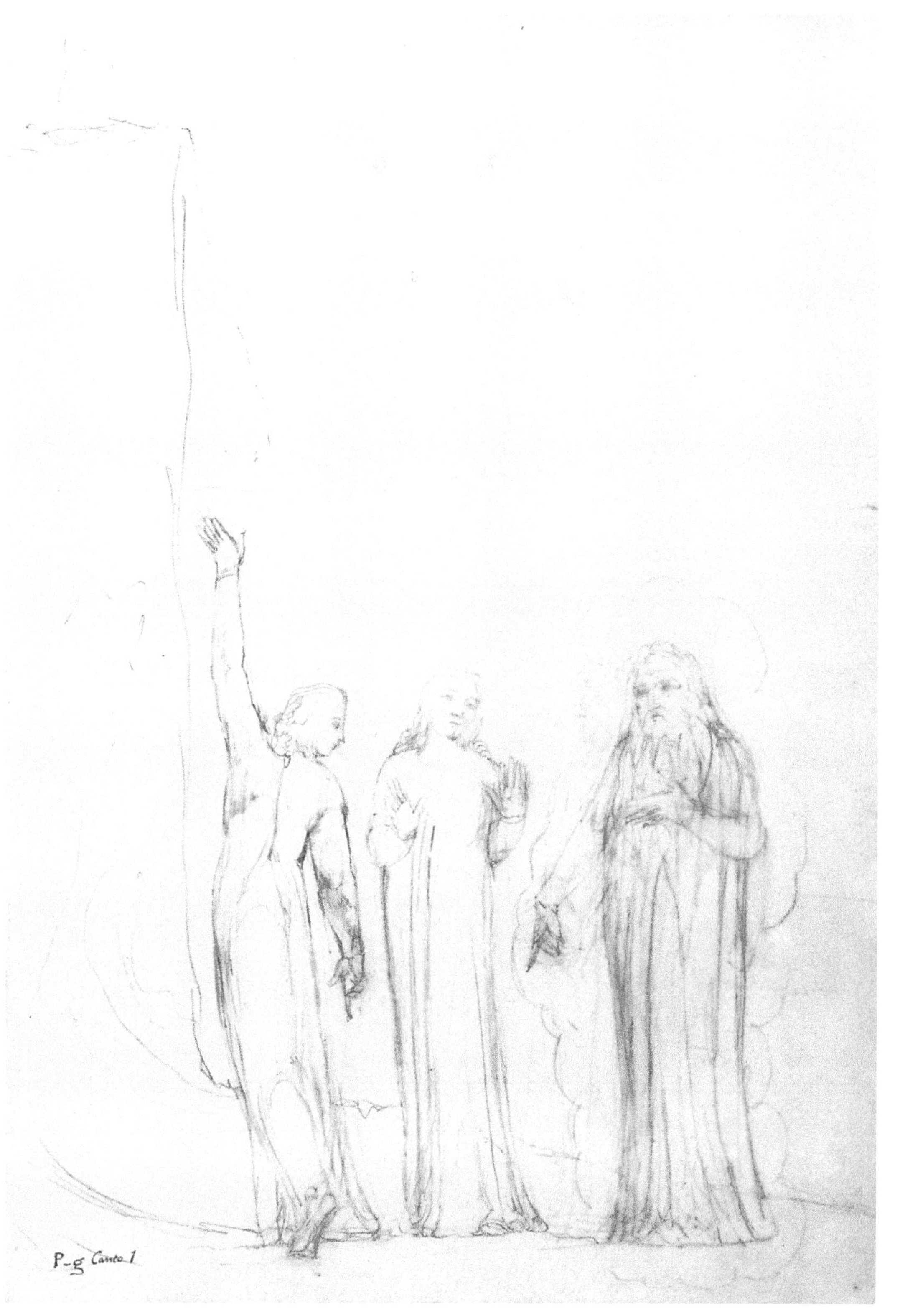

Plate 73

Now in Purgatory, the poets encounter the virtuous Roman Cato, who advises Virgil to cleanse Dante's memory. [*Purgatory,* Canto 1, lines 12–107]

PLATE 74

Bathed in the dawning light, Dante is freed from Hell as Virgil wraps his head with a cleansing reed. [*Purgatory,* Canto 1, lines 120–128]

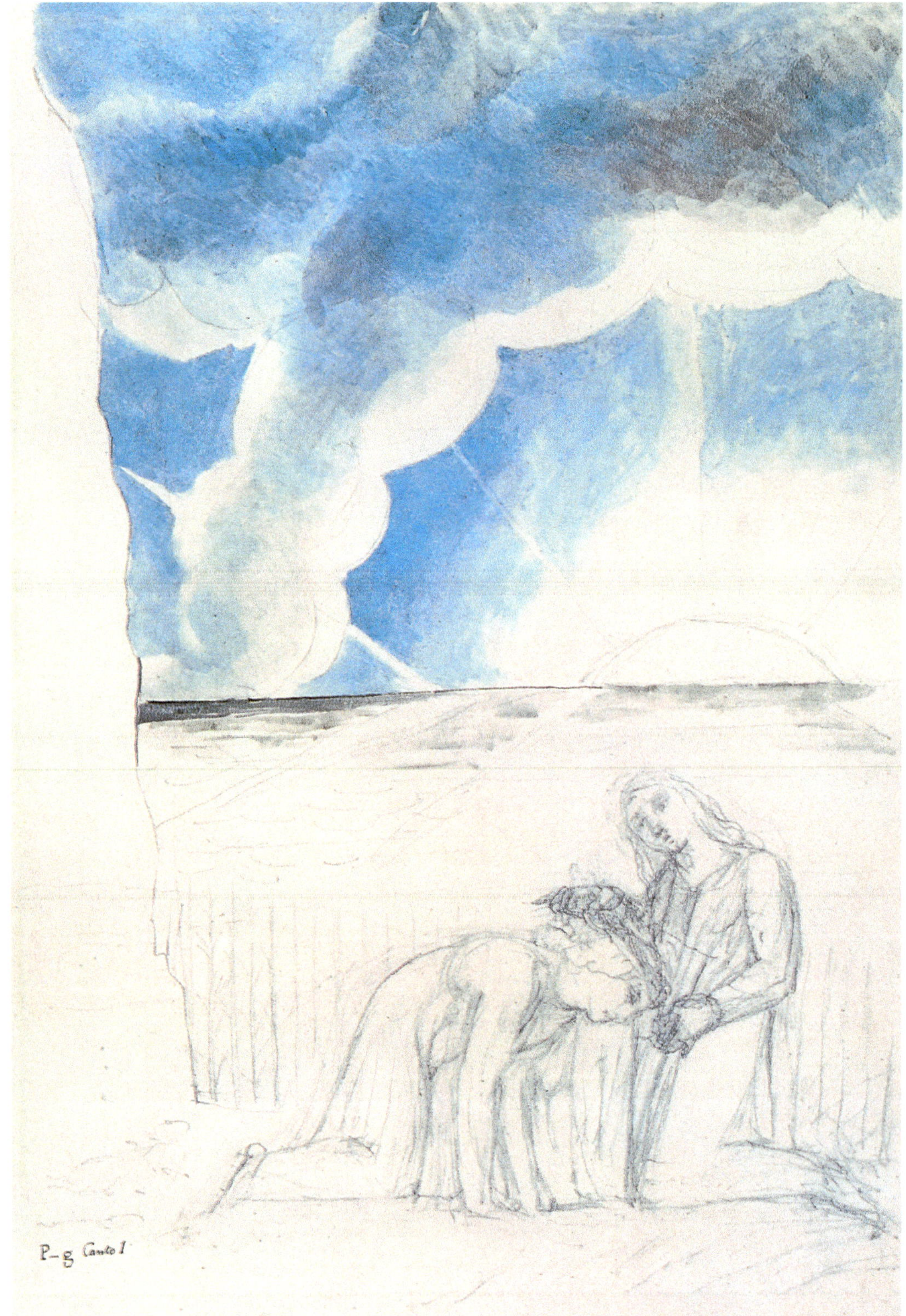

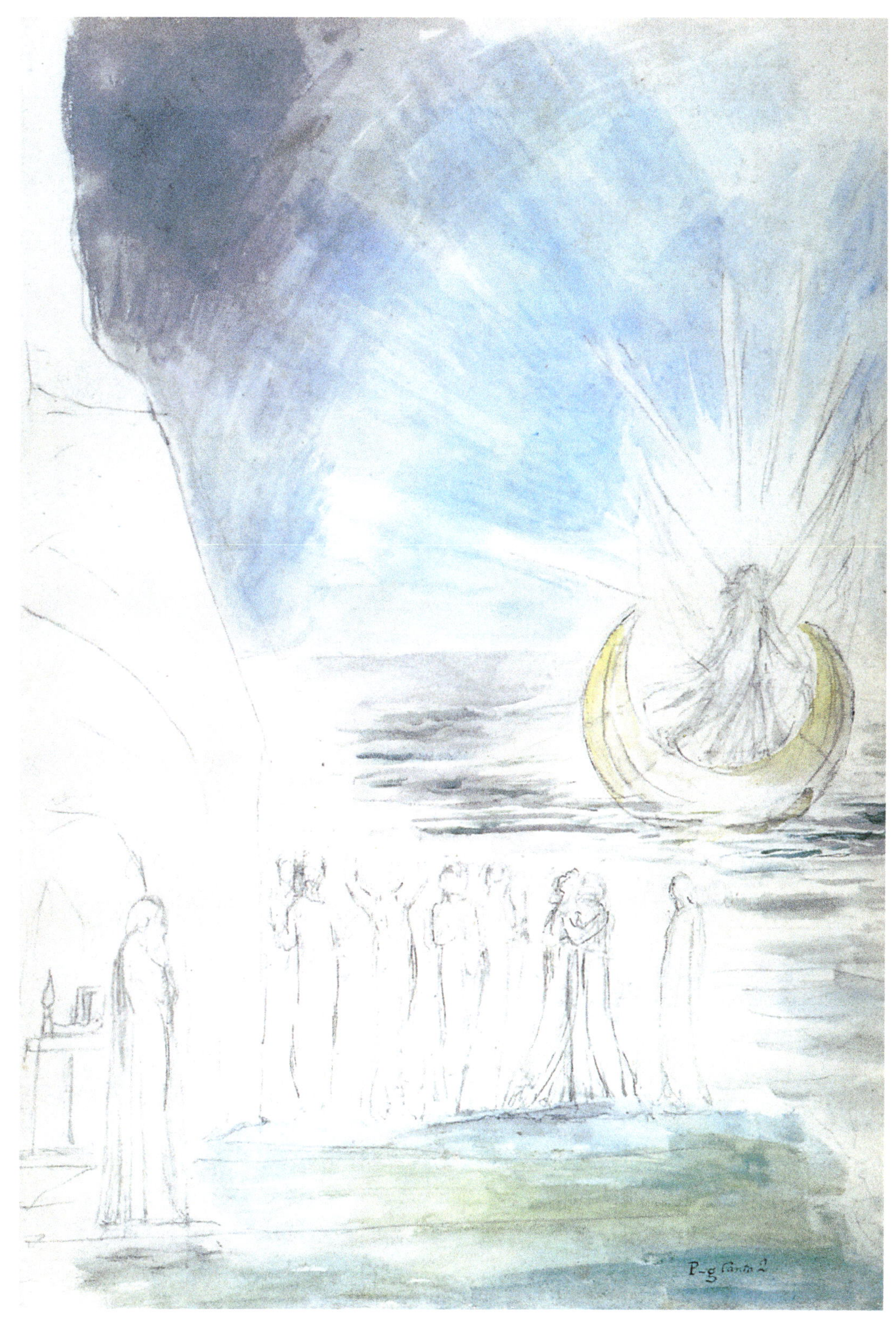

PLATE 75

On his way to the mountain of Purgatory, Dante meets an old friend who has come ashore after riding on the angelic boat. [*Purgatory,* Canto 2, lines 53–117]

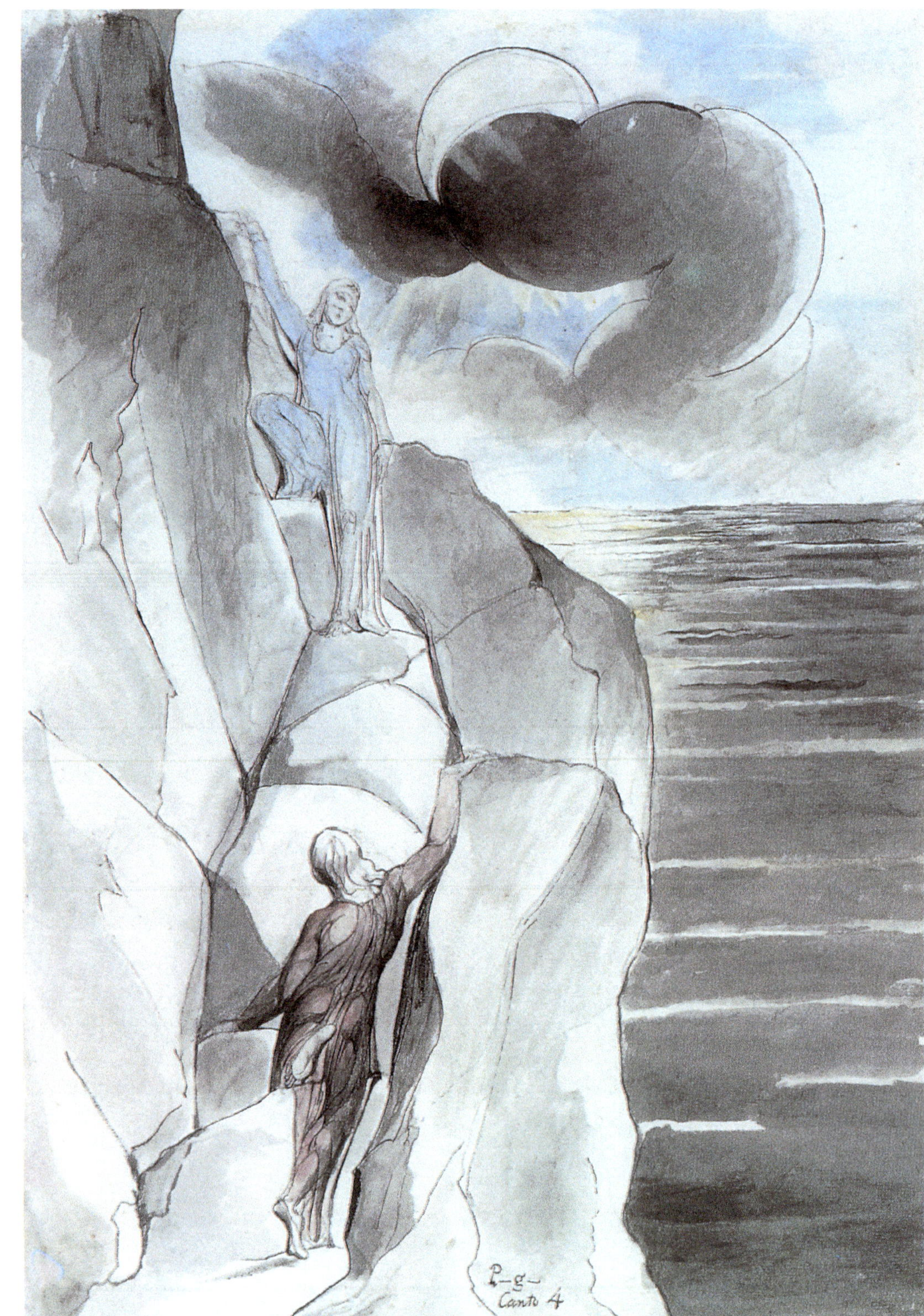

PLATE 76

The cloud partially obscuring the sun is a reminder that Dante must move forward on the road to repentance.
[*Purgatory,* Canto 4, lines 16–65]

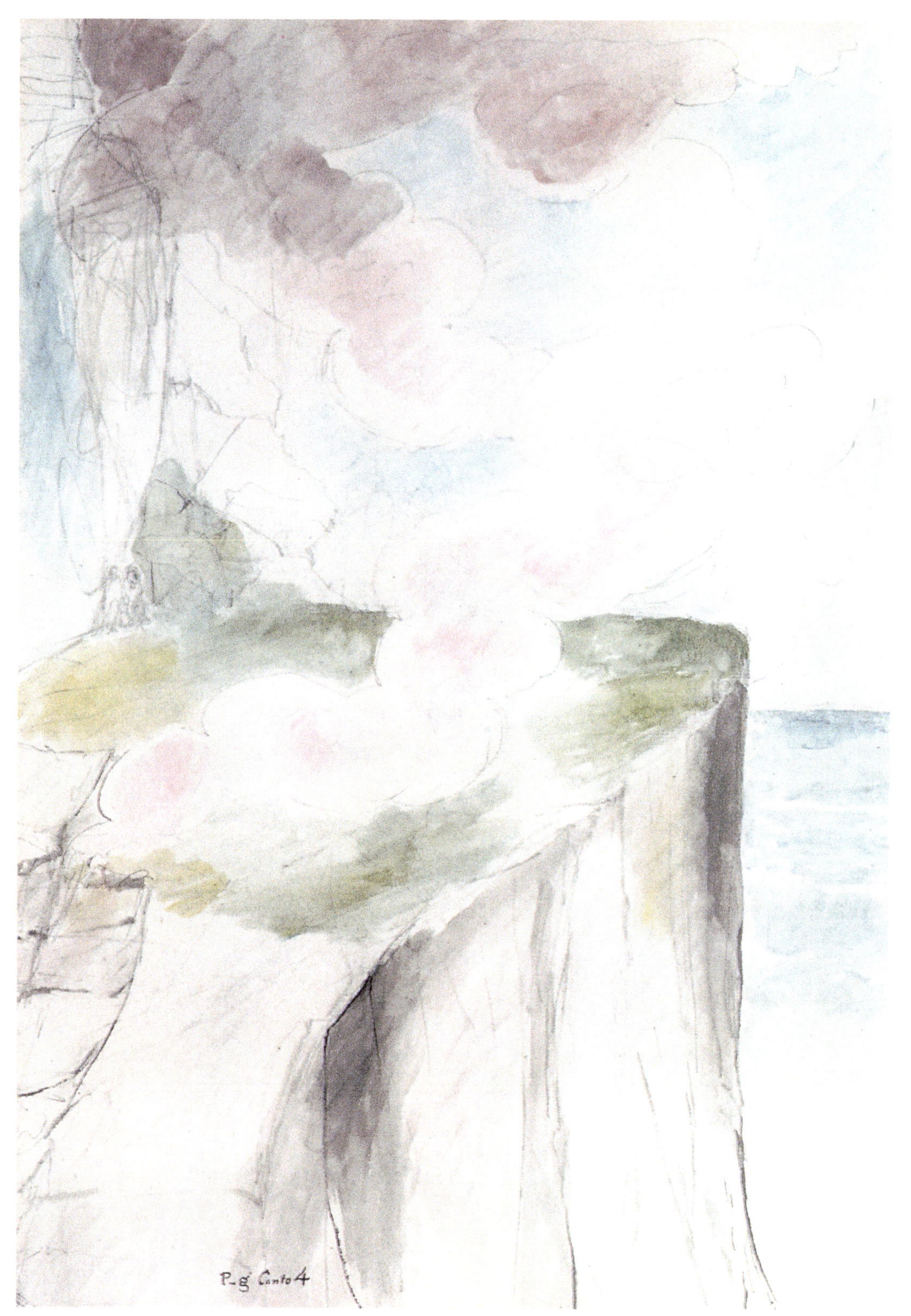

PLATE 77

Dante and Virgil, tiny figures in the landscape, are glimpsed resting on their way to Purgatory. [*Purgatory,* Canto 4, lines 42–47]

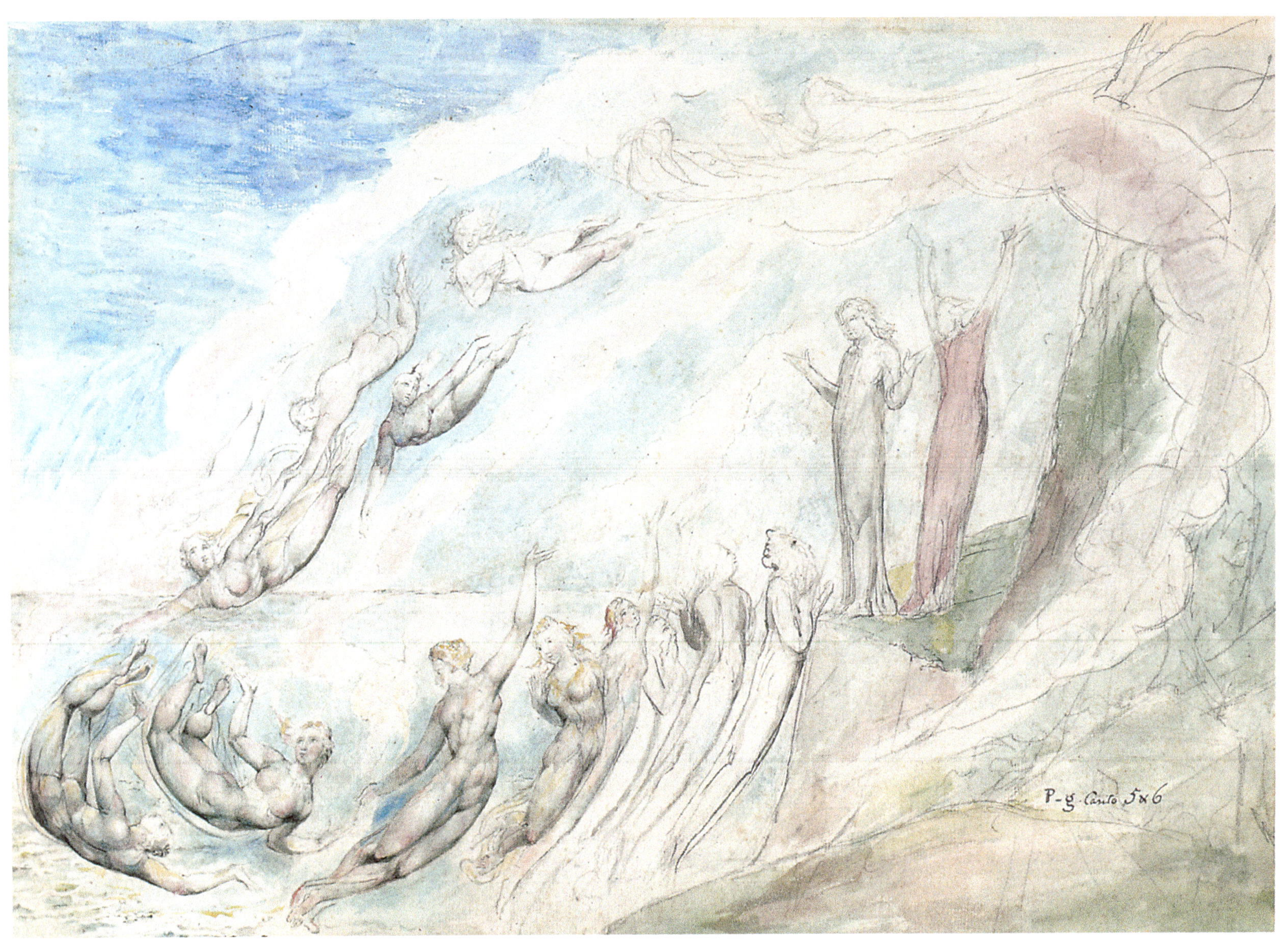

PLATE 78

The agitated souls of violent sinners who have repented appeal to Dante to intercede on their behalf.
[*Purgatory,* Canto 5, lines 22–62]

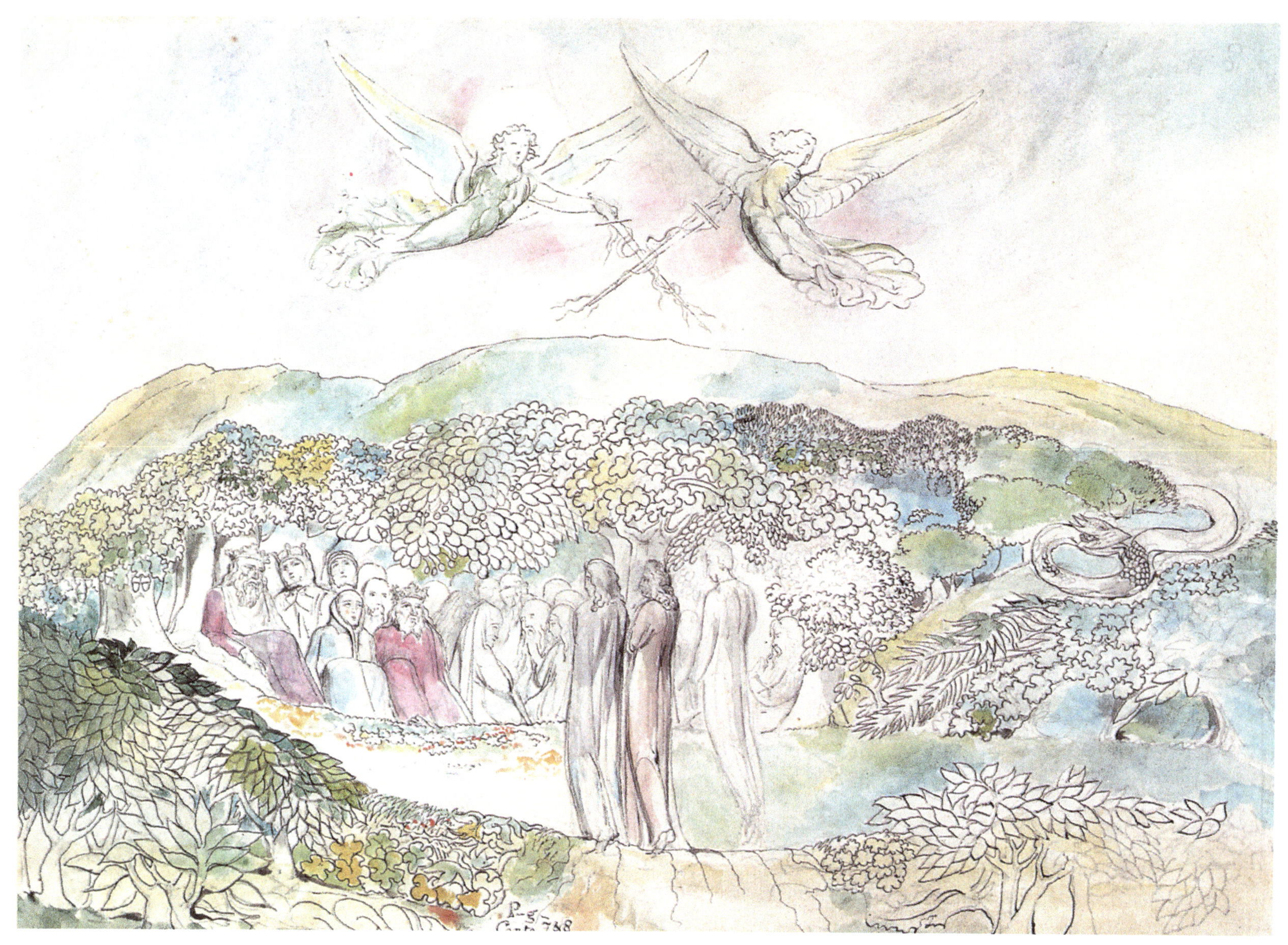

PLATE 79

As the serpent is held at bay by armed angels, Dante, Virgil, and the Provençal poet Sordello behold rulers who have been betrayed.
[*Purgatory,* Canto 8, lines 1–54]

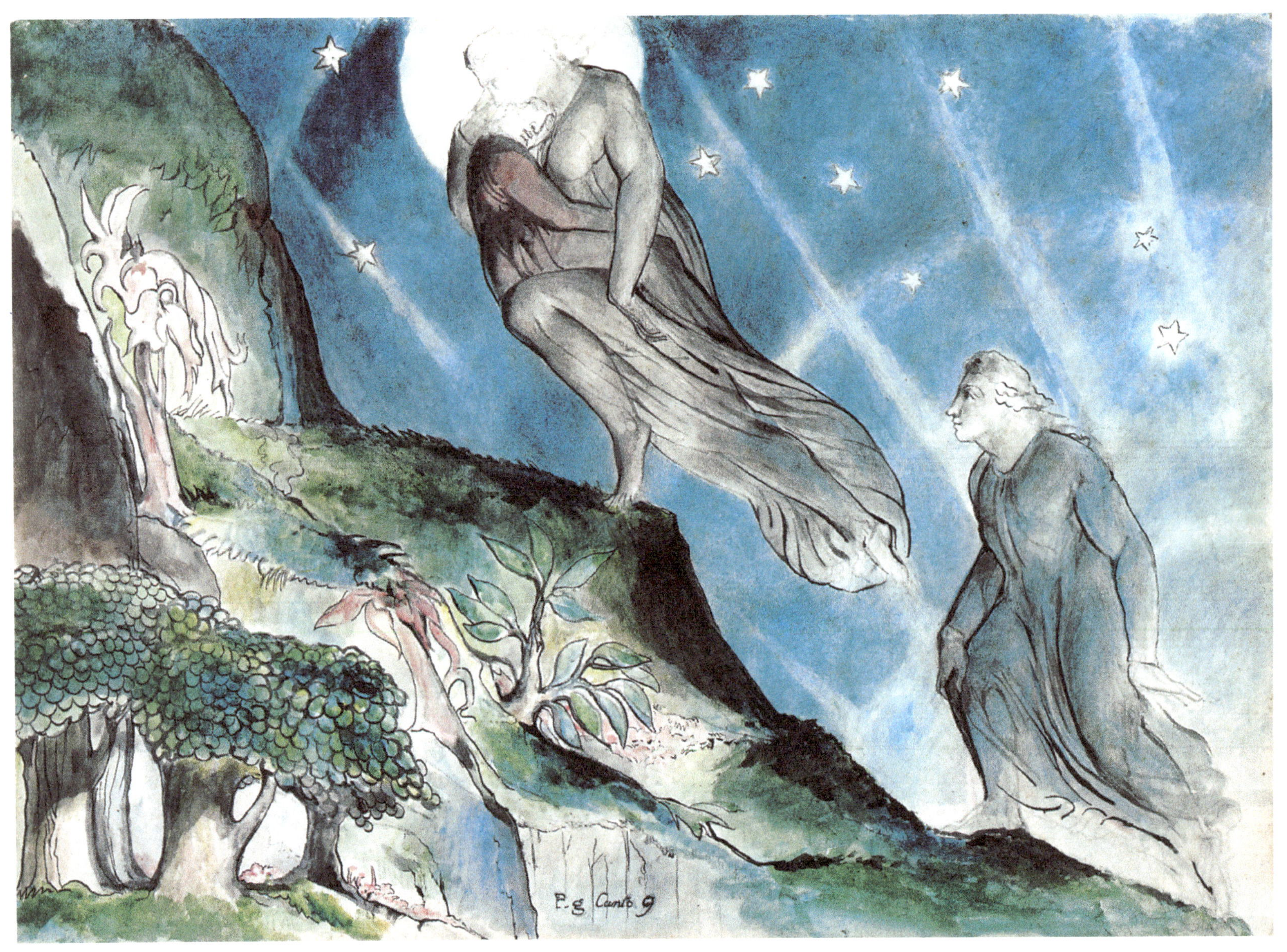

PLATE 80

Dante is borne toward the entrance to Purgatory by Lucia, a spirit sent by Dante's beloved, Beatrice, to guard the poet.
[*Purgatory,* Canto 9, lines 50–63]

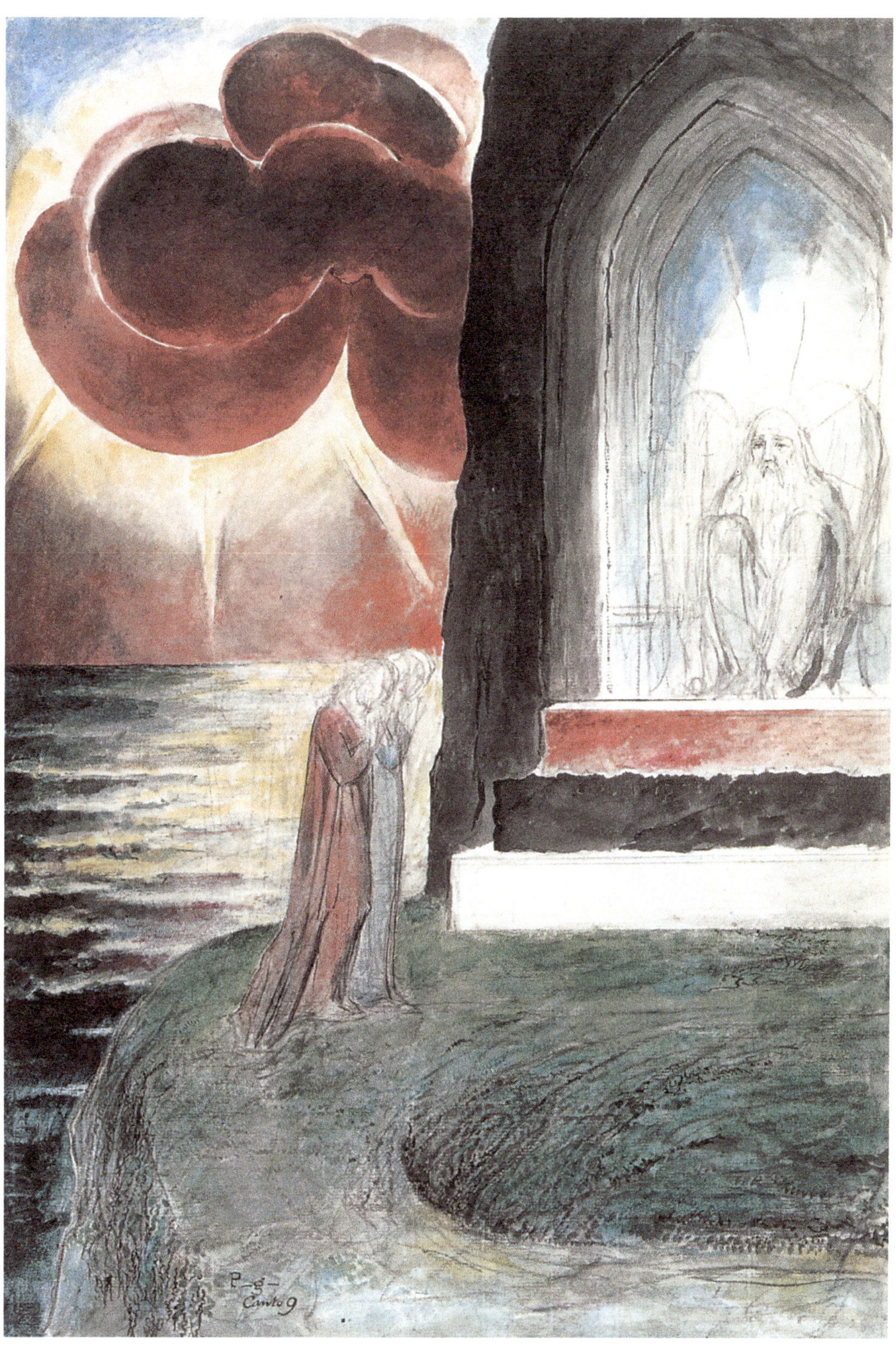

PLATE 81

Beneath an angry red cloud that suggests that they are still dogged by sin, the poets approach the entrance to Purgatory. [*Purgatory,* Canto 9, lines 64–101]

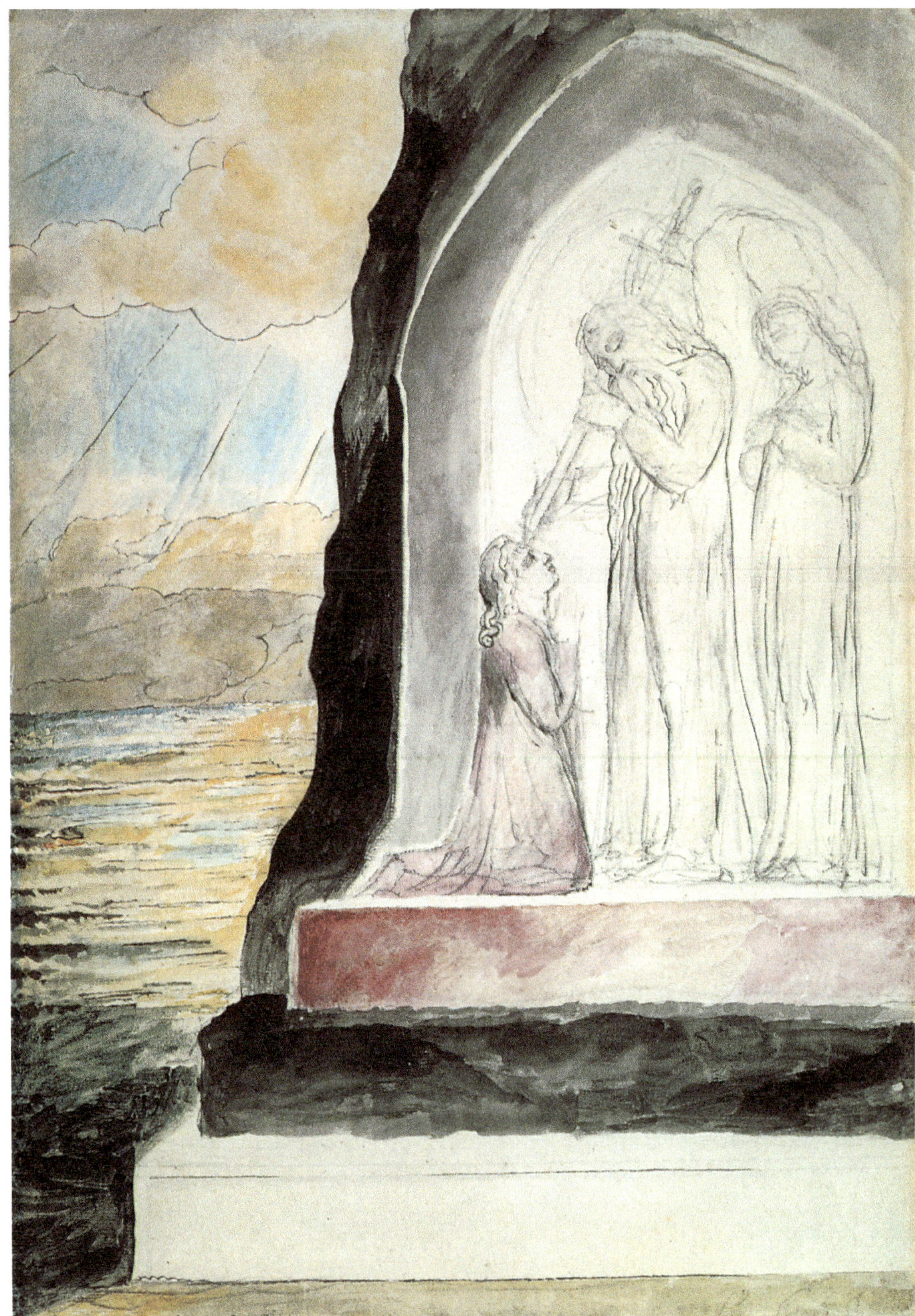

PLATE 82

As Dante kneels, the angel at the entrance to Purgatory inscribes the letter *P,* for *Peccato* (sins), on his forehead. The rising sun glows behind them. [*Purgatory,* Canto 9, lines 101–105]

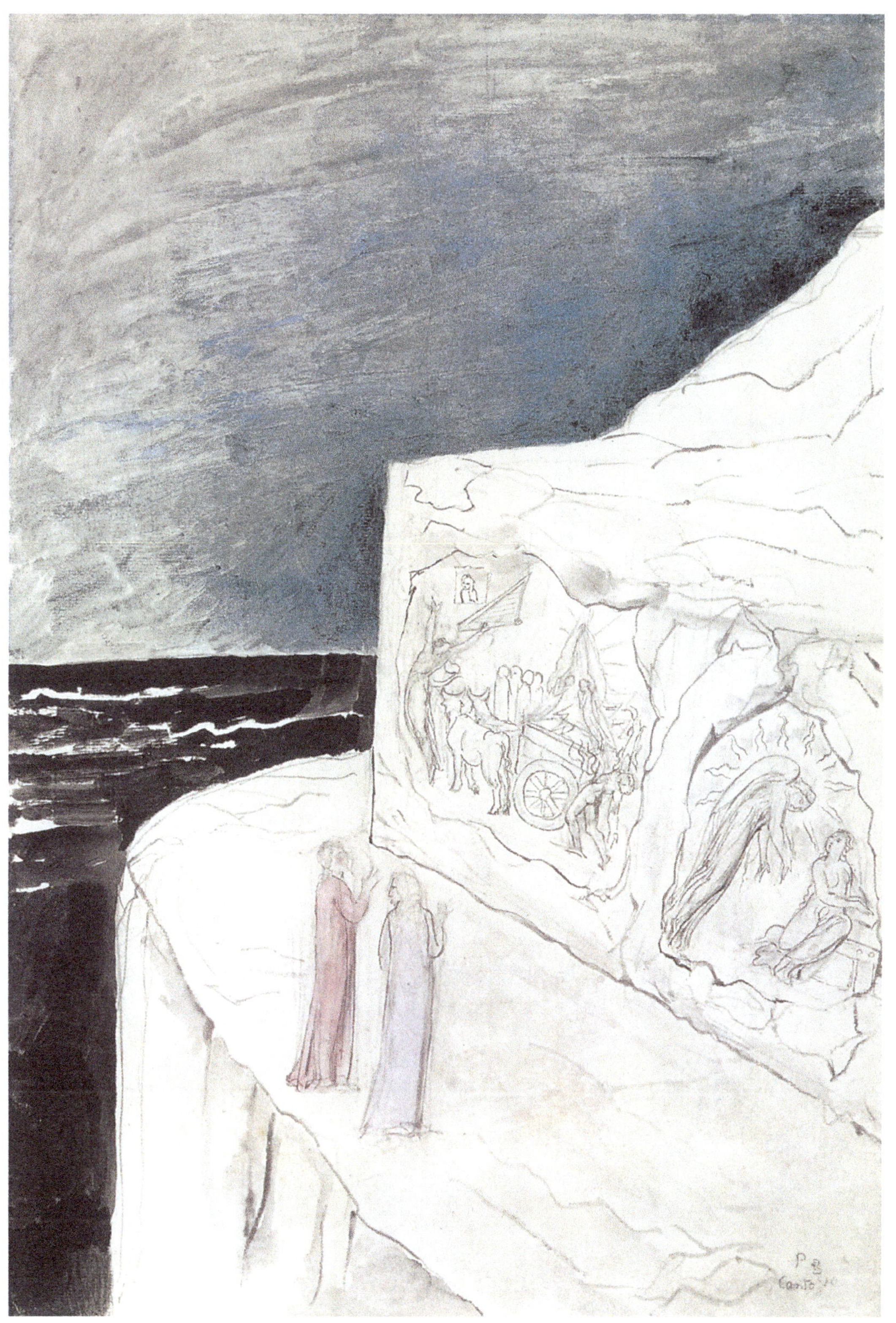

Plate 83

Dante and Virgil examine scenes from the Old and New Testaments inscribed in the rock, as they continue to ascend Purgatory. [*Purgatory,* Canto 10, lines 25–92]

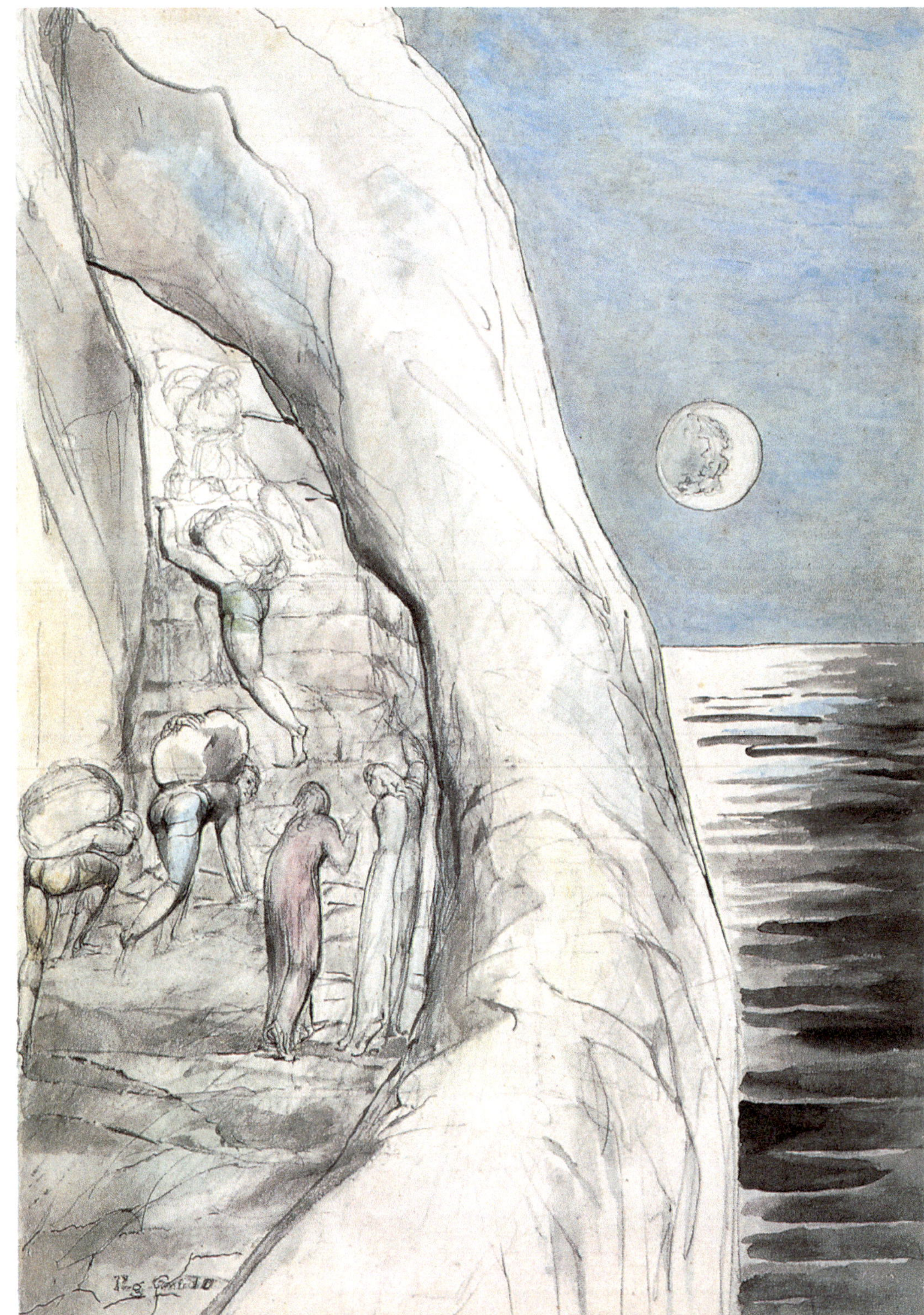

Plate 84

As the moon rises, the poets discover Christians burdened by their pride and ambition. [*Purgatory,* Canto 10, lines 106–127]

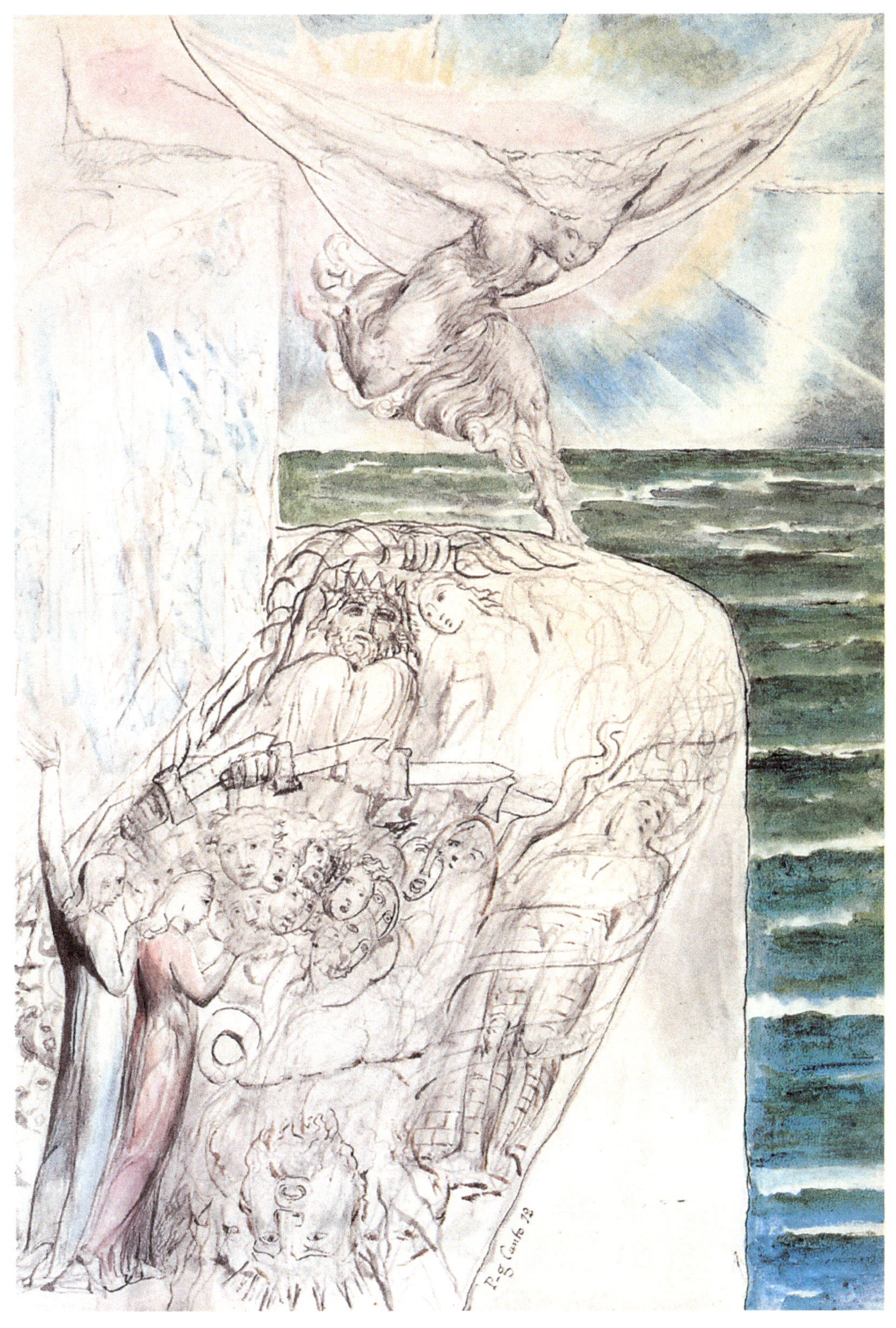

PLATE 85

Virgil shows Dante images of those whose downfall was caused by pride, including Lucifer and Nimrod.
[*Purgatory,* Canto 12, lines 14–64]

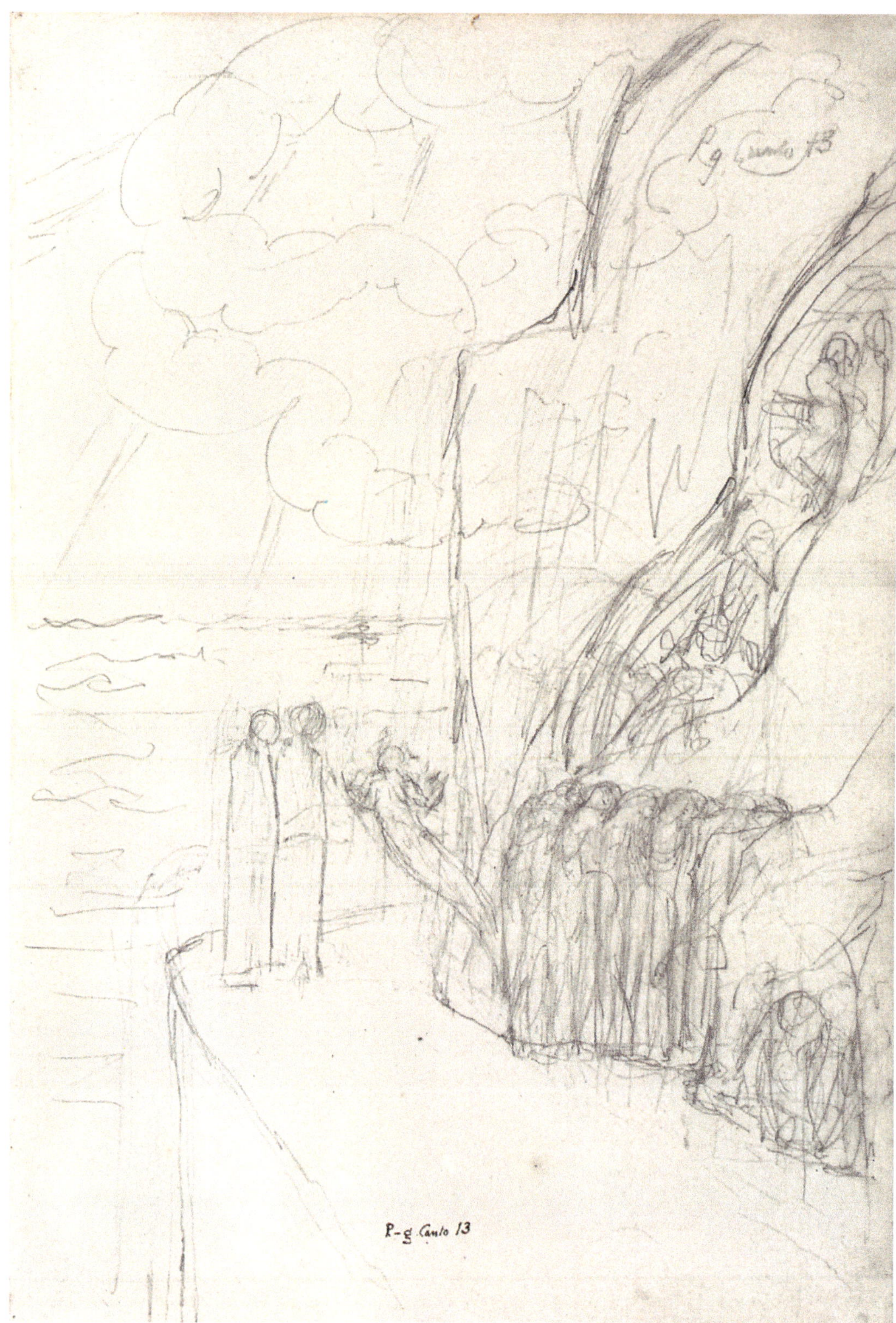

PLATE 86

Reduced to begging, the souls of those who succumbed to envy wander Purgatory. [*Purgatory,* Canto 13, lines 20–117]

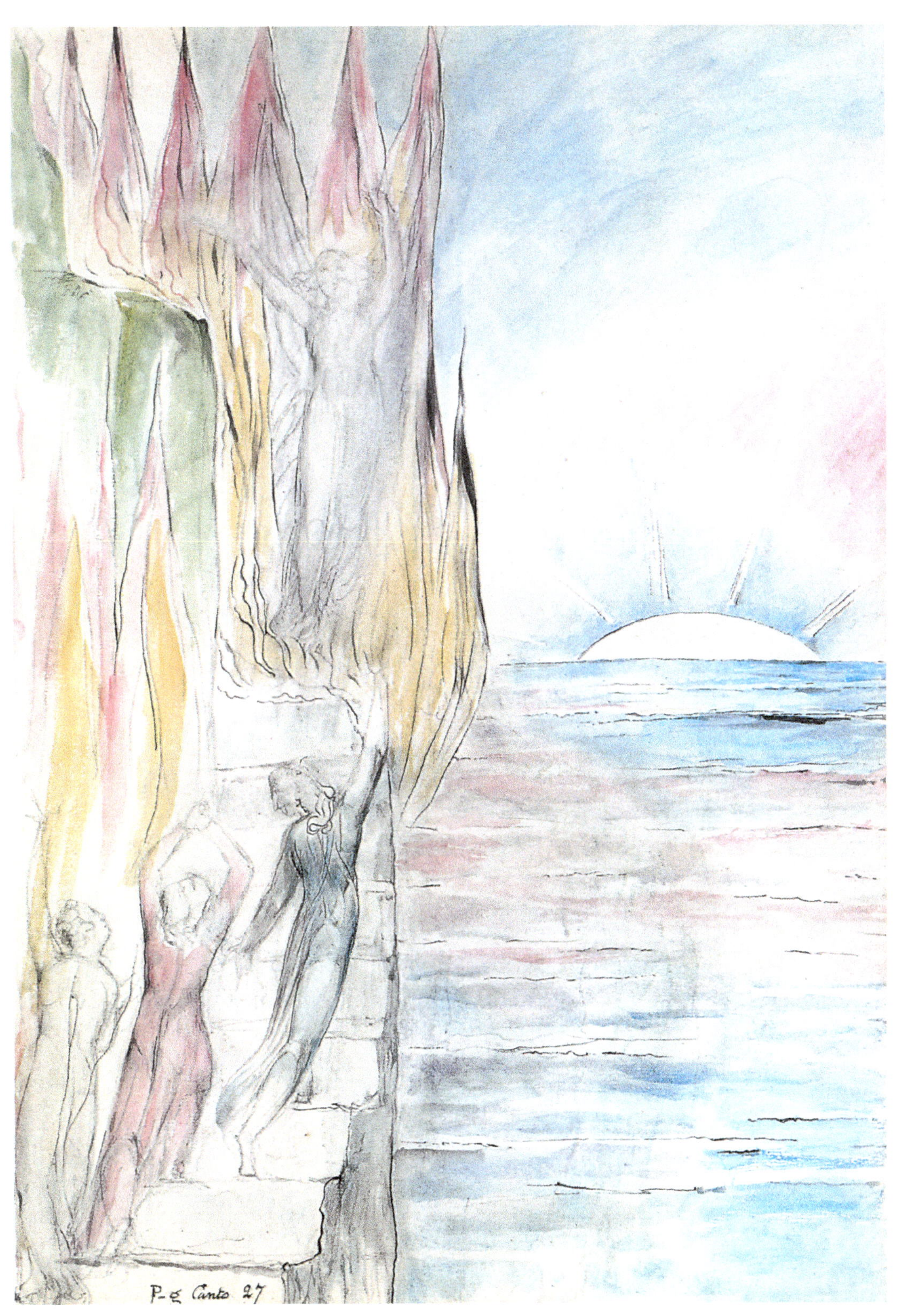

PLATE 87

Having been purged of sin, the fearful Dante is urged by Virgil to heed the angel and enter the flames. The Roman poet Statius joins them. [*Purgatory,* Canto 27, lines 6–19]

[Blake did not illustrate the content of Cantos 14 through 26]

PLATE 88

Still gripped by fear, Dante prepares to enter the flames.
[*Purgatory,* Canto 27, lincs 34–42]

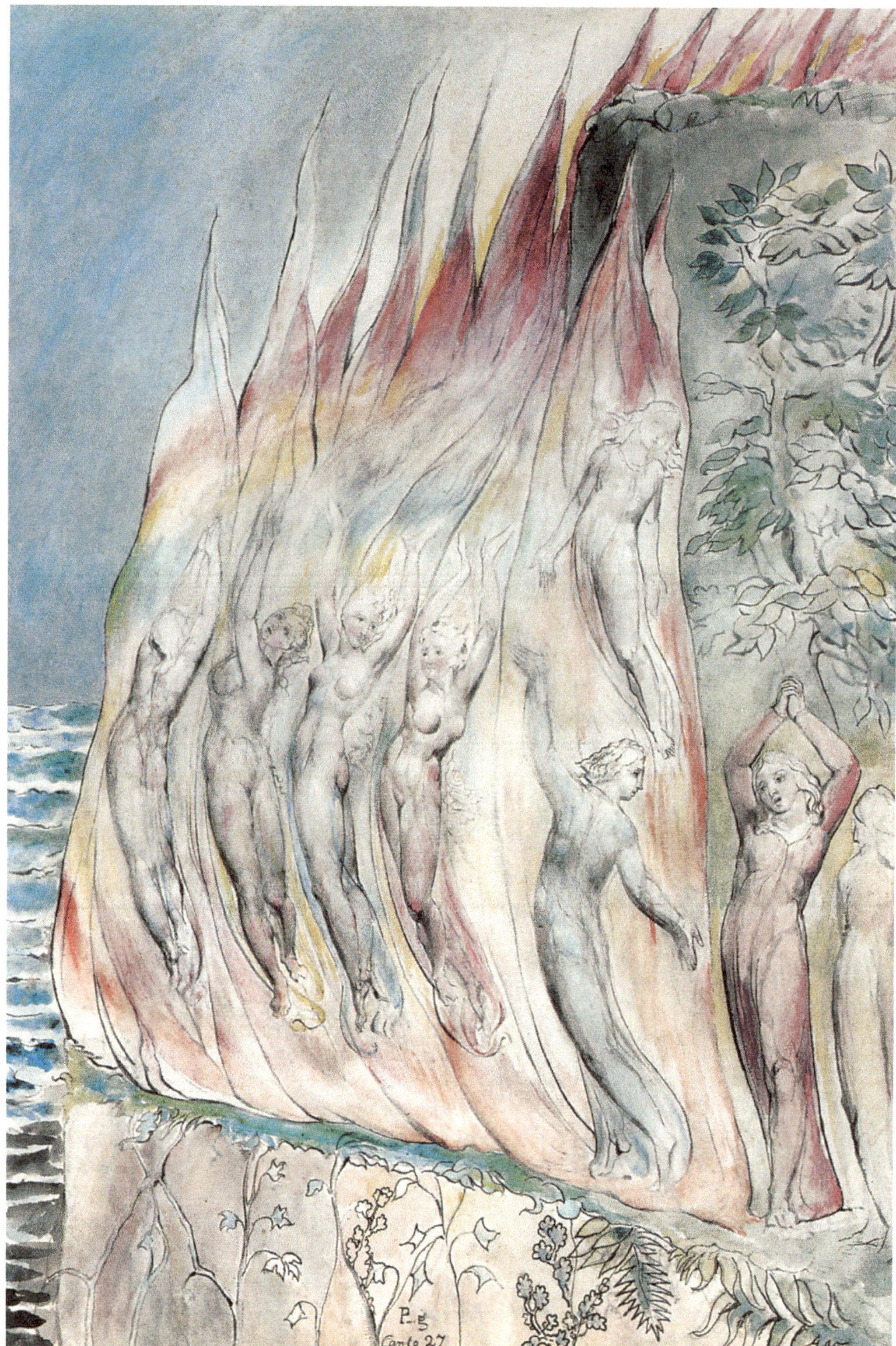

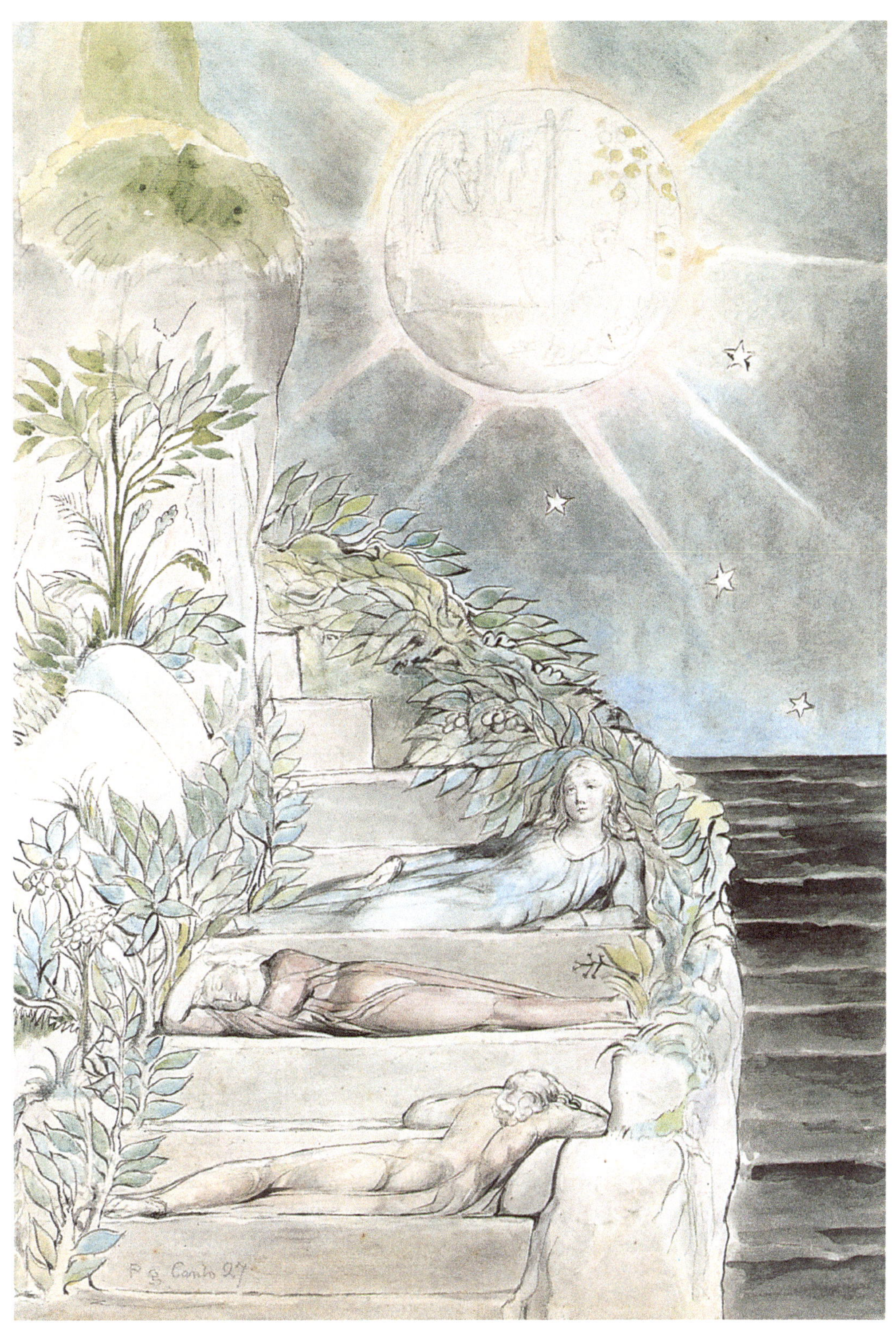

PLATE 89

The three poets rest under the starry sky, as Dante dreams of the action-seeker Leah and the deliberative Rachel. [*Purgatory,* Canto 27, lines 85–109]

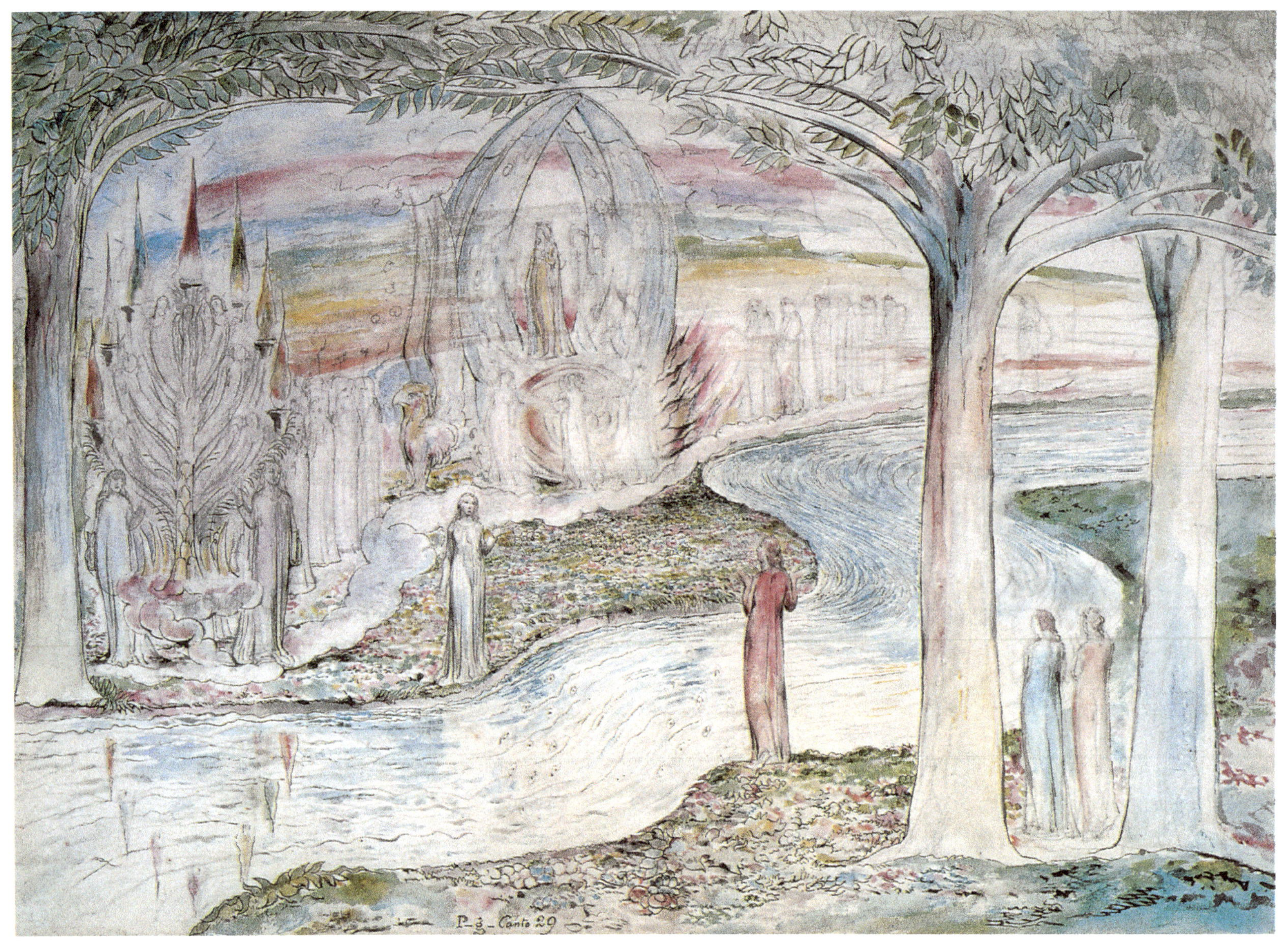

PLATE 90

At last, Dante beholds Beatrice, on the other side of the river Lethe, in Paradise.
Virgil, a pagan, cannot accompany Dante to Paradise.
[*Purgatory,* Canto 30, lines 9-54]

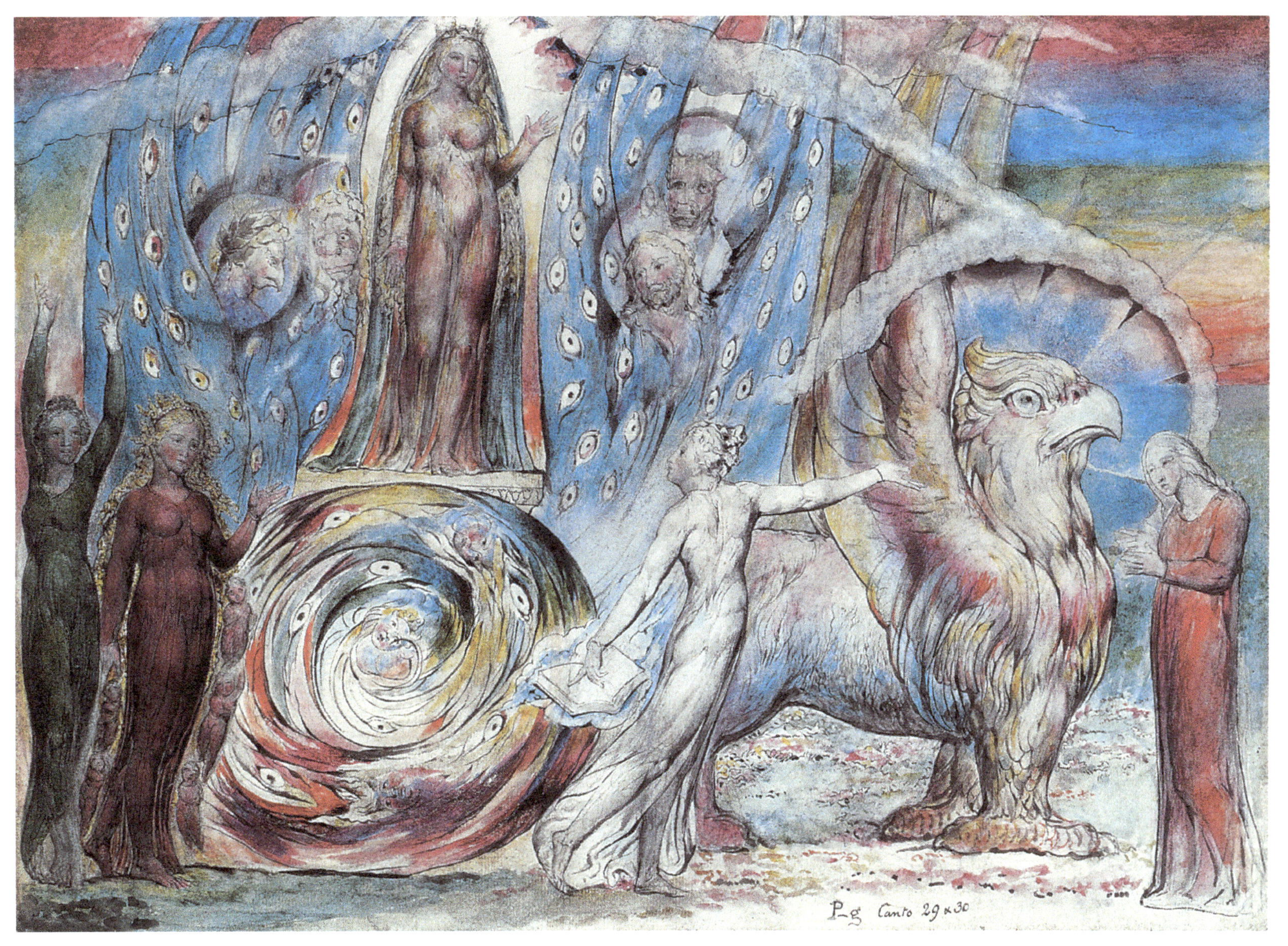

PLATE 91

Beatrice rides atop a car that represents the Church; a submissive Dante is confronted by a gryphon symbolizing the Saviour.
[*Purgatory,* Canto 30, lines 60–146]

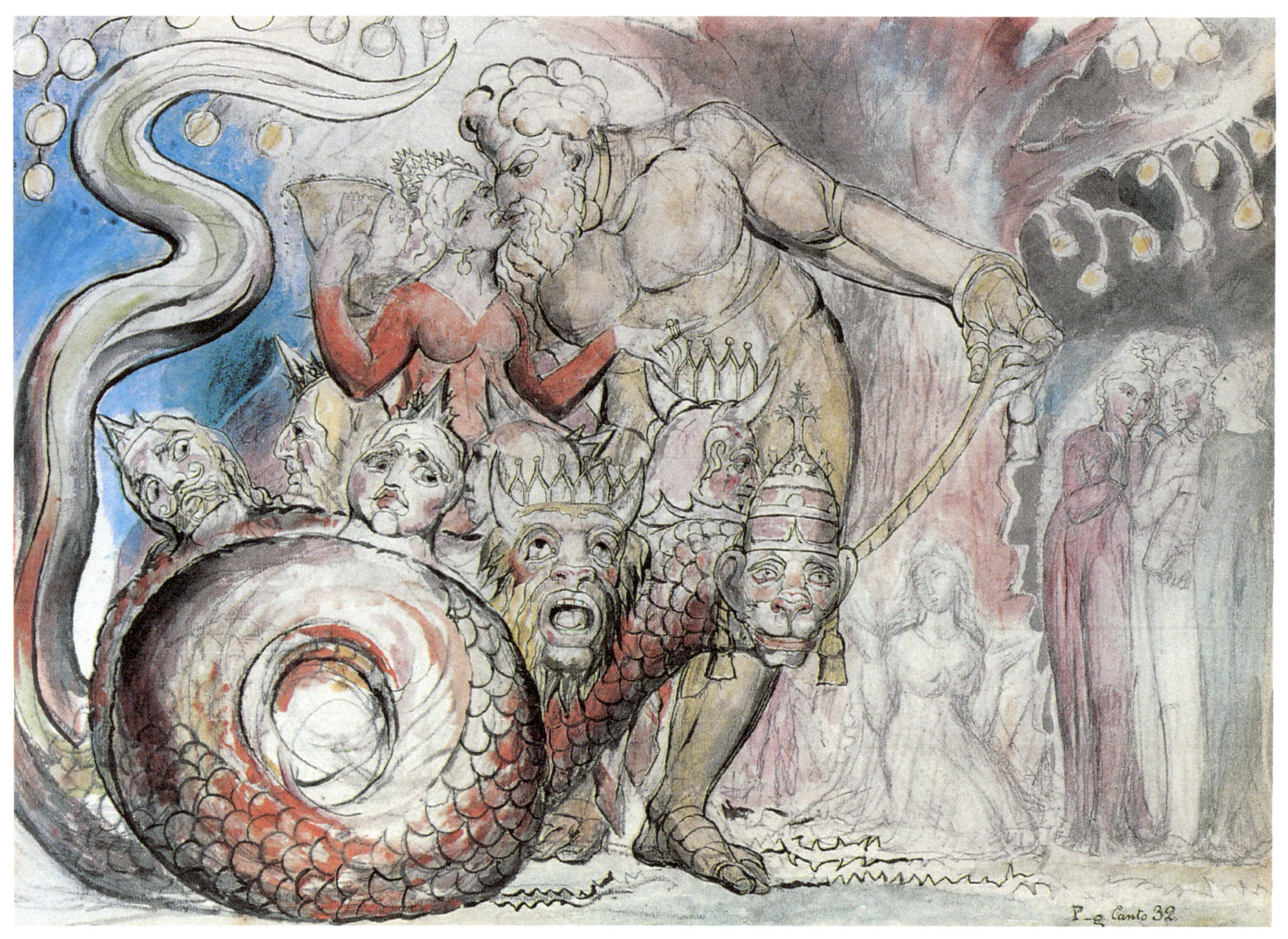

PLATE 92

Now, the Whore of Bablyon rides atop the Great Beast of Revelation, replacing the pure Beatrice with a suggestion of the corruption of the Church. [*Purgatory,* Canto 32, lines 129–157]

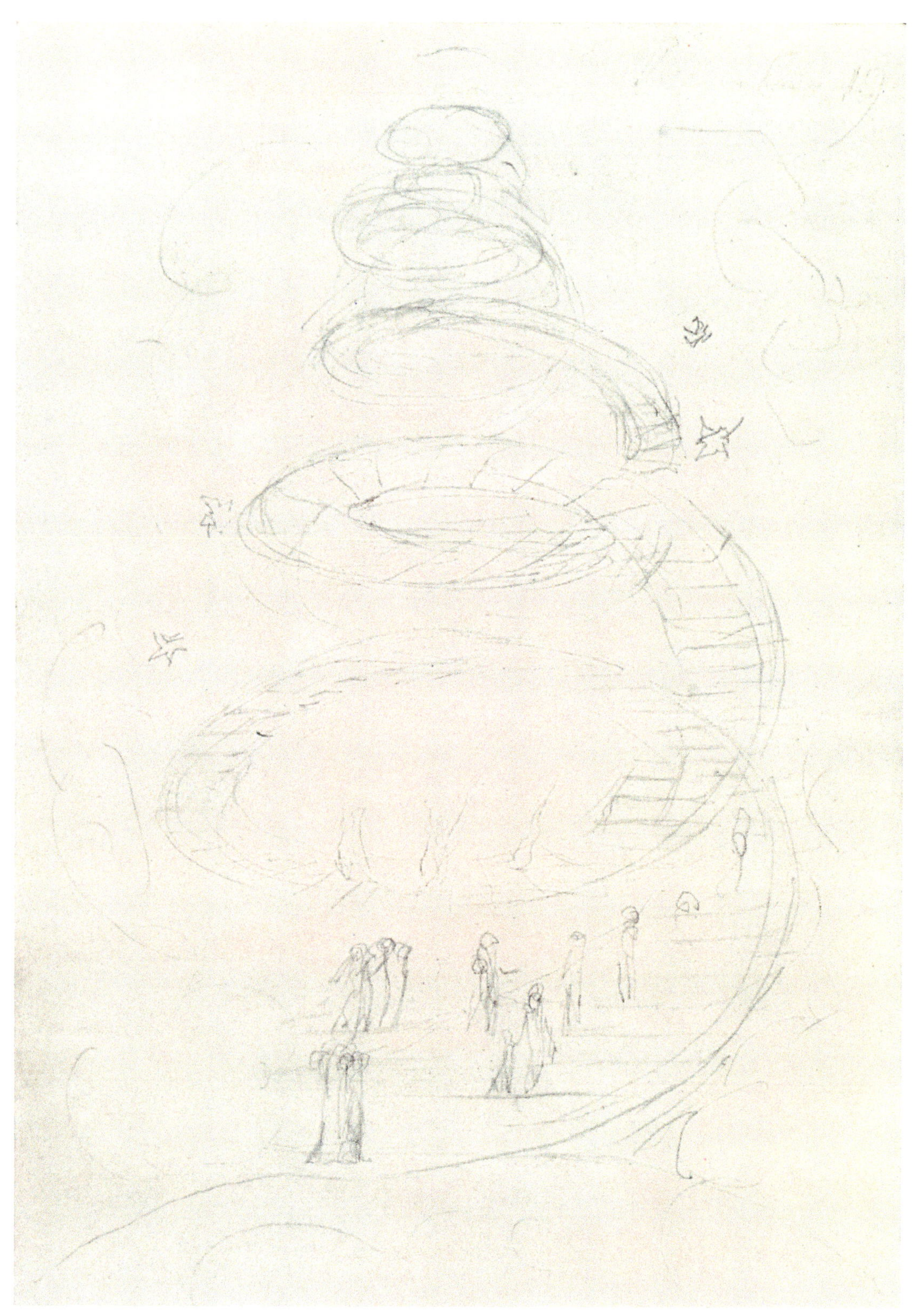

PLATE 93

Roughly sketched figures ascend the stairways of Paradise. [*Paradise,* Canto 10, lines 72–87]

PLATE 94

Dante kneels before a magnificent vision of the crucified Christ. [*Paradise,* Canto 14, lines 96–109]

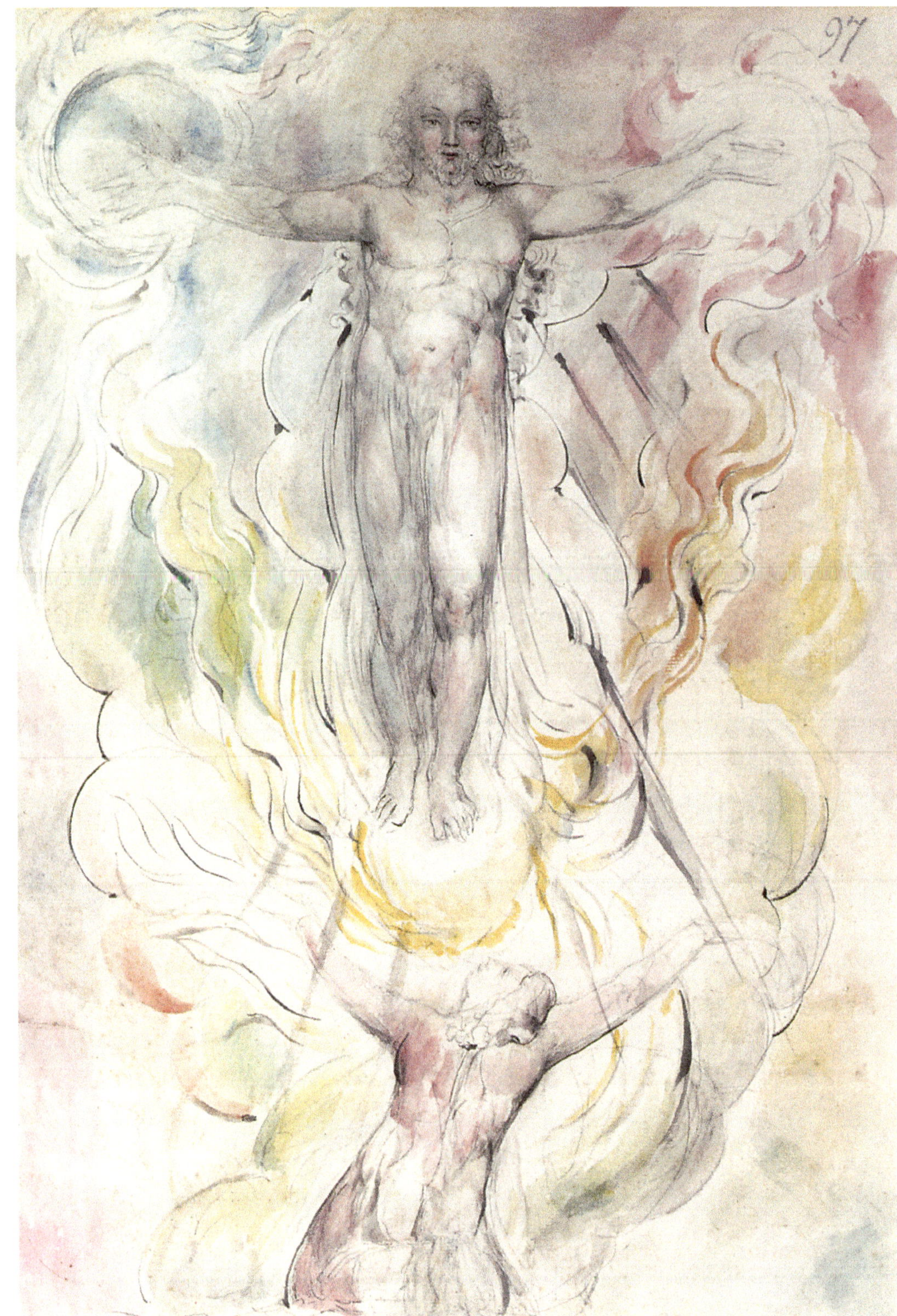

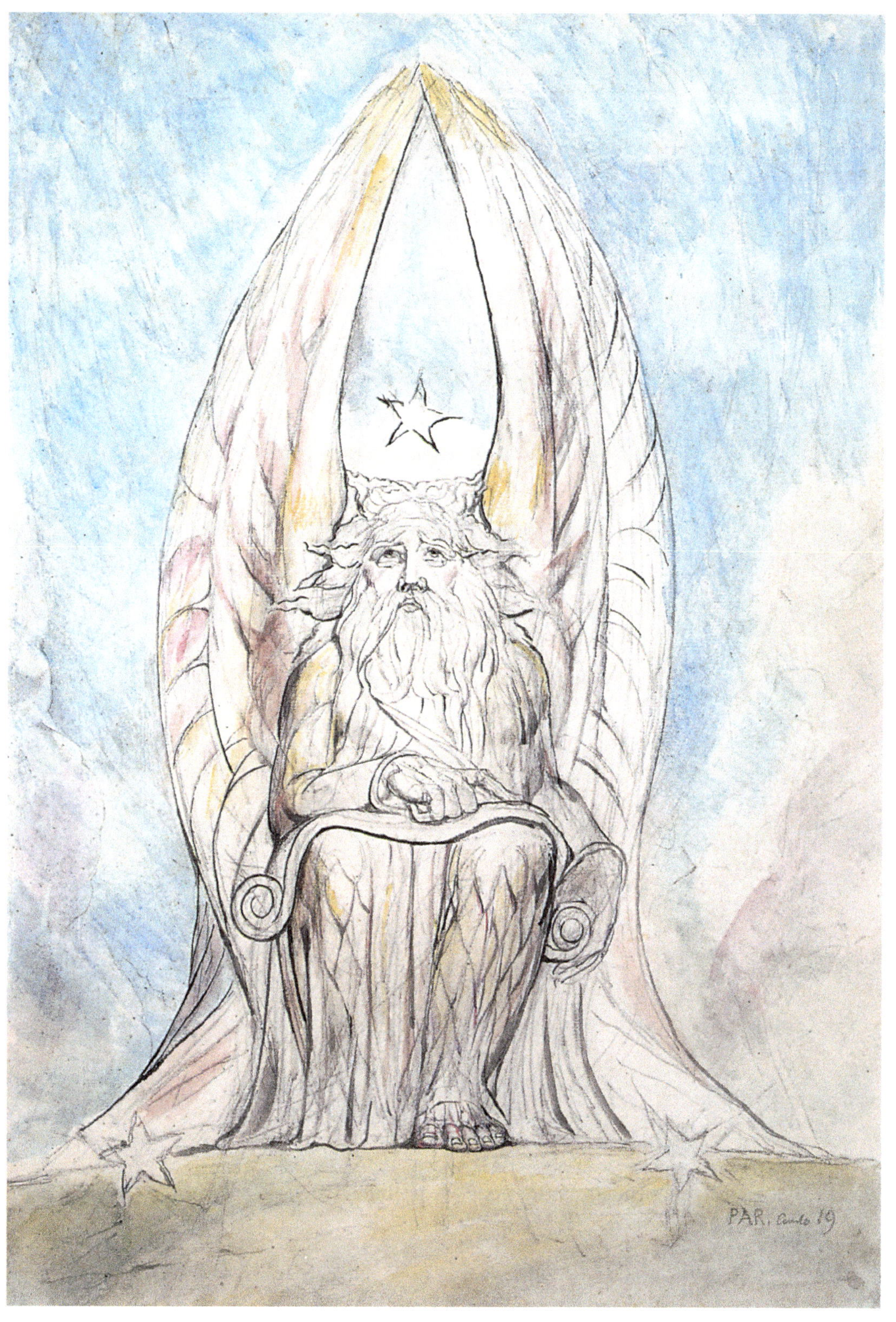

PLATE 95

The Recording Angel—absent in Dante's text—here may represent the stern God of the Old Testament.
[*Paradise,* Canto 19, lines 74–82]

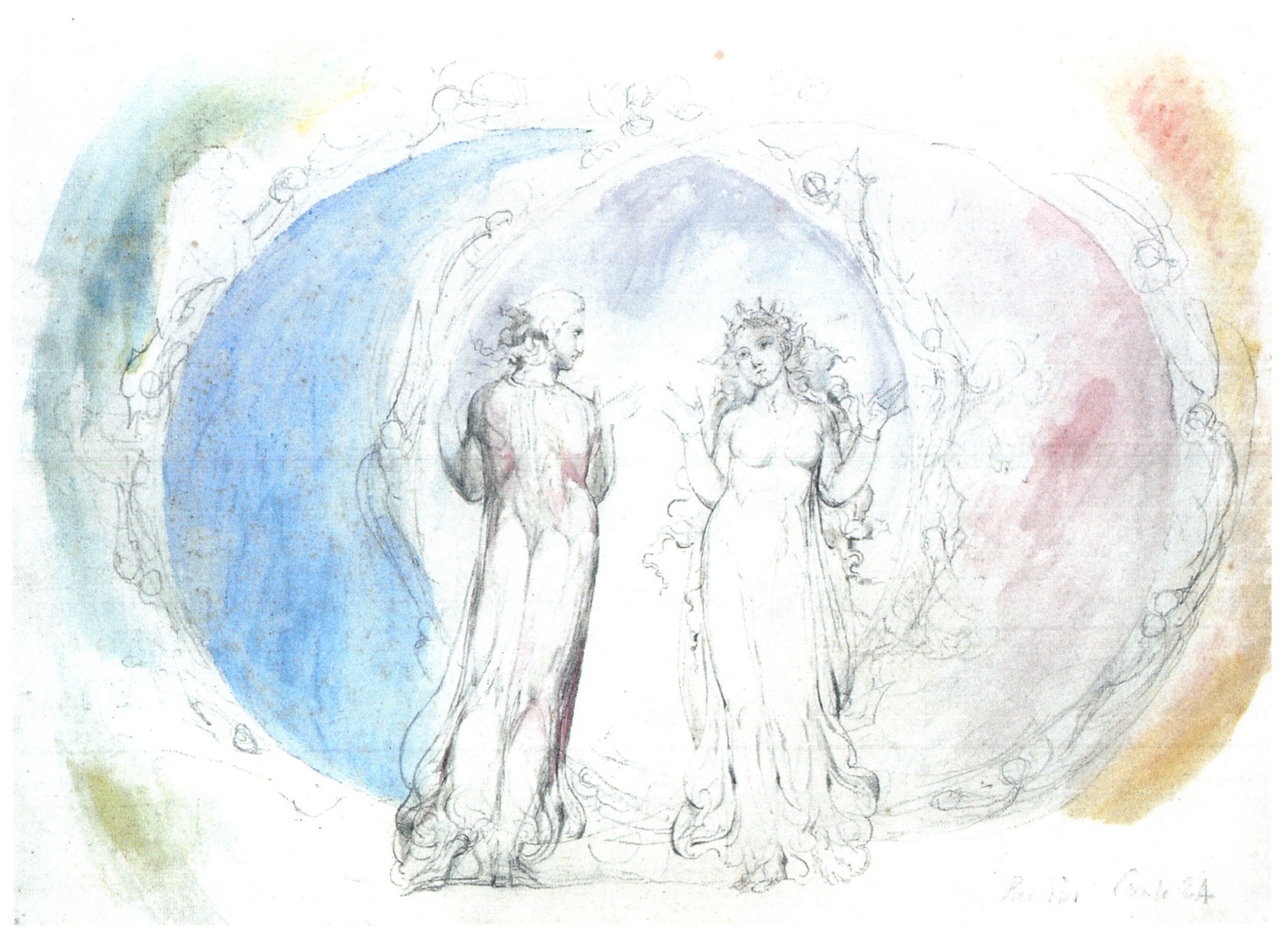

PLATE 96

As she stands near Dante in a contiguous sphere, Beatrice proclaims the poet's worthiness to seek redemption.
[*Paradise,*, Canto 24, lines 20–31]

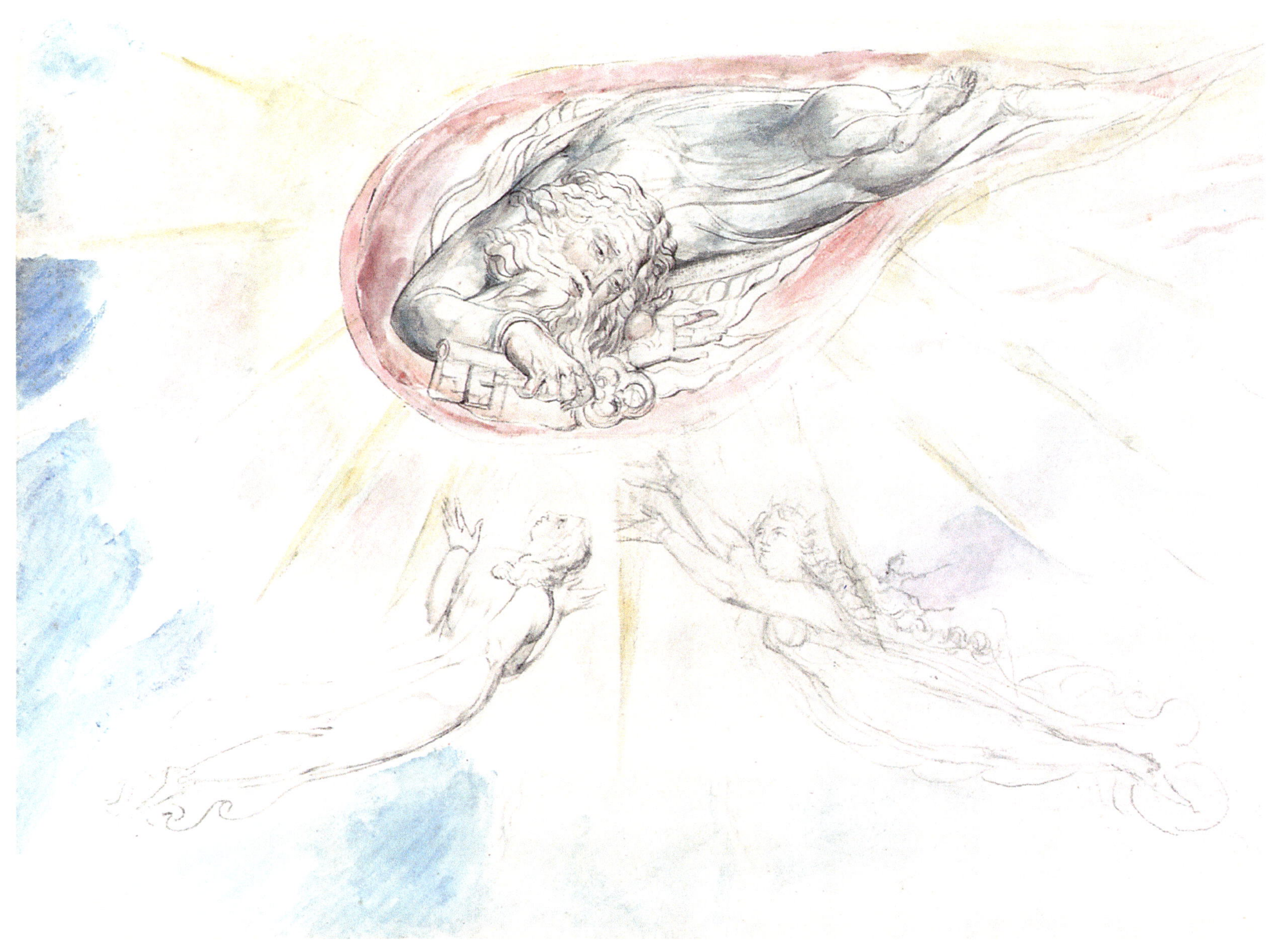

PLATE 97

St. Peter, his key in hand, asks Dante for the meaning of faith; Dante responds by "raising my forehead to the light."
[*Paradise,* Canto 24, lines 32–110]

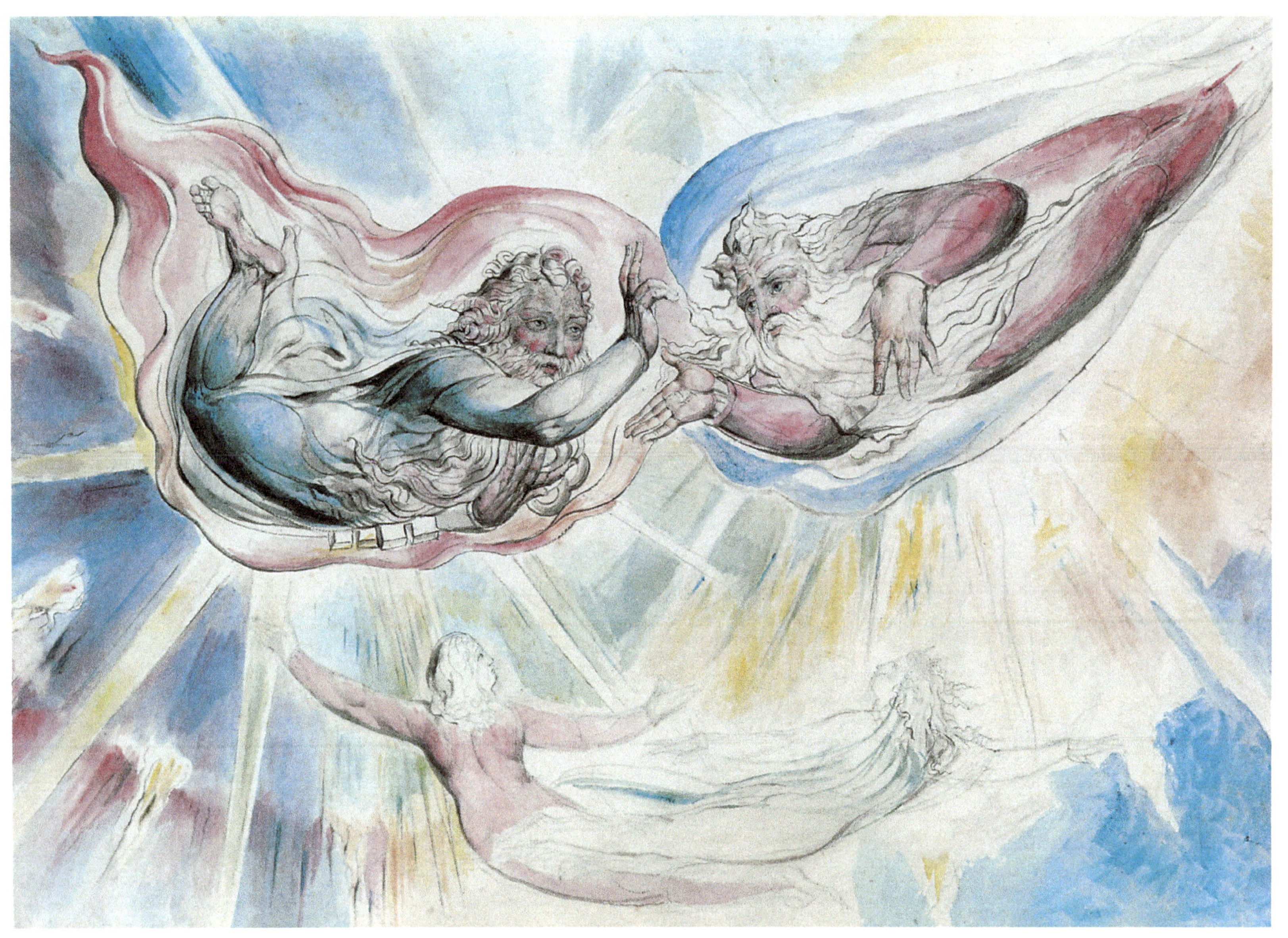

PLATE 98

As Beatrice intercedes for Dante, the poet is queried by St. James of Compostela regarding the meaning of hope.
[*Paradise,* Canto 25, lines 15–102]

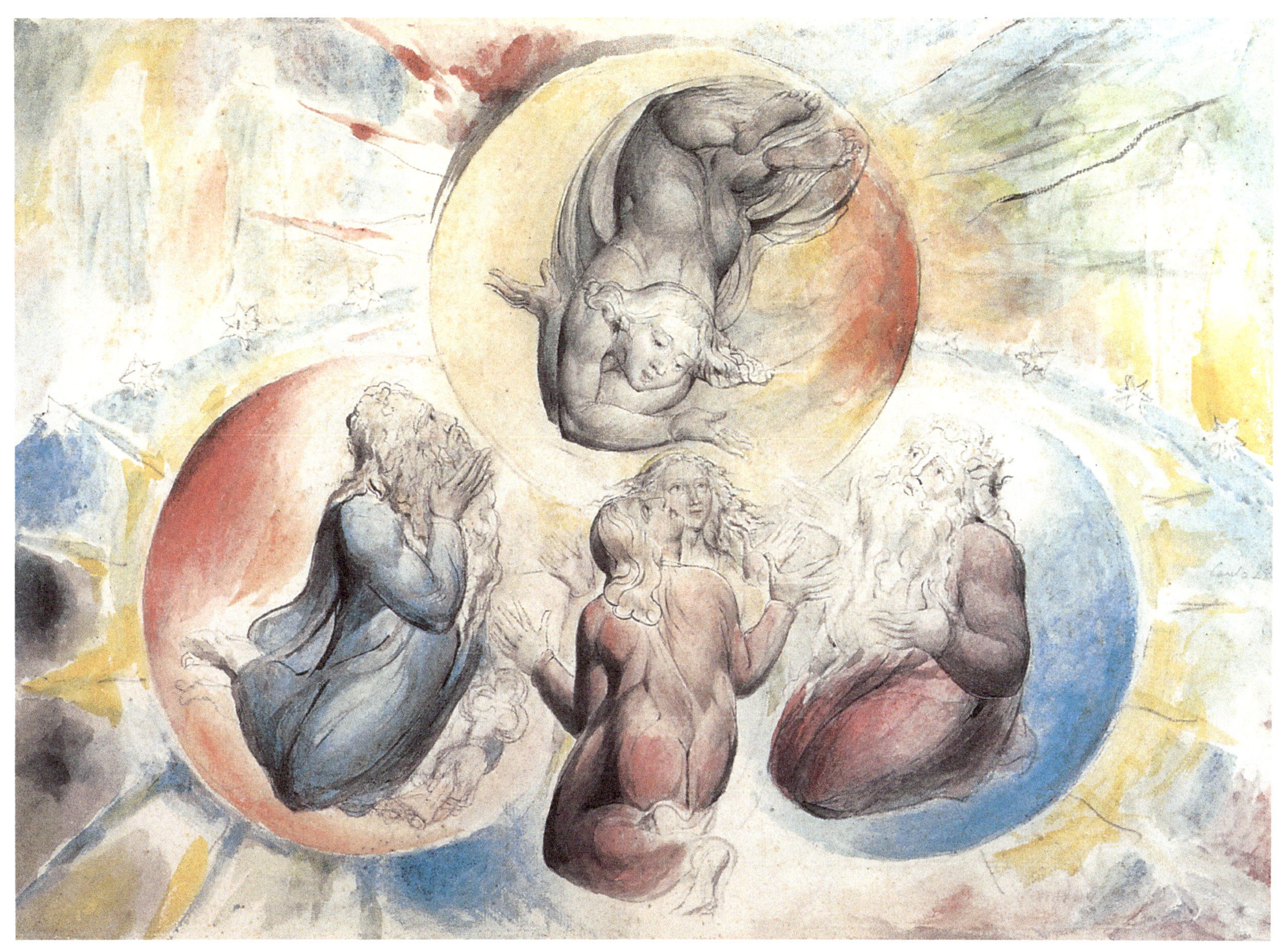

PLATE 99

Finally, after St. John the Evangelist asks Dante for the meaning of love, the poet meets Adam and is ready for salvation.
[*Paradise,* Canto 26, lines 103–139]

Plate 100

In the ninth portion of Paradise, Dante beholds the Divine Essence, as well as the angels, arranged in hierarchies. [*Paradise,* Canto 28, lines 18–53]

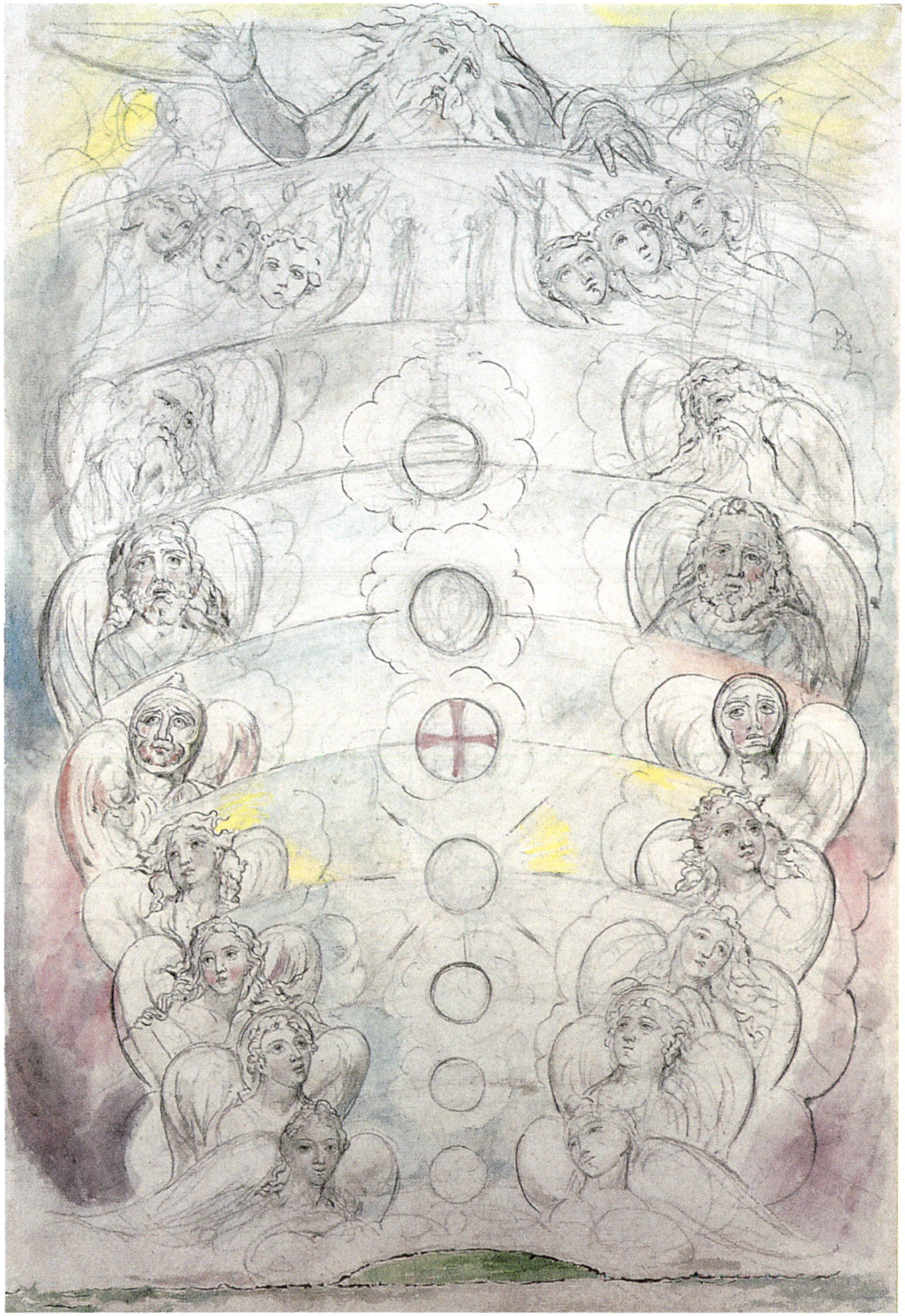

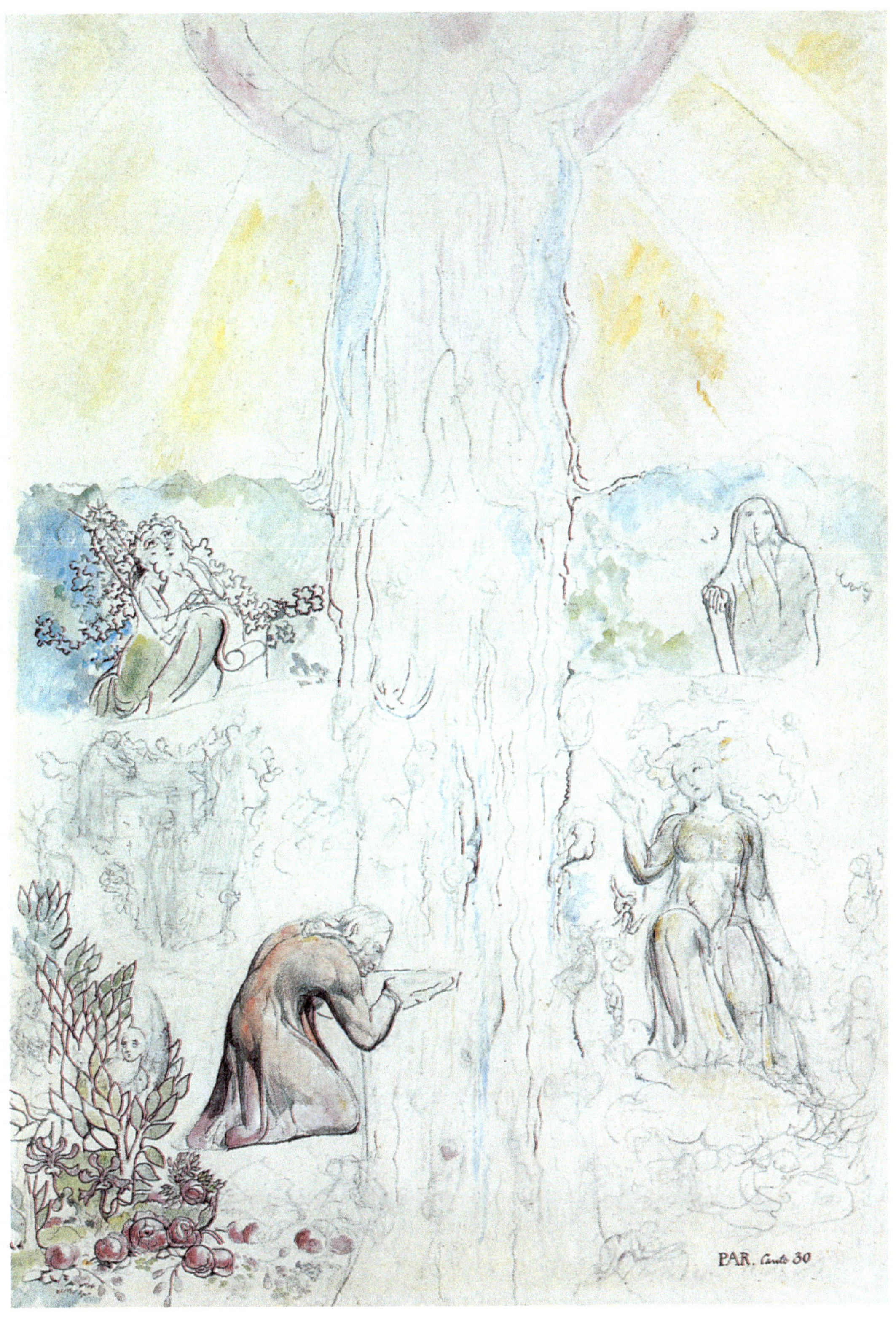

PLATE 101

Having rejected false religion, Dante, in the Empyrean with Beatrice, drinks from the River of Light. They have been released from their bodily existence. [*Paradise,* Canto 30, lines 55–91]

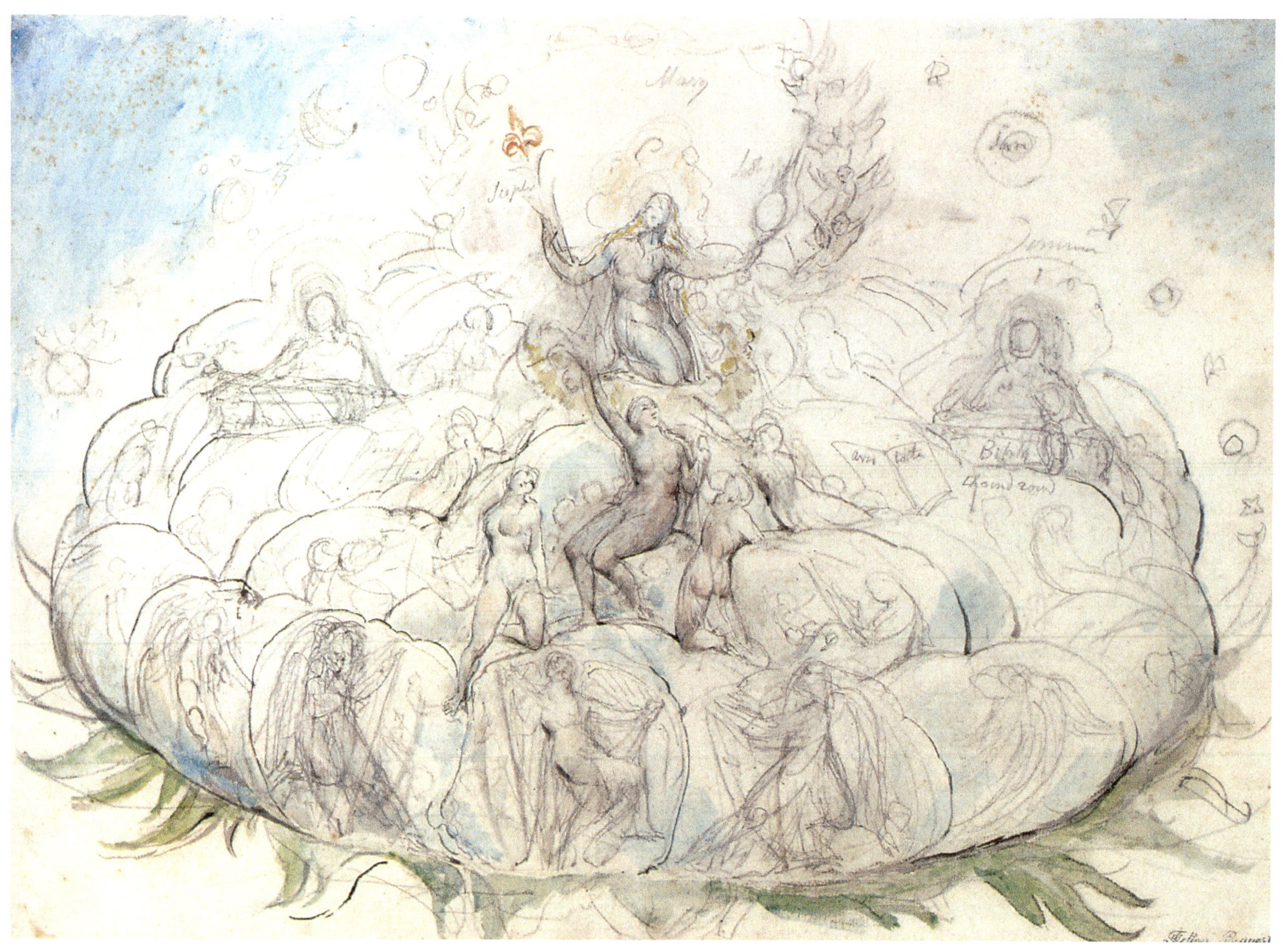

PLATE 102

Dante beholds the Virgin Mary—as well as Eve, Rachel, and Beatrice—in Blake's final plate. The Virgin Mary holds a scepter and a mirror, symbols of power and vanity. [*Paradise,* Canto 31, lines 106–132]